Daughters of Madness

Daughters of Madness

Growing Up and Older with a Mentally Ill Mother

Susan Nathiel

Women's Psychology
Michele Paludi, Series Editor

Westport, Connecticut
London

Library of Congress Cataloging-in-Publication Data

Nathiel, Susan.
  Daughters of madness : growing up and older with a mentally ill mother /
Susan Nathiel.
     p. cm. — (Women's psychology, ISSN 1931-0021)
  Includes bibliographical references and index.
  ISBN 0-275-99042-7 (alk. paper)
  1. Children of the mentally ill. 2. Mothers and daughters—Mental
health. 3. Mental illness. I. Title.
  RC439.N384 2007
  616.89′00852—dc22   2006038809

British Library Cataloguing in Publication Data is available.

Library of Congress Catalog Card Number: 2006038809

ISBN-10: 0-275-99042-7
ISBN-13: 978-0-275-99042-8
ISSN: 1931-0021

First published in 2007

Praeger Publishers, 88 Post Road West, Westport, CT 06881
An imprint of Greenwood Publishing Group, Inc.
www.praeger.com

Printed in the United States of America

The paper used in this book complies with the
Permanent Paper Standard issued by the National
Information Standards Organization (Z39.48-1984).

10 9 8 7 6 5 4 3 2 1

To Ellen Clare, Howard,
Christopher, and David

Contents

Foreword

A wise woman once said to me: "There are only two lasting bequests we can hope to give our children. One of these is roots; the other, wings."

—Hodding Carter

I was reminded of Carter's quote each time I read a woman's powerful account of her relationship with her mentally ill mother in Susan Nathiel's book. Through Nathiel's sensitive interviewing and demonstration of caring for them, these women were able to find their voices as "daughters of," dispel myths about how all women make "good" mothers, and reveal truths about their mothers, and their own lives. Nathiel acts as a developmental psychologist, providing interpretations of how the women's mothers were not able to handle various developmental tasks with which their daughters were dealing, including their daughters' identity development during adolescence. It is through their discussion of their mothers' illnesses that these women come to understand their own life stories—the choices they made and how they dealt with friends, family, and romantic relationships.

Through their discussions with Nathiel, these women speak about their mothers' mental illness, something their mothers couldn't do, especially given the era in which these women were entering young adulthood. In a way, these women become their mothers' voices and break the silence about mental illness that existed in their families. It seems appropriate for the daughters to tell their mothers' stories—they share many issues as women with their mothers. Yet the mothers couldn't make certain choices, in prefeminist times, that their daughters could make twenty or so years later, including availing themselves of mental health facilities, abortion, or feminist health care, or remaining single or raising children by themselves.

Unfortunately the illnesses robbed the mothers of the ability to speak out. But they wanted the stories to be told and knew their daughters were the ones to share them. And in this book, those daughters share them with us.

Michele Paludi
Series Editor

Acknowledgments

First and foremost, my deepest appreciation goes to the women who volunteered to be interviewed for this book. Revisiting some of the most painful parts of their lives, and keeping at it for a number of hours, was not easy for any of them. Their willingness to tell their stories, and their ability to do it so well, are at the heart of this book. They hoped that others would find familiarity, comfort, and help in their stories.

As a psychotherapist, I've been listening to all kinds of stories for several decades now, and I must acknowledge the contribution of all my patients over these years to teaching me how to listen. My understanding of the stories in this book, told by the daughters of mentally ill women, is deeply informed by my hearing many painful stories about the experience of being an outsider. Thank you all for sharing your lives with me.

This book was slow in coming to fruition, and many people heard about it as an idea long before it became a reality. My good friends Beth Culler and Jeanette Gross have been loyal supporters of my ideas for more years than I can calculate and never lost faith that I would complete the project. Judy Davis was an early supporter as well, inspiring me in important ways to start, to keep going, and to enjoy the process. Katie Nuro has given ongoing encouragement and insight into the whole project.

Other friends have given encouragement, put me in touch with women to interview, and have come through in reading drafts of the manuscript: Janet Brodie, Maria Tupper, Janet Rooney, Patty Harris, Steve Bittner, Karen Meyer, Dana Cervone, and Rachel Hart. My longtime women's group colleagues have been steadfastly supportive, and the weekly breakfast crew has cheered me on over the last couple of years, especially Cherry Czuba, Bev Byrd, and Ann Coward.

Some friends have provided more support and help than they might realize, as they helped clear the path for my writing time, and fully expected me to get the book finished when I was in doubt: Evie McGuaghey and Joy Murray stand out in that regard.

My editor at Praeger, the indefatigable Deborah Carvalko, has provided enthusiasm and support, and must be the fastest editor in the business. Her shared excitement when things went unusually well, and her deft and timely smoothing over of rough spots, made the project come to completion more quickly and easily than I thought possible.

Julie Silver, who presented the first Harvard Medical School Conference on publishing for healthcare providers, provided the springboard for bringing this project into the world of publishing, and gave me encouragement and guidance.

Of course this book could not exist if not for my family, who have made time, made excuses, made room, and given unwavering support for the project from beginning to end. My love and my thanks to you all.

Introduction

I was in my early fifties and visiting my father several hundred miles away when, after breakfast on the last morning of my visit, he asked if I would take a drive with him. Sure, I said—this was not such an uncommon request from him. We drove around aimlessly for a while, then he pulled the car into an empty parking lot, turned off the ignition, and said, "Maybe we should talk about your mother's illness." That was the first time he had ever directly acknowledged that my mother had been mentally ill, despite her intermittent psychotic periods and several psychiatric hospitalizations. We had lived it, all of us in the family, but never talked about it. I don't know why he chose this time to bring up the subject, but it struck me how taken for granted it was that we would never mention it openly. I guess it was predictable that even in this conversation we didn't acknowledge the forty-plus years of silence.

I had already been mulling over the idea for this book, and if I had any doubts about the need for it, they were erased by that conversation. Grown-up daughters of "mad" mothers haven't had a voice, and growing up as a daughter in such a family, with such a mother, does not make for a story that's easy to tell.

Why is this such a hard story to relate? There is, of course, the stigma of mental illness, as Victoria Secunda so aptly recognizes in her book *When Madness Comes Home:* "Telling someone that there's mental illness in your family, and watching the reaction, is not for the faint-hearted."[1] Telling someone that it's your *mother* who is mentally ill certainly ups the ante. The bond between a mother and her children is an idealized one in our culture, and that bond is assumed to be strongest and most mutual between mothers and their daughters. Sons are expected to grow up and away from their mothers, but a daughter is expected to stay close, to learn from her mother, perhaps to become her mother's friend and confidante, and certainly to share important life events with her even if the relationship is strained.

We all know that the mother-daughter relationship is not so easy as the idealization would have it. Few mothers could ever live up to the enormous and contradictory expectations of motherhood, yet most muddle through. There are high expectations of daughters, too: in the airbrushed image, a loving daughter looks up to her mother with appreciation of her mother's wisdom and warmth, and hopes to be like her. Few daughters can claim that kind of relationship, yet most daughters muddle through as well, coming to some acceptance of their mothers' limitations as they come to appreciate the durability of a loving if imperfect connection.

Between the idealization of mothers and the stigma surrounding mental illness, there is not much ground for a daughter of madness to stand on. Many of the women in this book grew up in the 1950s, 1960s, and 1970s when no one had even heard of a "dysfunctional family," much less grown up in one. Now that "telling" is more socially acceptable, these women have much to say. However, almost all had a hard time telling the story in a straight line, for a couple of reasons. One is the tendency of most people in crazy families to keep as far down in the foxhole as possible, living from emergency to emergency and not having much sense of the flow of time. A second reason is that the story has to be rewritten so many times. Families with secrets do a lot of rewriting, as bits and pieces of history emerge like old shrapnel over the course of years. New disclosures explain old mysteries, and some new disclosures completely blow the old history out of the water. One woman I interviewed learned in her thirties that her mother had "run off" for a while with an elevator operator in the family's apartment building when the children were quite young. It took a while to digest that, she told me, but ten years later she heard the *whole* story: her mother had been gone not "for a while" but for two entire years! For a young child, two years is a lifetime. Having this bit of truth, finally, meant not only that she understood herself better but also that she had to revise her understanding of family history yet again.

It's not surprising that these women had a hard time telling a story that made sense from beginning to end; in fact, they had never actually been asked to do so. The questions I asked began in childhood and went forward along each woman's life trajectory, always with the focus on what was happening in the family and with her mother at each specific period. There was something very intense and compelling about this process, as some things seemed to make sense and fall into place in a way that hadn't happened before. Story lines emerged out of discrete incidents, like a series of snapshots being transformed into a video. Sometimes we speculated about the mother's diagnosis, something often avoided in therapy.

The chapters are organized chronologically, from childhood on, paralleling the interviews, so that the reader can see how the stories unfold, beginning with the earliest memories. In each chapter I'll begin with an overview of the development tasks of the period covered in that chapter (early childhood, middle childhood, adolescence, and so forth), then let the women tell their stories of what happened to them during that period. In this way, it's clearer how early experience shapes later development. The women begin their interviews remembering childhood, and we end with their mature reflections about their lives today.

Each woman who volunteered was interviewed at least twice, for about an hour and a half each time. They were between the ages of thirty-five and sixty-eight, and most had fared relatively well in their adult lives. All had been in therapy, and about a third were therapists themselves. They all expressed the hope that their words would reach people who have been marginalized and silenced by growing up with a mentally ill parent. Telling the whole story was a new experience for all of these women, and it provided a sense of closure for some. Some knew little of their mothers' histories and were inspired to find out more, if possible. A few reflected that they never called their mothers Mom, and one woman asked me not to refer to her mother as Mom because it seemed "too intimate." That's a sad comment on a relationship that's so fundamental to how we begin life. Jerri spoke for most of the women in her comments after her last interview.

> I think what I greatly appreciated was the ability to say my story to someone, not just without interruptions but because somebody was truly interested to find out what it was like. I never really had a chance to discuss it when I was growing up, and it was unthinkable to talk about it. Even good friends can't really appreciate what I went through and what it felt like. Quite honestly, nobody ever asked me these questions before.

Serious mental illness usually lasts a lifetime, but it ebbs and flows like other chronic illnesses. Sometimes it is full-blown and requires drastic measures like hospitalization. Sometimes things seem to be fine, and everyone relaxes their vigilance. Women I interviewed told story after story of how the family "managed" their mother during holidays, birthdays, graduations, social events, and so forth. They all seemed to know when their mother was "on something," although they rarely knew what medications were prescribed. In some cases the medications helped, and at other times their mothers turned into groggy, blank zombies who could barely function. "How will she be" at this or that occasion, when this or that happens, becomes a major question in families with a sick member, no matter what the illness. When the illness is mental, the ill person almost invariably denies the illness and therefore cannot help with planning how to cope. In fact, for family members, coping with the denial is a huge part of the problem. With a chronic physical illness, it's common that the ill person is the one making contingency plans along with the rest of the family, anticipating that they might need extra medication, a wheelchair, a place to lie down, an early departure. The mentally ill family member can be expected to deny that anything is wrong, to be insulted if anyone implies that something bad might happen, and to actively fend off help if it's needed. In this, it's like having an unpredictable alcoholic in the family, either conspicuously absent at every family function or the focus of anxiety if present. And because a mother is an expected participant in all of her daughter's life events, her illness becomes a factor as well. The women in my study talked about the difficulty of explaining, as children, why "my mother isn't here" or "my mother couldn't come"—to the PTA meeting, the game, the school play. As adults, they still had to offer explanations, mostly vague, about why their mother wasn't at the wedding, the birth of a grandchild, the winning of an award, the funeral of a family member. (And why can't she be there? Maybe she doesn't comprehend what's happening. Maybe she's "not doing well" and would act inappropriate or hostile or outright crazy. Maybe she's in the hospital again, or just released and unable to tolerate any stress. Maybe nobody has the energy to deal with her unpredictability.) So out comes, "Oh, my mother? She's not here." And most times, there is no reason one can offer for why that would be. The response is often a blank stare. "But she's your *mother*." Translation: "That bond transcends everything, doesn't it? How could your own *mother* not be here?" Motherhood is supposed to trump mental illness, just as it's supposed to trump alcoholism or drug addiction or abuse. That's the idealization. The truth is, often it doesn't.

I don't intend to portray daughters of mentally ill mothers as a group unto themselves. Some of what they experienced is common to children of mothers with other difficulties: alcoholism, drug abuse, chronic victimization, and so forth. Yet there are some unique features, as well. The kind and degree of stigma associated with mental illness is high, which affects early recognition and treatment and affects the patient's own willingness to accept and deal with her diagnosis. And psychotic mothers have, I think, a unique effect on their children. Unlike some other impaired mothers, they cannot simply stop being impaired. There's no detox program or safe house for schizophrenic or bipolar or borderline personality–disordered or obsessive-compulsive mothers.

In her memoir, Minrose Gwin says it beautifully:

There is such a thing as crazy-mother bonding. This can occur unexpectedly any time two women who have crazy mothers are having a conversation. It happens when one realizes the other also has had a crazy mother.... Oh, she will say to you or you will say to her, your mother was, uh, mentally ill? Yes, she was crazy, you will say. Really crazy, she will ask ... yes, you will say, really crazy ... I had to commit her twice. A flash of recognition across the table, a sigh. So was mine. Yes, mine was too. What follows is a conversation that no one else can possibly follow.[2]

What has been compelling to me about the women who volunteered to be interviewed for this study is how curious they still are, how eager to put more pieces into the chaotic jigsaw puzzle that is their life story, and to keep rearranging them until they make sense. And above all, I was deeply touched by how determined they are to find the mother in the madness, how tireless they are in searching for the best bits, the moments of wholeness, the fleeting times of reprieve, comfort, emotional connection, and nurturing. In almost every interview there would come a point, somewhere in the middle, as we moved from childhood memories to adult experience, when the woman I was interviewing would look at me wistfully and say, "My mother was so pretty. I remember when I was little, she was so pretty." That memory of a pretty mommy is still alive despite what came later for these women. What transpired was invariably ugly, shaming, often terrifying, not at all what the little girl would have wanted from her pretty mommy. But that memory, that inner picture of a mother who was so pretty, seems to have sustaining power even decades later.

Chapter 1

Mother's Role in Our "Self" Development

A bewildered man sits in my office with his wife, who had grown up in a violent home, and asks me why she can never really let down her guard with him. He's kind and gentle, and he had hoped that their relationship would help her heal from her chaotic childhood. She had hoped so, too. Neither one of them can understand why she doesn't enjoy their life more, why she can't relax.

A successful doctor with two thriving kids is similarly frustrated by her inability to enjoy her family and her career. No matter what she does or what she achieves, the feeling that she is somehow a "bad person" haunts her. She's afraid she will carry this feeling forever. If being a doctor hasn't made her okay, and being a good mom hasn't made her okay, she fears nothing ever will. What's wrong?

The fact that someone you know has trouble trusting other people or trouble asking for help, or seems to be on guard or tense most of the time, is understandable if you know that her parents were abusive and rejecting. When that person is close to you, however, understanding isn't quite enough. You begin to think to yourself: "But I'm trustworthy. I'm not abusive. I go out of my way to be understanding, because I know what they've been through. Why can't they get over it?" The answer that I hear in my office is often an apologetic, anxious "You're right. I don't know why. It's not you, it's me." We believe very strongly in the power of the present to heal the wounds of the past, and we don't know what to do when that's not enough. Because I've been a therapist for more than thirty years, I have a deep respect for how tenacious the grip of past experience can be. But it can be hard to convey that tenacity to patients and their families, and in truth, there's always a bit of mystery about why some wounds heal and others don't.

I love my work, and I'm honored to have been companion and guide to a great many people who've put in years of hard work in therapy. The results are usually not very spectacular from the outside, but the ability to be in the present, to live in one's own body, to know who one is and honor what one knows—those can be huge accomplishments. These patients and I have some understanding of what makes the difference, what helps, what loosens the grip of old terrors. But none of this erases the feeling I've always had that part of what I'm doing is putting a jigsaw puzzle together in the dark. I'm generally confident that I've got the pieces in approximately the right places, and that a whole picture will emerge from those pieces, but it has always been frustrating that the "why" of some healing has been so elusive.

Recent research into the early development of the mind and the brain removes much of that frustration. It also enables me to explain much more clearly to patients about how old feelings and experiences are wired into who they are today, and how this gives us a better road map to help us reach a place of change.

Such research makes a difference in understanding not only the stories of women raised by mentally ill mothers but also the stories of anyone growing up in severely traumatic or neglectful early environments. Early maternal failure has a deep and lasting impact, and although the stories of the women I interviewed are moving, they don't tell the whole story. ("Maternal," throughout this book, refers to the primary caregiver, whether male or female, parent or guardian, other relative, or anyone else.) The aftershocks of early maternal failure often appear only in adulthood, and often in the form of an absence of something important. For example, a child wouldn't be able to say she doesn't feel "whole," but when an adult articulates that feeling, she may be referring to something or some things that didn't happen very early in childhood. At a time when stigmatized and otherwise marginalized people are speaking out about their experiences, I believe we have a responsibility not only to hear the stories but also to understand why they matter. Talking about the negative impact on self-esteem barely touches the surface of the long-term effects of abuse, neglect, and other forms of early maternal impairment.

It's a truism that everyone has problems. Many mothers may seem crazy at times. But I'd like to argue—vehemently—that there's a fundamental difference between people who got enough of the basics as infants and children and people who didn't. People who got enough of what they needed, on enough fronts, have a baseline and a response to threat that are different, and they simply don't have to struggle with such things as believing that what they see and feel is real.

How your "self" feels to you and how you feel about yourself are two different things on two different levels of experience. If you had good enough (not ideal) experiences before your memory system became functional at eighteen to twenty-four months, you will not be aware of any particular feeling of your "self," of who you are. You might have feelings about yourself—for instance, you feel you're not smart enough or pretty enough, or you have trouble with certain situations or people—but that's different from the feeling of not having a self to begin with. As Daniel Stern says, the core sense of self refers to something we live inside of, not something we talk about.[1]

At about six months of age, we lay down the template of our earliest experience of being ourselves in relation to the world. Our core sense of self is physical—it's the background of what we feel like living in our bodies. This sense is indescribable, and we don't even think about it. Its absence, however, gives us an uncanny sense of reality being shifted: if your arm goes to sleep and you touch it, it doesn't feel like it belongs to you anymore. Try putting that into words. Stern says: "Sense of self is not a cognitive [idea]. It is an experiential integration."[2] Trying to explain this is like asking a healthy person to explain what it feels like to be healthy. If you had to do so, you'd do it in terms of what you don't feel: nothing hurts or aches, you're not nauseated or exhausted, your mind and body function the way you expect them to, and so on. But the state of being "healthy" is very complex and takes a huge system of organs and other body systems, all running smoothly, in order to have that taken-for-granted sense of being healthy.

The same thing applies psychologically. Think of the difference between standing on your own two legs versus standing on stilts. Legs, as part of your body, don't require that you be aware of standing on them or having them balance and support you or move under you when you need them. Stilts, although they also provide support, require a level of awareness and effort that legs don't—even for an expert stilt walker. Walking on stilts might become relatively automatic, as long as the terrain is smooth. But although even people on their own feet can fall, falling from stilts is more likely to happen, the descent is longer, and it's more difficult to get back up. Being a resilient survivor of early maternal impairment is like walking on stilts.

When a child is raised by a mentally ill mother, we need to understand how the mother's illness can affect her mothering ability, and how her problems interfere with her response to her baby. "Good enough mothering"[3] requires a steady attention and response to an infant, an ability to "read" and understand the baby's signals and to have a sense of what the baby needs. It requires that the mother be able to attune herself emotionally to the baby, to play with her by sharing and amplifying excitement, and to comfort or quiet her down when she becomes overstimulated. It requires that a mother love and enjoy her child. None of us really has that information about our own upbringing firsthand, because we simply weren't able to process or remember it. We have to rely on stories told to us, or on our own sense of emotional resonance. Sometimes a person has to piece it together from emotional reactions to things later in life. These reactions are subtle, hard to put into words, and it seems like we're groping through the fog to get our hands on something firm.

Research confirms what common sense already tells us: that all those thousands of times someone comforted us when we cried (or didn't), all those times we were held (or not) and sung to (or not) and washed and changed and put down to sleep (or not), are all important. We do remember them, but we remember them more by the body/mind sense of what it was like to be there, not because we have memories of specific events. Did Mother smile at us with her eyes, did she enjoy laughing with us, did we bring her pleasure? Or were we a burden, seeing ourselves reflected in her tired, distracted, depressed gaze? Even worse, did she see us as the cause of her unhappiness? Did she treat us as though we were the enemy, out to get her, out to cause her trouble? Did she glare at us, frighten us, hurt us, or just look through us as though we weren't there?

Infant and child psychologist Urie Bronfenbrenner said, "A child needs at least one adult who's irrationally enthusiastic about them."[4] If we think in adult terms about what a child might feel when there isn't that adult, we might suppose the child would feel unloved, disappointed, sad, and misunderstood. But that's pretty advanced language and thinking for a child. The real question here is how does an infant process all this? What's happening in the mind and brain of an infant who has these experiences? Where does the memory go, and what is it like when that memory is evoked?

The first few years of life, the years when we form our "working models"[5] of the world, are years we can't remember. By the time we know what's going on, we're well into the second act of a three-act play, and we have to start figuring things out backward from there. It can take quite a bit of clever detecting to figure out what went on before we were really "there," with the capacity for explicit memory. For people with significant deficits in their very early life, these wordless "working models" push against their rational adult view of the world. That accounts for what I hear so often in my work: "I know it, but I can't feel it." That statement—which I've heard from countless patients who have tried as hard as they could, but come up short in the end—may be the single most potent factor in failed or incomplete therapies. All the knowing in the world won't affect those early feelings, because in "adult" knowing, the brain/mind works very differently from the way a very young child's brain works, and the communication link between the two is often virtually nonexistent.

Sometimes a survivor is able to say, "My family was crazy, but now I'm with people who care about me and won't treat me badly. Now I can let down my guard and enjoy life." If only it were that simple. That kind of reaction is what one writer calls a "high road"[6] response, and it comes from the part of our brain with the best read on current reality. That's the part of my mind that, for example, reminds me that airplanes are extremely safe when the rest of me is clutching the armrests. I can laugh at myself in that situation and recognize that the high road is correct, but the "low road" reactions don't always shut up and go away just because the high road has spoken!

Human beings can't help striving for some consistency and understandability in the world. We can laugh at our irrational reactions to things like airplanes, but sometimes we try to bring all the layers together into a coherent whole. There are times when I'm clutching the armrests in the plane, and the irrational voice has gained dominance, saying to the rational part of me, "Hey—you should be nervous, too. Listen to that weird sound the plane is making. What if this is one of those rare planes that does crash?" In this case I'm trying to get all the parts of me to agree with one another.

The low road has some different operating principles from the high road, and often they're completely out of our awareness. You'll blink your eyes in a split second at a baseball thrown in your face, because part of your brain is wired to respond instantly to danger before you have time to process it rationally. A child who's been hit, especially in the face, will instantly flinch if the abusive parent lifts his or her arm unexpectedly. In fact, an adult who was hit as a child may still flinch if her best friend or loving partner lifts his or her arm unexpectedly at a particular angle. It happens too fast for the high road to get a word in edgewise. That low road has different operating principles, and those principles are etched deeply, saying: "arm lifted at that angle = danger = duck." It's not very nuanced, to say the least. But it's a fast and protective early-warning system. And, no, it doesn't necessarily go away, even if a hundred—or a thousand—lifted arms don't hit, because it doesn't work that way! By the time the high road gets around to saying "There's no danger," it's way too late. The reflexive behavior might be set very early, before language, and the most likely or most frequent behavior pattern is what becomes the working model. Then the neural pathways are laid down, the "danger" signal is set, and off we go. That part of our brain is not logical and calculating, and it doesn't think in terms of past and present. Everything is "now." So if one hundred nonhitting arms are raised, it really doesn't matter much—the signal is set on automatic, and when it's triggered, it goes off.

When these old fears and reactions keep resurfacing in close adult relationships, it can be both frustrating and painful for all concerned. We want to be able to comfort and heal the people we love. If we were dealing with the parts of the brain and mind that develop a little later in childhood, we could expect that changing the circumstances would change a person's feelings. After all, that's the part of the mind that has a sense of past/present/future and can make changes based on new information. When we experience the world as a dangerous place before we have language, our brains wire us to shoot first and ask questions later. If the learning is not encoded in such early layers, though, we can more easily understand with our more logical mind that a new environment is not so dangerous and change our responses accordingly. Severe trauma even in adulthood is stored in the brain much like very early childhood experience, however, and without language, which explains why severe trauma also repeats in the form of flashbacks and doesn't fade away with experience.[7]

Allan N. Schore, renowned researcher on infant neurological development, says, "The question of why the early events of life have such an inordinate influence on literally everything that follows is one of the fundamental problems of psychology."[8] His work, like that of many others, has given us a window into the brain and mind development of infants and very young children, as well as into the very early, moment-to-moment interactions of caregivers and infants. These two realms—brain development and relationship development—are not so separate as we once thought. The brain is not some isolated hunk of gray matter sitting inside a skull, slowly getting itself online as we grow. And our very early relationships are not just pleasant or unpleasant interactions with caregivers. It turns out that brains are primarily social organs, and they develop in some very different ways, depending on the context in which they live. The infant's brain shapes how she responds to the world, and the world in turn shapes some aspects of how her brain is going to develop. It's reciprocal, co-creative. Our infant brains sort out what the world offers, and prepare us for life in this world, by developing some potential capacities and inhibiting others. The brain/mind grows and develops in the world that the infant experiences, and takes that world as the instruction manual for what's to come later. One child's brain/mind might have the kind of experience that prepares her for a world in which it is safe to play and be spontaneous; another child might be prepared for a vastly different world by developing the capacity to keep a low profile, damp down feelings, and avoid eye contact.

The real-life stories that follow in chapters 2 through 7 tell us, in many voices, what happened, how it felt, and how it seems connected to the present. Those stories can be understood in their own right, without knowing any more about how mothers and babies interact and how babies' brains and minds develop in the context of that interaction. In my admittedly biased view, however, the research into these areas is exciting and informative and deepens the understanding of what's really at stake when impaired mothers are raising their children. The reader may choose to move ahead to chapter 2, at this point; reading what follows here is another option, and coming back to this section at some other point is a third option.

THE RESEARCH: BONDS AND BRAINS

The recent research in infant and child development is taking place on two fronts. The first has to do with "bonds"—that is, attachment bonds, the emotional relationship between the infant and her mother. The second has to do with how an infant's brain develops neurologically when the infant is being cared for.

In school you most likely read about the baby monkeys who preferred a warm, fuzzy, cloth "mother" rather than a cold, metal "mother" that provided food from an artificial nipple. Although these baby monkeys all grew up to be very maladjusted adults, the point was made that food, or physical nurturance, isn't the be-all and end-all of a baby's development. Sigmund Freud said that this was a major drive and that babies originally cling to their mothers because the mothers provide milk, but another researcher has center stage in our understanding of child development these days. John Bowlby, a British researcher who started out studying young animals, saw that in addition to being fed by their mothers they also seemed attached or bonded to their mothers, clinging to them, running to them when there was danger, and checking back on their whereabouts when they went off to play and explore; the same, it turns out, is true for human infants.[9] Our survival in the wild depended on this sense of attachment between infant and mother, since neither we nor young monkeys would survive long on our own. Bowlby also observed during World War II that infants raised in war orphanages, even though they were fed and changed on a regular schedule, weakened and sometimes died from the lack of emotional connection with a caregiver. This knowledge has become more prevalent these days; as more people adopt children from foreign orphanages—many of which do not provide a nurturing environment—and there has been a growing recognition of the importance of early caring if an adopted baby is to thrive.

Bowlby is the father of attachment theory, which has been elaborated and brought to new levels of sophistication in the past fifteen to twenty years.[10] People interested in his theory have done very-long-term studies of attachment between children and caregivers, and those studies now add weight to the written theory.

In a twenty-year study conducted at the University of Minnesota's Institute of Child Development, researchers have examined the relationships of hundreds of young children and their primary caregiver, most commonly the mother.[11] They've been able to see four different ways that children relate to their mother in a mild stress situation involving the mother leaving and then returning to her child two times while the child is in a room with toys and, at times, a benign stranger. Some children show distress when their mother leaves, but are able to go back and play with the toys until she comes back, at which time they run to her, greet her happily, and want to show her the toys. These children are securely attached. Some children are very distressed when their mother leaves, can't play with the toys at all, and when she returns, both seek her out and reject her, either by pushing her away as she holds them or by asking to be picked up but not appearing to be soothed or comforted. These children are anxiously attached in a "preoccupied" way—that is, obviously preoccupied with their mother and where she is. A third group of children shows little feeling when their mother leaves, and little, if any, when she returns. All their attention seems to be on the toys, and they seem to be very independent. However, monitors show that their heart rate, blood pressure, and respiration all increase when their mother leaves and returns, so they're not as independent as they might seem. These children are also anxiously attached, but in an "avoidant" way. The fourth response, disorganized attachment, is hard for investigators to observe without becoming pretty uncomfortable. Children who fit this description have odd or contradictory responses to their mother's return after an absence: they might move toward her, crying, then veer off to one side and avoid her. Or they might approach her and then just sit down, staring straight ahead.

More investigation and lengthy interviews and home studies show us the connection that's already intuitively obvious. Mothers of securely attached children were tuned in to their children, comforting in times of stress, pretty predictable, and caring. They provided what Bowlby called a "secure base."

Mothers of the preoccupied and anxiously attached kids tended to be inconsistent—sometimes caring and comforting, and sometimes rejecting and unavailable. The child's insecure attachment showed that he wasn't sure if or when Mom was coming back and whether he could confidently expect to be comforted when she did. The preoccupied kids worried about where their mother was and when she would come back, but for the securely attached child, Mom seemed like a secure base of operations: She could be counted on to come back and to be interested and available when she did. That made it okay to go off and play with interesting toys, to explore what was out there.

The mothers of the insecure/avoidant children were generally rejecting of their kids' need for reassurance or comforting, and the kids clearly felt there wasn't much point in going to them after they'd been gone. Most of their attention was on the toys, although the monitors tell a story of more anxiety than meets the eye. The monitors say that even if the child acts independent, the attachment needs are still in operation. It's still stressful when Mom leaves and when she returns, but the child has learned that it's not safe to go to her for comfort or reassurance. These are mothers who also tend to use abandonment as a threat to control their children's behavior; consequently, these kids expect to be rebuffed and to have to cope on their own.

The mothers of kids with disorganized attachment seemed to be mentally disorganized themselves. They had a hard time attending appropriately to the children, either neglecting them or paying too close attention in an out-of-sync way. Some of these mothers frightened their child, either on purpose or inadvertently. When the source of comfort and safety is also the source of danger and threat, a child is in a bind with no real escape. So these children act in strange and contradictory ways, directly mapped onto their mothers' strange and contradictory ways. Obviously if a mother were psychotic or delusional, her behavior could be very frightening to a child. The mother wouldn't even be able to recognize that the child was there or that she was having an impact. Even worse, she might have the delusion that the child was her enemy, or the devil, and might act accordingly.

What's rather remarkable is how enduring these attachment patterns can be. At age six, a child with an anxious/preoccupied attachment style shows some insecurity at home and at school, seems fearful, may want closeness but show hostility at the same time, or may try to be cute or charming in a way that seems artificial. The six-year-old with the anxious/avoidant style continues to keep his distance, doesn't seem to be very talkative, and keeps busy with toys or activities, seldom seeking out the mother. A six-year-old with disorganized attachment tends to try to control the mother, either in a mock-parental way, by bossing her around, or in a solicitous and protective way, as though she's the parent and the mother is the child. A securely attached child at six seems pretty relaxed and friendly, talks freely with her mother, goes to her for comfort or help, and also has fun playing and exploring without much anxiety.

As we'll see in some of the stories later on, a common theme is the mother's unavailability for comfort or help, at least on a consistent basis. Bowlby says that insecurely attached children "no longer express to their mothers one of the deepest emotions or the equally deep-seated desire for comfort and reassurance that accompanies it ... because a child's self-model is profoundly influenced by how his mother sees and treats him, whatever she fails to recognize in him he is likely to fail to recognize in himself."[12]

Research also shows that young children of mothers with psychotic disorders are more likely to have insecure attachments by the time they're two, and that in adulthood, more than half of the children of a mentally ill parent have either a mood disorder or a substance abuse problem.[13] This same research shows that a child of the same gender as the mentally ill parent is at much greater risk of psychological problems, and that boys are more likely to develop conduct disorders, while girls develop more internally focused problems. In a study using the "still face experiment," infants of normal mothers became distressed and cried if their mothers, in the middle of playing with them, suddenly became expressionless, but children of depressed mothers didn't show any particular reaction.[14] They were evidently already accustomed to "losing" their mothers in this way.

How do these attachment styles play out in adulthood?[15] First, it is possible to change, to make a more secure attachment in adulthood than one had as a child, and therapy often plays a role in that change. It also can happen that having a very secure "other" adult during adolescence or early adulthood can help an insecure person develop a more secure attachment style. Secure adults find it comfortable to be close to others, to be interdependent, and they don't worry about being abandoned or being too close. Anxious/preoccupied adults tend to want to be too close, and worry a lot about their relationships and about being left out or left behind. They sometimes scare other people away, since they appear needy or dependent. Anxious/avoidant adults don't like to get too close in their relationships and don't like to depend on others. They like a fair amount of distance from others and can easily spend time alone.

These new findings in attachment research mesh with a new field, virtually invented by Daniel J. Siegel, called interpersonal neurobiology.[16] Siegel's been interested in how the infant's and child's brain develops in the context of the ongoing mother-child relationship. Remember the debate about nature versus nurture? It turns out to be nature and nurture, of course, and it seems now that the nature-nurture relationship is far more complex than we imagined. "It is not a matter of nature versus nurture, but rather it is that nature needs nurture. Experiences shape the brain connections that create the mind and enable an emerging sense of a 'self' in the world."[17]

The brain as a whole grows and develops after birth, but different parts of the brain develop at different speeds and come "online" at different stages. (We know something about this from infant research showing prime periods for development of musical ability, mathematical ability, and so on.) A crucial discovery, in this age of the brain, is that the brain is profoundly social, not just an isolated organ running our lives from command central. An infant is born with a brain that is already working a mile a minute but still has enormous potential that will unfold at an amazing rate for the first few years of life. In order for this potential to be realized, the infant must be immersed in an attachment relationship with a primary caregiver, most often the mother.

Although there are many duplications of function in the two sides of the brain, and this isn't an absolute black-and-white division, it's an important one. The right side of the brain is dominant during the first two to three years of life. During this time it develops rapidly, sprouting neurons and connections and generally lighting up like a Christmas tree when Baby is playing with the mobile over the crib or listening to Mozart tapes, but especially—most spectacularly—when playing with Mom. The right brain is impressionistic and visual; it makes holistic images. It's the part of the brain that registers tone of voice, gestures, and facial expressions. It's the part that picks up on feelings and is responsible for the "feel" of things, for the "sense" of self and others, and for subconscious processing of social and emotional cues from the environment. The right brain doesn't experience things with words and doesn't have any sense of past/present/future; what happens is a total experience, body and mind, and it's all happening right now. The right brain soaks in the whole feeling of the world around it, and its first learning environment is in the communicative environment between the baby and the mother. It's as though the mother and infant were in their own bubble, creating a communicative web of connection. The baby comes programmed to take in the world, make intuitive sense of it, in a whole body/mind kind of way. Just as every baby comes into the world without language but with the potential for language, every baby comes into the world without an imprint of the world but with the potential for that imprint. Any language is possible for any baby, but the language a particular baby learns depends on the language in which her mother speaks to her. The brain with infinite potential forms its linguistic ability around the language it hears. The same thing is true with a "feel" for the emotional world. The brain is poised to develop in an infinite number of ways, and the way it will develop—its particular personal shape, so to speak—will come about in the relationship with the mother. This will become the dominant and preferred mode of operating, just as the original language learned will be the dominant and preferred language spoken, even when other languages may also be known and spoken. Researchers looking at heart rhythms and other physiological measures see that the mother and baby are in sync on all kinds of levels. Their two brains are resonating with each other, as the more mature mother's brain both responds to and leads the child's brain, literally teaching it how to work properly, how to connect with another person, how to disengage gently, how to reengage.

The rich growth medium of the mother-child interaction is where we can see how children take in the world, make sense of it, and respond to it according to that understanding. This happens from the day of birth, if not before. The whole sense of the world, the feel of it, begins to generate the growth of neurons in the brain, with all the connections and synapses and neural networks. When an experience happens repeatedly and predictably, the neural anatomy reflects that this is a strong experience, and those connections grow stronger, whereas other competing possible connections don't get made. At a certain point, when the tremendous growth spurt slows, the brain actually gets rid of some of the unused neural possibilities, so that the brain is now primed to see, hear, feel, and know the things it is accustomed to and has somewhat less capacity to respond to new experiences.

Schore calls this the "coherent, continuous, and unified implicit sense of self."[18] Our sense of self needs to have some coherent shape or contour, and it needs to be continuous, not fragmented. "The implicit self is the key to a deeper understanding of personality and the problems of normal and abnormal behavior."[19] The implicit self is the self built up from billions of moments of living and being and interacting, moving, seeing, hearing, feeling, sensing, initiating, responding, and so forth. This is all before we have real "event" memory, and have only this kind of holistic body/mind memory.

What Schore is saying, of course, is just what my patients were complaining about earlier in this chapter: that the deepest and most troublesome feelings they have seem to come from a much earlier time, leaving a stain that seems impossible to eradicate.

Another important job for the right brain is to run the autonomic nervous system (as opposed to the central nervous system, which governs muscles and nerves). The autonomic nervous system governs what is generally called arousal, and it has two parts: one steps on the gas pedal (intensifies and speeds us up), whereas the other hits the brakes (decreases intensity and slows us down). Infants are born with only very gross ability to work the gas and the brakes, as we can see when a baby gets so excited it turns red and starts screaming or crying. But each infant has an inborn preferred range of arousal, below which it feels bored or lethargic, and above which it feel overstimulated and uncomfortable. One of the main jobs the brain has to learn in the first few years is how to keep things in the comfortable range—how to jazz things up when too low and calm them down when too excited.

Self-regulation and how it is learned is the focus of uncounted volumes of research. Some researchers say that problems in self-regulation are at the heart of all emotional difficulties, and though that may be going too far, it's certainly a major issue in most emotional problems. The very term "emotional problem" states that there is a problem with the emotion—the feeling and expression of affect. The job of our psychological defenses such as denial, rationalization, and so forth is to defend us against the too-intense emotion that would be aroused without the defense. So when we learn that emotional regulation is learned pre-verbally and in the context of the mother-infant relationship, it becomes apparent how dependent we are on what we "learn" in these early years and specifically what we learn from our mothers. And if Mother is dysregulated in a major way herself and has trouble modulating her own emotions, this certainly spells trouble for the developing infant—and all before there is any objective memory or language to capture what the trouble is. Again, keep in mind this is all visceral, whole-body experience, without the ability to filter anything out.

It's obvious that infants shouldn't be left in very uncomfortable emotional states for long periods of time, and not just because that can become a painful memory. If pain or intense distress continues for long without comfort or soothing or repair, it overwhelms the infant's limited capacity to cope. What the infant is "learning" is that negative states are intolerable and overwhelming and must be defended against. Negative states will always occur, but the infant brain needs to learn from a comforting mother that distress can be followed by soothing. Being able to tolerate a moderate amount of anxiety, distress, and discomfort is a hallmark of mental health, and this is where we learn it: in early infancy, before we even know what's happening.

Under high stress the baby's brain starts to overproduce cortisol, which actually begins to kill brain cells. This is an emergency response to what the organism reads as an emergency. For infants who are left in this state for long periods of time, their brains are always on "red alert"—with all systems on high activation. And a situation that makes a well-cared-for child feel uncomfortable might make a neglected child respond as to a crisis, an emergency, calling for the most high-level defensive actions. The actual neural pathways that lead to comfort and

deescalation, an emergency stand-down, are not present in the brain of
these infants, so once red alert gets activated, it perpetuates itself.
When such infants become young children or adolescents (assuming
nothing happens to improve the situation), it's easy to see that they
overreact to any stress and are constantly in a state of crisis, or chronic
numbness, which is the brain's other response to overwhelming stress.
But by the time these children are adolescents, telling them that they
are overreacting isn't going to do much good. It's too little, too late.
They might be able to understand intellectually that their response is
out of proportion, but there's no place to go with that awareness. Imagine hearing a fire alarm blaring in your ears from five feet away and
how you might react to someone who calmly says, "There's nothing to
worry about." It's hard to discount what every nerve in your body is
telling you, even if it's incorrect. Again, there's that dilemma—you
may know there's not an emergency, but your feelings say that there is.

It seems that, as developing infants, we need a pretty high proportion of good stuff to bad. Negative states are inevitable and normal,
but if they outweigh the positive states, there's going to be trouble
ahead. Putting together "bonds" and "brains," it seems that we need a
secure attachment, with plenty of positive feelings, comfort, and stability, in order for our brains and minds to develop as they should. So
this is not just about having a nice childhood with pleasant memories
or the opposite, it's literally about how well the brain develops and
what working models, or templates, the infant brain is constructing in
the midst of all these experiences.

Certain parts of the right brain are where we experience fear. When
these parts get set off, there's a full-body response that's experienced
physically as "overwhelming, irrational, uncontrollable fear."[20] This is
the home of the "low road" reaction. Infants need their mothers to
comfort and soothe them when they have this reaction, since they don't
yet have the capacity to evaluate what's out there. This fear response is
crucial to an infant's survival, since it signals to the mother that something's wrong, and signals loudly, like a fire alarm. This part of the
brain cannot calm itself down any more than a fire alarm can shut
itself off. The mother's job is to do the evaluation and provide comfort
or protection, whichever is needed. Ideally, the young brain learns
from the mother how to turn the alarm off, how to evaluate the situation, and how to calm down. If the mother cannot provide this external
help, however, the infant brain is left to its own devices: go on permanent red alert or just shut down. Either response seriously compromises the child's development.

At about age two and a half or three, the left brain begins to catch
up to the right brain. The left brain has to do with language and logic
and time. It reasons, figures things out logically, compares things, and

decides things based on thinking. If there's too much of this left-brain action, things might seem two-dimensional and dry; too much of the right brain, and we're awash in impressions and senses and feelings, all in the "now." (To keep track of which side does what, I think of the right brain as rivers of rich irrationality, and left brain as logical linear language.) And of course, our brain is designed to be used all together, in an integrated way: words and music, color and form, present and past, logic and impulse. Siegel thinks of the right brain as providing the music, and the left brain as bringing the words.[21] Together, they form a whole that is greater than the sum of the parts.

In the following vignettes, researchers can process these films on a second-by-second basis and run analyses that tell them exactly what's happening between a mother and infant. But if we simply look in for a few moments, the whole of the experience is easy to grasp. Here's one mother and her baby.[22]

This mother and her baby are smiling at each other, and Baby is becoming excited and wiggling around, while Mom encourages her with her tone of voice and "mom talk" in a high-pitched voice that rises and falls. They laugh together, and the excitement is high, especially for the baby, although the mother clearly enjoys her baby's exhilaration. Then, at some point, the baby peaks and turns her eyes or her head away, and Mom relaxes and calms down, too. They are quiet for a few moments, the baby gazing away into space, the mother gazing fondly at her child.

Then Baby reengages, first with her eyes, ready for another round, and Mom joins with her at just that moment, and they follow the same pattern as before: engagement, being in sync, revving up, then disengaging and quieting down. This is Mom attuned to her baby, Mom in sync. Baby is learning that she can initiate her action from inside her own body, that Mother will join and follow in a way that matches Baby's own feelings, and that Mother will slow down and rest when Baby needs to step on the brakes a bit. The baby is feeling her own internal rhythm and seems to feel in charge without feeling alone. The mother seems content to follow Baby's lead and keep her company in an encouraging way, and to enjoy the game. Her whole gaze and posture and voice convey her delight in her baby. Notice the ebb and flow of activity and connection, and notice, too, that although they are in sync, their movements will not happen at exactly the same instant. There will be a little lag, possibly a little jerkiness, to their connecting. Perfect synchronization isn't the ideal here, but being in sync and able to move through the out-of-sync moment is just fine.

Contrast this with another mom and baby who also start out by laughing and giggling. This mother, too, encourages baby with her tone of voice and high-pitched mom talk and clearly enjoys the baby's excitement. Then Baby calms down and averts her eyes or head, the universal baby signal of disconnection, saying, "I need to regroup." But this mom moves around so she's looking directly into Baby's eyes, and with a pressured high voice, keeps up the patter and encouragement. Baby turns her head to the other side, looking away from Mom and turning a little pink. Mom leans over again, catching Baby's gaze on the other side, and again going full force with her voice and her urging to smile and laugh. Baby turns away a third time and now starts to whimper and move around in a way that signals some discomfort. As Mom follows her yet again, Baby starts to cry, turns red, squeezes her eyes shut, and is obviously in mild distress. Mom finally calms down, picks Baby up, and, using a calm voice, pats her back until Baby calms down. (The researchers report anecdotally that when research students observed this interaction behind a one-way mirror, several of them became so uncomfortable that they had to leave the observation room.)

What is this baby learning? Because these out-of-sync, unattuned interactions will happen thousands, if not millions, of times during this baby's early years, and because they suggest that Mom will be poorly attuned in other ways, this baby may learn, by age three or four, not to show excitement or make much eye contact, and to disconnect when the arousal level begins to increase even a little bit. Her mother might say, at that point, that her daughter is shy, but this wouldn't be correct. This may be a child who's learned to damp down her own intensity. She may be cautious about letting others connect with her, because her early implicit experience—of which she will have no memory—is that other people will somehow push her to an intensity level that's uncomfortable. Connecting with and making eye contact with her mother "feels" to her a little chaotic, a little uncomfortable, and she doesn't have an internal sense of confidence that other people can be in sync with her. She may have to protect herself, not rely on others to calm down with her as well as share excitement with her. (There can be many mitigating factors—other important figures who are more attuned to the child, for example—but for these purposes we're just drawing the line out straight, as it might happen if Mother were the only attachment figure.)

As an adult, this person won't be able to explain why her affect is rather flat or why she has trouble connecting. Her mother, if she doesn't change in the meantime, will no doubt be out of sync in other ways, perhaps a little driving, a little controlling, a little emotionally invasive. And if this grown-up child sees her mother interacting with other children, she may be able to put two and two together. But there will be no memory. There will just be her necessary reaction to her early world, laid down as a template for what's to come. If she were talking to a therapist, she might say she has "trouble trusting people" or that she just doesn't feel "connected" the way other people seem to, but it's obvious that talking about trust and connection on an adult level isn't going to help very much, if at all. Her experiences are too early and too much part of the emotional wallpaper to be grasped in this way. The adult patient might learn to stand up to her mother, or not let her intrude so much, but all of that adult behavior change still won't touch that early experience.

It may be too simplistic to draw this straight line, saying, "If your mother did thus and such when you are six months old, you will end up with this kind of problem when you're twenty-five." In fact, that kind of reasoning is some of what gives psychology a bad name. But in defense of this simplicity, consider the effect of a million interactions with one person, when the vast majority of those interactions have the same emotional tone, intensity, rhythm, and feel to them. There's really no doubt that this furrows into your mind, much like years of rain running a course through sand and dirt will wear a deep furrow in the soil. Many things can change what happens, of course, and especially for resilient people, many things do change. There are other caregivers besides the primary one, other experiences, other people—a multitude of things that modify and change the direction of what happens between a mother and her child over the course of time. If the mother has periods of time free from her own distress, this helps a lot. During those good times, other capacities of the mind can and do develop, given half a chance. It seems that, up to a point, our brain and mind are eager to make the best of everything and take advantage of every opportunity, no matter how small, to find some good caretaking that can ameliorate the impact of impaired parenting. But this may only mitigate, not erase, the tenacious grip of early maternal impairment.

What makes the new research compelling is that it resonates with what I see in my office. It makes intuitive sense to me and to many of my clients. It doesn't seem theoretical or far-fetched, and it seems to fill in missing pieces of the puzzle. The very early years of childhood, so often lost in the fog that we can only guess what might have happened, seem to become more visible, clearer. My guesses about "what might have happened" are clearer to me and make more sense to me and to my clients. At the very least, it gives us a different lens through which to look at how people come to be in pain, and what we might do to help.

Chapter 2

Early Childhood

I would have to say that the biggest effect of my growing up like I did was that I've spent my whole life wondering—is it really me? Am I really the bad one? Am I so bad she had to treat me that way? Is that why I get depressed and angry—I'm just no good? I can eventually pull myself out of that, but it's still there.

—Juliana, successful art director, married, two children

Young children ask questions with their whole being, and take in the answers with their whole being. For the first few years, before they have words, they absorb the "is"-ness of their own particular world. An impaired mother may be having trouble with her moods—she may be depressed, or her moods may fluctuate from one extreme to the other. Her connection to reality may be frayed, or, in the extreme, nonexistent, or she may be unable to see her child as a separate person. A self-centered mother may have trouble recognizing that a child has needs that are unique to him, but a psychotic mother may be unable to see the child as psychically or physically separate. One mother of a patient of mine said to her (when my patient was five years old): "I cut my finger while I was cutting up the carrot—you must have been having evil thoughts about me." Seriously impaired parents are usually so preoccupied with their own thoughts and feelings, or their own delusions, that they cannot tune in to the child or respond in an attuned way to the child's emotional or physical needs. As we've seen, the child needs someone to be in sync with her, to match and join her in her ups and downs of excitement and rest, to help her comprehend her own body and mind, as well as the external world of reality. An impaired parent is very unlikely to be able to do this at all consistently, although some try.

But these are not things a child can remember when she grows up. It's all stored as implicit memory, templates of "how the world is." These templates are formed, laid down neurologically, then become the lived-in foundation of everything else built upon them. The templates are like a pair of glasses, but permanently affixed to the child's vision of the world. Whatever distortion there is is built into the lenses, and the child does not see it—she sees the world through it, shaped by it, altered by it. It's the way the world is.

Because we don't have "regular" memories—explicit memories—of things until around age two and a half or three, we don't remember how we were treated, how our parents were, what Mother was like, or what happened to us. We may have vague ideas, but more likely we have what I call resonances of things in the present. We may react to something that doesn't seem to belong to present reality. Or, as in some of these examples, we find out something as adults that seems to make pieces of an internal puzzle fall into place.

Eleanor: My mother told me that when I was an infant, she thought it was important that I have a lot of freedom. She didn't want to control me the way she thought her mother had controlled her. This was one period when she was very paranoid, I found out years later. So when I cried or moved around in the crib, she didn't pick me up or hold me, because that would have seemed like control to her. So she thought she was giving me good care. My core experience of being in the world is of being alone. There's no one there. It's pre-verbal, and I struggled for years even to articulate it. When she told me that, I could feel the click in my brain like the tumblers in a lock when you have the right key.

Juliana: I was in my thirties when I found out that my mother had left for some period of time when I was quite young. I thought it was maybe even as long as a couple of months, which would be an eternity to a baby. But a few years after I found this out, my father let it drop accidentally that she had run off with some guy in our apartment building and hadn't come home for two years. When he told me that, it was like someone kicked me. I have this very intense fear of being abandoned, of being left, even though I'm very self-reliant. As soon as my father said that, I had this panic in my body that felt exactly like how I feel when my husband goes on a long business trip.

Pat: The first time I was in therapy, in my thirties, I described my childhood as "there was no center to my house." There was no center to the home. She looked at me and said, "You should have been the center." In my family, my mother's depression and pain, and the fights between my parents, were the central things. Everything revolved around those things. Somehow that all made sense in a way, because I always feel peripheral to things, to people, to organizations I've worked for. I always feel I'm over here on the side, not really important. It's not that the child has to be the star, but it was more like the center was hollow, there was no one there.

Another way to fill in the missing pieces is hearing stories when we get older, or asking questions. This can be a tricky proposition, because the stories can change over time, as Juliana's did. Some seem pretty factual, though, and make our story more coherent. Being able to make sense of our own life story is extremely important and is a process that often goes on for a lifetime—for some of us, anyway.

Eleanor: I know from what I learned later that she was psychotic for a while after I was born and used to go downtown in a nightgown and robe, or dressed strangely in some other way, and the police would pick her up and call my father at work, and he would tell them to take her home. He was a doctor, so I guess they thought they should do what he told them. She told me once that she remembered hallucinating during that period of time. When I was three or four, my older brother would walk me over to the neighbor's house in the morning to have breakfast and get dressed, because evidently she couldn't manage it. I don't remember any of this.

Cecily: I don't remember any specific incident early on. I think she was ill for a long time, and then she had shock treatments, and then she was well for a long time, like maybe eight years. I think during that period they had me, and then she became ill shortly thereafter, so I don't really remember. It was just a part of life.

June: My older sister remembers my parents "playing house"—my mother making dinner and serving it on a plate at a table, and my father going off to work in the morning in a car and coming home at night. And they lived in a condo, and they had a car. She was pissed, because she remembered having parents, and then they were gone. She lost more than me and my middle sister did in that way.

Alice: When I was in the hospital it came out that she used to pinch me to wake me up, because she wanted to feed me when I wanted to sleep. So even the most basic things, like being able to sleep when you're tired, or not eat if you're not hungry, those things didn't belong to me— they belonged to her. For years I didn't pay attention or even notice when I was hungry or tired; it just didn't register. I had to learn how to notice those things.

The author of *My Mother's Keeper*, Tara Elgin Holley, found out in her early twenties that her grandparents had received a telegram from a psychiatrist in New York City saying, "Your daughter [Holley's schizophrenic mother] is acute paranoid schizophrenic. Needs hospitalization."[1] By then she had had Tara, who was a few months old. The reports said her mother was hearing voices, seeing the angel of death, and believed that the FBI, police, and spies were constantly following her and watching her. Holley's grandparents, who were Christian Scientists, refused to accept this. They insisted that all illness was an illusion. Holley says she realized as an adult that her mother was afraid of hurting her and so allowed others to take care of her for many years, on and off. She also found out that her mother made many suicide attempts, and that when on medication she was barely able to function and always ended up throwing it away. Holley also knows that, in the care of her grandparents, she wasn't toilet trained by the age of five and that her life was very chaotic. "I learned, probably very early, that the mommy for whom I yearned might be there for me, and then again she might not. A sad mother, preoccupied and distant, might take her place.... It would be difficult to make up a word with a more jagged edge to it [than] schizophrenia."[2]

Laura Love, author of *You Ain't Got No Easter Clothes*, whose mother was schizophrenic, found her absent father when she was in her twenties. She and her sisters had been raised alone by their chronically psychotic and suicidal mother. She knew nothing about her early years, other than what she could piece together on her own. When she finally was able to talk to her missing father, he explained that her mother, "during one of her breakdowns, had cut up or burned every picture of us as infants for some reason known only to her. I realized ... how odd it had been that she had never shared favorite baby stories with us as mothers often do, and that she seemed to have no fond memories whatsoever of anything we had ever done as small children."[3]

Sometimes the adults in a family deliberately choose to withhold information from the children. However, they may also simply be trying to forget or minimize painful realities that they themselves have trouble facing. Holley came to realize that her schizophrenic mother's family was deeply ashamed of her mother, and they conveyed to Holley that she shouldn't ask questions about her mother. This active avoidance paradoxically coexisted with their covert anxiety about any of Holley's behavior that seemed to be an early sign of the illness her mother developed.

Holley, living with her aunt, was occasionally punished, but only years later was she able to figure out why her aunt had once beaten her severely, and with anger. Her aunt had thought Tara had looked at a "dirty" magazine and blamed her mother's mental illness on her being too sexy and too interested in men. Holley felt her aunt was trying to beat the badness out of her, the same kind of badness that had made her mother sick.

Other adults sometimes tried to protect children from knowing of their mothers' illnesses. There's plenty of room for argument about when and how to tell a child about serious problems within the family.

Jerri: I was maybe four years old. All I can remember is that I had taken a bath, and when I was done, I was in my pajamas. It had to be colder out because my dad bundled me up in my overcoat and a hat, and he handed me to my aunt. My aunt took me to her car, and I stayed overnight at her house. That was very unusual. I really didn't know what was going on. I didn't ask any questions. Then, all of a sudden I realized my mom had disappeared. Of course, when I was older I realized she had gone to the hospital, but I didn't know that for a long time. I stayed with my aunt overnight, then my dad took me home. It just seemed to me like she disappeared for a few weeks. She was at a private hospital. Much later on, my dad told me she had a nervous breakdown.

I don't remember her acting in bizarre ways. I think I heard her crying at times at night. I guess there were definitely strange things going on, but I didn't see anything and I wasn't told anything. I know she had a series of five nervous breakdowns between that time, when I was about four, and when I was ten. Once I asked my dad, "What's wrong with Mommy?" I remember my dad said to me that she had problems sleeping. That's all he said to me.

SOMETHING'S WRONG WITH MOM

In all my interviews, I began with the question "What's the first time you remember thinking or knowing that something was wrong with your mother?" For a few women, there was a clear memory, something that stood out as strange or different or "wrong."

Eleanor: The first time I knew something was wrong, or different, was when I was in first grade. My teacher told me the principal wanted to see me, and he told me my mother wanted me to come home. I walked home—a couple of blocks—as I usually did. When I came in the door she was waiting for me with a strange expression on her face, and I remember sensing something was not right. She took me in my room and told me I left a sock on the floor and asked me what it meant. It seemed sinister, although I didn't know the word at that time. I said something like "I forgot to pick it up," but that wasn't good enough. She had this really suspicious look on her face, and she just seemed weird. She acted like I was lying or trying to trick her somehow. I remember walking back to school thinking, "Something's wrong with Mama, but nobody should know." It just seemed like it was secret, and I didn't want to think about it anymore.

Pat: It's one of my first memories of my mother. I was five, and I had gone to morning kindergarten and then come home and taken a nap. My mother was out in the yard doing laundry, and I came down and told her that I napped. She said I must be lying, and then she told me that she was more sensitive than other mothers and that these things really hurt her. There was this sense that what I did could make her ill somehow, that she was fragile and I could hurt her, and that I was supposed to take care of her, not the other way around.

June: When I was about four I noticed her not remembering me, responding to me as though she didn't know who I was. Sometimes she would play with me like a playmate. I might not have known it was wrong, but I had a feeling it was different—it was different from my father. There were times she was very loving, very motherly. She would read to me, stuff like that. Other days I just wouldn't be there, as far as she was concerned—she would just be sitting there smoking and looking at her nails. Didn't even notice me or pay the slightest attention to me. Like she didn't see me or I wasn't even there.

WHAT'S REAL?

Part of a child's development includes learning how to connect her own internal sensations, thoughts, and feelings with external reality. Children need to hear, thousands of times, "That's right, that's a dog" or "Ouch, that stove is hot" or any number of verbal statements that connect what the child is seeing, hearing, and perceiving with a trusted adult's picture of reality. When adults distort reality significantly for their own reasons, it is not just contradictory, as it might be for another adult. Being told that something is true when their own ears and eyes say otherwise is quite confusing for children, and if it happens often, and about major things, it's profoundly disturbing. It disrupts their ability to understand themselves in the world that they perceive around them.

When episodes of cruelty or abuse are disavowed by the mother, this becomes a problem in itself. Even an angry mother who occasionally slaps a child in fury, for example, could not be seen as "disturbed" if she's able to come back later and reflect on the experience by herself or with her child. "Reflection" ideally might be a conversation between the mother and child about what happened and why, and an ability to make up and repair the problem. But reflection could also just be, "If you act up that way again, you're going to get smacked." This isn't ideal, obviously, but it does acknowledge that the behavior happened, that the parent was the author of it, and that she had an understandable reason to do it. This is a hallmark of integration: the ability to reflect later on one's feelings and behavior, even when they're less than exemplary. When a mother is able to talk to a child about how angry she got—and why—then she isn't disavowing the experience and is not asking the child to do so, either. Even furious behavior is part of "who mother is" and is acknowledged by the mother to be part of her.

This doesn't mean that being able to reflect in this way makes the action okay. Parents can be abusive, cruel, or otherwise very damaging to a child in a way that is clear to the child, and this doesn't mitigate the damage from this abuse—but adding disavowal adds a different twist.

John Bowlby wrote movingly about disavowal, describing it as what happens when a parent says either that something the child saw or heard didn't happen or that the parent wasn't the one who acted, or gives a bizarre reason for what happened.[4] When a mother acts as though her behavior never happened or that she is incapable of such behavior, then if the child wants to stay connected to mother—which is a biological imperative up to a certain age—the child has to agree with her, and therefore deny her own reality and her own perception. This is not to say that such denial of reality doesn't happen normally from time to time. "No, Aunt Agnes didn't pass gas. It must have been the dog," happens in all families, as well as, "I just had my eyes closed. I wasn't sleeping," or "I didn't run that red light, and don't you go telling your mother that I did."

When the disavowal is frequent and persistent, though, rather than occasional, it raises havoc with early development. At the time when internal templates should be integrating and becoming more complex, they become fragmented and contradictory. What we would be aiming for, once infancy has become early toddlerhood, is a view that "Mother" is a person with many moods and ways of being, that they are all "Mother," and that most of the time she is safe and protective and supportive, even though she is also capable of being angry, distracted, rejecting, mean, and neglectful. But when a mother disowns her own experience and behavior, the child learns to disown her own experience as well, to match the mother's states of mind in order to track her, stay close to her, and anticipate danger. Children who learn to do this tend to see other people as potentially extremely changeable, and perhaps to experience themselves in the same way. Developmentally we want to continue making a lot of little islands of different experience into one continent, so that moving from one experience or mood or feeling to another feels smooth and natural, not as though we're jumping from one disconnected place to another. But if the mother is jumping from one place to another, and not acknowledging that they are connected in the sense that they all belong to her, then the child learns to do the same thing. For the child to be able to be with or rely on the parent, she has to stay alert to these abrupt changes and has to be able to make a parallel switch instantaneously.

Bowlby stresses how difficult it is to convey the power of this disconfirmation, because it goes way beyond and is fundamentally different from having a difference of opinion, or even from being told someone else is right and you are wrong about something. Children can hear plenty of this and still hold onto an unspoken sense that they can trust their own eyes and ears. When a mother is psychotic, however, and she is the primary attachment figure, a distrust of one's own ability to see and hear and feel reality can be deeply woven into the development of one's very personality and one's own memories, both implicit and explicit.

> **Eleanor:** I spent years as a kid trying to figure out what was real. My mother was suspicious and always looking for hidden "clues," even when she wasn't psychotic. My father was a respected scientist with an important job where lots of people listened to him, and he was extremely logical. But my mother, despite being paranoid, or maybe because of it, was very intuitive about emotional things. She was tuned in to the emotional undercurrents of any situation, and I could feel that she was often picking up the very same things I was picking up on.
>
> On the other hand, my father had a way of making things simple and obvious and on the surface. Just follow certain logical steps and the world will be something you totally understand and manage.
>
> So I went back and forth between them, all the time. They were both right. Neither one was right. They were alternately right and wrong. And they absolutely never agreed, and never said that a person could blend their two viewpoints and get a three-dimensional view. It was an underground war.
>
> Either you were a smart, logical person who could figure things out like my father—and from that point of view my mother was a crazy person who saw shadows lurking everywhere and was always suspicious for no reason—or, if you saw it from her perspective, my father was this simple-minded, overly logical person with no emotional "sense," who could only see the obvious, while she was able to figure out the real story of what was going on underground. Even explaining it makes my head spin!
>
> **June:** I came in from school one afternoon and saw my mother lying on the floor. I asked her what she was doing on the floor and she said, "Who the hell are you, and how did you get into my house?" Then she got up and said she hadn't been on the floor, and what was I talking about? But I had seen her lying on the floor. That just made me feel like my brain was turning inside out. I saw her on the floor, and she says she wasn't on the floor. What am I supposed to do with that?

The movie *Gaslight* is based on exactly this kind of confusion about reality. In this movie from 1944, a husband systematically tries to disrupt his wife's trust in her own senses and perception of reality. (The title comes from his turning down the gas lights in their apartment and, when his wife comments on the dimness of the lights, claiming that there is no difference and implying that something's wrong with her memory and perception.) Eventually, she begins to go crazy. Imagine when the person being "gaslighted" is a child, trying to build a basic sense of what's real and what isn't.

One thread running through the interviews was the daughters' need to hear me confirm that what they were saying was indeed strange and frightening and not the usual childhood experience. I was surprised by this at first, since these women were not patients of mine and almost all had had a lot of therapy. They certainly weren't grappling with this stuff for the first time. But even in telling some of these very bizarre stories, it's as though they still needed some reality testing. I thought the answer was obvious when they asked, "This really was crazy—right?" but recognized that they needed to hear it confirmed again, decades later. This is the power of early disconfirmation of consensual reality.

A less destructive but still disconfirming kind of interaction is when a parent simply refuses to listen to a child or reflexively says the child is lying. When it turns out the child is in fact pointing out something important, there's no repair, no one going back to say, "I'm sorry I said you were lying. You were actually right." In fact, sometimes the situation goes from bad to worse, and the child is blamed for the situation she is trying to report.

> **Rachel:** I looked out the back door, and there was a barn right on the side of our house that was on fire. I kept saying, "Mom, there's a fire, Mom, there's a fire." She just said, "Stop lying." I had never lied in my life. Finally she listened to me and looked over and saw it herself and called the fire department. She ran us outside, and my father went back in to get us blankets, and she was screaming the whole time, thinking our house was going to catch fire and my dad was going to burn to death. I was four years old and trying to calm my mother down, while I'm scared to death about my father and listening to her screaming about the horrible things that could happen to him in the fire. I just kept talking to her to calm her down.

AM I BAD?

Juliana's mother was not psychotic, was never hospitalized, and was never even seen as mentally ill. Yet her behavior was so systematically and deliberately destructive that her daughter's story belongs here. Almost everything Juliana said about her mother pointed to what's called malignant narcissism—a severe personality disorder characterized by an inability to empathize with others, a need for excessive admiration and attention from others, and a sadistic streak. Juliana's mother went out of her way to undermine her daughter's sense of herself and systematically humiliated, demeaned, and physically abused her daughter.

In talking to Juliana about her early years, she recalled the years when she felt her experience was "just the way it was," as children tend to see the small world in which they live.

> **Juliana:** By the time I went to elementary school I was already like two different kids. One was the kid who could go down the hallway and

function and smile and all that, and inside I was this whole other kid who felt worthless and like a piece of shit. And it got proved over and over again that I shouldn't ever tell people what the real reality of my life was. I always felt humiliated and awful. I didn't know there was any other way to feel. I was blown away when I got a little older and saw other kids with their mothers and saw that the mothers were nice, and affectionate, and didn't yell and hit their kids all the time. The mothers actually seemed to like their kids! That was amazing.

Relationships with siblings are important, and they can be critically good or critically bad. In Juliana's case, it was critically bad. It's common for personality-disordered mothers to divide their children into favorites and pariahs, even if the roles switch back and forth. Some people say that as a matter of course, one sibling is always on the outs with the mother, and the others are the "good" ones. The roles shift over the course of weeks or months.

Juliana's relationship with her brother was the focus of her mother's divisiveness. When Juliana was four, her mother left her in the care of the older brother, who took advantage of his privileged status to sexually abuse his younger sister. The abuse continued for several years, although never seen or acknowledged by Juliana's mother, who continues to deny it to the present day. Juliana recalls the particular time when she first understood how their relationship was to be.

> **Juliana:** I was about three and sitting under the dining room table. My brother had done something wrong and was being punished for it. They didn't know I was sitting there. She picked him up on her lap and held him and told him how much she loved him. She had never, ever done that to me. Then my brother saw me under the table and looked right at me, and I realized from that moment on that there was nothing I could do to ever have that relationship with her. I still can't. When I think back to what that look said to me, it was like, "Fuck you. I've got it and you don't." She never believed what I said, so he would blame everything on me, and she bought it. That was the game. Later on she would have him beat me when she was mad at me.

Often the favoritism develops because one child makes the mother feel particularly good about herself. Even the favoritism isn't necessarily about being more loving to one child than another, but another form of narcissistic bolstering required by the parent. In Juliana's brother's case, he had needed surgery as a very young child, and when his mother visited him in the children's ward, she saw him running in the halls unsupervised. She took him home, against medical advice, and that night the hospital burned down, killing many children and injuring others. She felt she had saved her child's life, and from that time on he was her favorite, and Juliana was the "bad one."

WHEN MOM IS MEAN, OR JUST DOESN'T CARE

It's easy to see the problem in developing a secure attachment if the attachment figure herself is dangerous.

> **Rachel:** I remember when I was really little, about three, my mother had an extreme anger problem. One time she took a radio and threw it across the kitchen and through the dining room, and it hit the wall and smashed. She was seeing a psychiatrist then—me and my brother had to sit in the waiting room while she saw him.
>
> By the time I was three years old I had learned to not argue with her. I could never say something was my brother's fault and not mine. I learned not to show tears, not to show anger, not to show anything to her, because it just incited her anger more.

It can be almost as difficult when the mother is not comforting or help-ful when the child is injured, and in fact is seen as someone who will make things worse either by punishing the child or ignoring her. Recall Bowlby's writing that by twelve months of age, insecurely attached children have already learned not to express themselves freely to their mothers and not to go to them for comfort when they're frightened or hurt. Because their mothers cannot see or respond to these feelings, these children may grow up not being able to recognize such feelings in themselves.[5]

> **Danielle:** When I was little I used to play with matches, and I used to get beaten for it. I remember coming back from the house next door, and I was playing with a pack of matches and it went off in my hands. I was blis-tered and burned, and I never told because I was afraid that I would get beaten. I was around six or seven. It really hurt, but it was easier to deal with that than to tell my mother I did it. She would have beaten me for it, and even if I told my father, he would have told her about it. He would have bowed down for her; he would never have kept a secret for me.

Another kind of danger is being neglected and left on one's own as a small child. There are countless children raised this way in impover-ished families and neighborhoods, and the results are much the same. In Alice's case, her mother was bipolar and simply seemed to follow her own whims, leaving her numerous children for Alice, the oldest, to take care of.

> **Alice:** I was four. I was four years old and I had free rein. The neighbors used to call my mother and say, "Alice is outside by herself again." My mother had no sense of parenting. She seemed to feel, "If you have a kid, what can the kid do for you?" not "How should you take care of your child?" We were there for her, not vice versa. She really didn't have

a clue, so as soon as we started doing that separation thing, she would have another kid.

At four I was crossing streets that I should not have been crossing. I went places like the penny candy store, and the adults would always ask me where my parents were.

When I was five, I took my younger brother and sister down to the park. We would go fishing down the river. We would go ice-skating. I would do things with them that neighbors again would say to my mother or to us, "You shouldn't be doing this without parental supervision."

Years later we found out that the woman across the street would watch us when we went to the park, and the woman down the street would watch us when we went to the river. So we kind of had these guardians.

Yet another kind of nonprotection of children, especially girls, occurs when the father uses the mother's physical or emotional absence to molest them. This was the case for Alice.

Alice: I can remember when I was like three years old, he would do all this cleaning of genital areas, and it was a combination of pain and pleasure, and it seemed weird and bad, but he would say he had to do it. I would be on the kitchen table spread-eagled, and he would be using Q-tips to clean me. I started remembering that stuff more later, and I remembered the red Formica tabletop and the Aunt Jemima doll on the counter.

WHY DOESN'T ANYBODY HELP?

Where are the fathers, the grandparents and aunts and uncles, the teachers? Where are other people who might help these families and these children? The mental health community is rarely mentioned in these stories as being a source of support, or even competent treatment. Personality-disordered mothers actively discouraged the girls from having independent relationships either with their fathers or with others outside the family.

Rachel: I could always talk to my dad, and my dad always knew where I was coming from, but my mother always told us how hard he worked and how he needed to be left alone. She always interrupted us if we were spending time together. A lot of times if she was home, he wouldn't really hang out with us anyway. Like when we had a pool or when we went to the lake, my dad enjoyed swimming and so did I, but he would stay back with Mom. She'd let him know that his place was by her side, not with us.

My father did come into my room once or twice when I was crying after Mother had yelled at me. He tried to explain that my mother kind of went overboard when she would yell, and that I shouldn't allow myself to get so upset. After, like, the second time that he had come into my room, my mother caught him and told him that if she ever found him in my room again after I had been yelled at ... I don't think she finished that statement.

There's a big difference between a mother who's pathologically controlling, like Juliana's mother, and a detached mother. Eleanor's mother, as we saw, left her alone as an infant because she didn't want to be over-controlling. Her psychological remoteness and detachment meant, however, that she was willing for her daughter to make attachments to other caregivers. This willingness in some cases comes from indifference, or from being overwhelmed, or from some awareness that the child needs more than the mother can give. Detached mothers may show minimal interest in or support of their daughters' other relationships, but they tend not to interfere.

> **Eleanor:** When I was quite young, my father hired a woman to come to the house five days a week. Several of the young professionals in the neighborhood had maids come in to clean house, but the wonderful black woman who came to our house five days a week was really the house manager, cleaner, cook, and child-care person. I was very attached to her. My mother did very little—mostly smoked and read books or magazines. I can't imagine what things would have been like if we had to rely on her to do things and take care of us. I was attached to my mother, but it was really Sarah who raised me and taught me things I needed to know. I look back and see my father was trying to make things as normal as possible, at least on the outside. Overall I think he provided as much protection as he could have.

Again, Juliana's mother is one of the mothers who put their daughters in danger even though they had reason to know that such danger existed. They seemed either not to care or to be so focused on their own needs that they couldn't be inconvenienced by an awareness of the peril their daughters might be in.

> **Juliana:** My mother didn't want to know anything bad about my brother. She didn't want to know that he was beating me up—not only when she told him to, but other times. She didn't want to know about the sexual abuse. But if your kid is sleeping with their knees tucked up under their nightgown and wrapping their blankets around them every night, don't you think you'd want to know why? It started the night she threw an ashtray at her boyfriend. I was four, and she took this guy to ER and left me with my brother, who was eleven or twelve. That's when he started sexually abusing me, and I think it was partly because he knew he could get away with it.

Mothers like this often actively undermine other relationships, saying, "You can only trust your family." In another case, a patient told me her mother routinely said, "No matter how nice your friends seem, they're probably laughing at you behind your back." Since there's no way for the child to disprove this, she's left going around in circles—no matter how nice her friends, she cannot trust them or feel comfortable around them. This kind of undermining comment sows the seeds of self-doubt on a very basic level: If you cannot trust your own sense about when people are okay and when they're not, your ability to build relationships is hamstrung. The mother who said this to her daughter had no adult friends of her own and relied on her children for company and support. The kids were close, and the mother was loving, but the message was that it should be this way forever.

In the mouth of a borderline mother, such a remark could be deliberate cruelty aimed at humiliating and confusing the child and establishing a sense of superiority. From a paranoid mother, it might be her own perception of the world as a humiliating place that would lead her to share this warning with her daughter. In that case, the mother might in some distorted way be trying to protect the child, even if the dangers were more imaginary than real. When a child grows up and sees the world as not so dangerous, it can feel like a betrayal to the parent who sees the world in this way. Paranoid people are quick to divide others into "friends" and "enemies," and it's all too easy to land in the enemy camp just by disagreeing about whether others are plotting against you or spying on your house.

KEEPING SECRETS

There seems to be an instinct among kids not to talk about what happens at home when it's negative. Home, which should be a refuge, begins to feel more like a secret prison. It's inconceivable to young children that there's anyplace else to go, and they usually resist attempts to remove them, even from an abusive home. For some kids, "telling" would mean destroying the family, or at least that's what they're led to believe.

> **Juliana:** The message was very clear to me that you didn't talk about our family stuff outside the home. If we didn't like it, we could leave, but of course there was no place to go. There was no doubt in my mind I was being told to keep my mouth shut.
>   **June:** My mother was desperate to keep us with her. I always believed that if we were broken up, I couldn't be with my sister anymore. My mother would tell me not to say anything to anybody. I was very much into keeping the secret.

In other families, there's just a pervasive sense that children shouldn't talk about family things outside of the family. This happens, of course, because there's negative or shameful stuff going on in the family. Families with close and affectionate relationships, with none of the pathology we've seen, don't transmit this message at all, and consequently kids from these families talk freely about family activities, their parents and siblings, and so forth. Some kids become adept at talking only about the "good" or "normal" stuff and leaving the rest out. This intensifies as they get older, as we'll see in the next section.

> **Jerri:** I always got the impression that it was very wrong to talk about anything that was private. So I was always afraid to talk about anything, not just my mother, but anything at all that was private or in the family.

MAKING THE BEST OF THINGS

In this section we'll look at how these kids coped, both positively and negatively. Most of the coping strategies they came up with worked, at least short term, but some seem to work better and be more easily converted into long-term coping strategies. These are attempts at self-regulation (see chapter 1)—attempts to calm themselves or divert their attention, either by changing their internal world or changing the external world.

It's unusual for a child to be so self-aware, but Rachel remembers clearly how she tried to handle her anger.

> **Rachel:** When I would get really angry, as a kid is, I would tighten every muscle in my body, because it was my way of expressing myself, of expressing my feeling, inside my own skin. It would exhaust me so I could sleep and escape that way, too.
>
> My mother would laugh at me and say, "Oh, look, she's doing the little chicken dance." That angered me, but it was better to have her laughing than angry at me. Afterwards I would be physically exhausted, and I could go and take a nap or go and hide. I would hide under my brother's crib. The side came down, so I could hide under the crib and feel safe under there.

Rachel and Helen also used their imagination to handle things that were too difficult or confusing.

> **Rachel:** I also had an imaginary friend that I could communicate with, and I didn't have to talk out loud to talk to her. She was exactly like I was, a mirror image, but she lived on another planet, so she didn't have to deal with life on Earth, and she didn't have parents. But my parents made fun of me about that, too.

I turned to just hiding everything and turning everything inside. I liked the Simon and Garfunkle song "I Am a Rock." From the ages of about five to seven I would go up to my room and cry. Then, finally, I said, "I'm not going to show her that she's hurting me this much."

Helen: I remember having this sort of fantasy that I had two mothers. That I had one that was nice, and then an impersonator would come, the mean one. That's how I handled it in my mind, because my mother was a pretty warm, lovely woman, but when she wasn't feeling well, she was angry and distant. I really kind of thought of it that way. I can look back and understand that allowed me to keep my image of a "good" mother, because the mean mother wasn't really the same person at all.

Jerri had an elaborate imaginary world in which elements of her real life were reflected in the lives of her dolls. She also came up with very creative ways to express herself secretly so that she could relieve herself of anger and guilt.

Jerri: I had a paper doll set. One of the dolls was named Mary, and she would have the perfect dollhouse and clothes, but there would always be a problem that she would have to take care of. I look back at it now and realize I was really doing play therapy with myself. I acted this out a lot. Then I had stuffed animals, too, and I always had my "feel sorry for me" animals.

There was a teddy bear losing his hair, and who had one eye. I felt sorry for my pink-haired doll. They all had to be included. One doll that I didn't like very much had to have some way to belong, so I took out his stuffing, and I used to put notes in there. I hid them all inside him. My parents never knew a thing about it. I would write out the bad feelings I had and put them in there. I was a very hopeful child, so I would think, too, that things were going to be okay.

The other thing I did is, if my mother got into one of her paranoid states and was angry and nasty, I would go in my closet and stand there and say, "I wish my mother would just go away." You weren't supposed to have these thoughts. But I did. She went away before [to the hospital]—why didn't she go away now and just leave us in peace? Then, when I was old enough to go to confession, I would go confess, "I had bad thoughts." Then I was able to dismiss it. It wasn't hurting anybody.

The resilience seen here and in the chapters to come is one of the mysteries of surviving and thriving despite very difficult early life experiences. The resilience literature is vast, but there still are unanswered questions in my mind about why some kids find a lifeline and other kids have so much trouble. Psychological resilience has been associated with having at least one person who's a positive force—even if the person is peripheral—being intelligent, being creative, and having a sense of humor. It's moving to hear how creative some children can be in finding ways to survive psychological abuse and neglect, and it does raise the question of what happens to kids who do not show this level of resilience. These are truly the unseen and unheard victims of severe family dysfunction.

Chapter 3

Middle Childhood

When we think of being a kid, middle childhood is usually the time we're remembering. We're old enough to have "explicit" memories— such memories start at about age three—and by that time we have a store of memories of events and of specific things that happened to us. When we remember them, we have the feeling of "I'm remembering this happening," which is quite different from the feeling of the implicit memories we have from birth to about age three. If things are going pretty well, our memories may be episodic (more like snapshots than videos) but come fully equipped with sights, sounds, feelings and sensations, tastes, and smells.

Kids this age have a daunting number of developmental tasks as their brains keep growing. They learn how to think logically during this time, and about how others think and feel. They build on their ability to relate to other people, connect with them, play, work together, and form friendships. A core sense of social identity begins during this period, to be modified during adolescence. Kids are learning about morality but haven't yet moved from black-and-white, right-and-wrong thinking. At five or six they begin going to school, inhabiting for the first time a world of their own outside the family and home. They relate on their own to new adults and other children, and their intellectual and cognitive abilities begin to take center stage.

Ideally, kids this age can explore the world on their own, while also knowing there's a safe place to go home to, literally and figuratively. The best case is when parents can, from a distance, support their children's move out into the world, being ready to back them up, provide comfort and support, and encourage them to keep going. Children this age also need to be protected from being taken advantage of, whether by adults or other kids, and they need to know that their parents are paying enough attention to notice when things aren't right, to ask questions, to sense significant changes. This doesn't mean shadowing kids and protecting them from everything, no matter how small; there's a broad range of okay parenting between the extremes of neglect, on the one hand, and the worst stereotype of yuppie overparenting, on the other.

When kids from dysfunctional families are old enough to start seeing the inside of other people's families, it's usually something they don't forget. This may be the first time they've ever seen a more "normal" family in action, and it may be the first realization that what goes on in their family is not the way it is for everyone. This age is often the beginning of a decades-long search for answers to the question, "Why did things happen the way they did in my family?" Ask anyone who grew up in a very dysfunctional family how they felt about things when they were four or five, and you'll just get a blank look, even if family life was violent, crazy, or bizarre. "It's just the way it was. I didn't feel anything in particular" is the usual answer. No, they don't feel any particular way "about" it because that usually comes later, when they're old enough to reflect on their experience and when they've seen other possibilities. Kids who lose a parent to death, divorce, or abandonment very early on don't usually have a sense of missing that parent—life without them is just the way it is. Later on, they can reflect on what they missed, how things might have been different, but at the time, the way daily life unfolds in the family is the way reality is taken in by the young child.

First let's look at daily life in families with mentally ill mothers. For almost all the women interviewed, their mothers were symptomatic during this period, if not before. The women's recollections are clearer for this time period, and they can tap more easily into their childhood thoughts and feelings. The interview questions first covered mundane topics, such as: Who got you up and ready for school in the morning? What happened when you came home from school? How were things with brothers and sisters? What were mealtimes like? We then moved to experiences more out of the ordinary, such as what life was like when their mother went to the hospital, who explained what was going on, and so forth.

MOM AT HOME

When we get a look at what happened behind closed doors in these families, the differences among various kinds of mental illness become relevant. Mothers with serious depression typically feel inadequate and very self-critical, in a way their children find distressing. These mothers are often relentlessly self-accusatory, struggling with their lack of energy and what they see as their worthlessness and incompetence. The following recollections are from women whose mothers were depressed, passive, or otherwise preoccupied with their own difficulties. Depression may be accompanied by suspiciousness, irritability, and social isolation, and Cynthia's, Jerri's, Pat's, and Eleanor's mothers fall mostly in that category.

Cynthia: Mealtimes at home were horrible; it was always a scene. We never knew if Mom would be furious at herself because things weren't perfect, or furious at one of us, or would burst into tears. All you could pay attention to was her mood and how bad she felt. You couldn't do anything to make it better, there was no way to ease her pain—she would just attack herself and call herself names, or she'd be mad at one of us. It was like the end of the day at dinnertime was the time all of her self-hatred just came bursting out of her.

Jerri: You never knew what was going to upset Mom. You had to keep to the routine, no exceptions. Everything had to be the same, every single day. She had a routine at home, and that was it. But if something bothered her, she'd get into a paranoid state and be muttering to herself about why people were against her. She would get really angry and nasty. She would make remarks about everybody, and it seemed to make sense to her, but it didn't make sense to anyone else. We never wanted her to get like this, because then it would take forever for her to get back to normal. It was like the only thing that kept her together was this rigid routine.

I can remember from my earliest times asking to use the phone. I would have to ask my father if I could use the phone. It was always a look from him: "What do you have to use the phone for? If we let you use the phone, she'll get very nervous about you using the phone." But I didn't know why, I could never figure it out, except that it was an interruption in the routine, and she would be worried about who's going to be listening, what are people saying, anything like that.

Pat: She would take the whole day to dust two rooms, and when she showed me how to do it, it was this major project. With my mother everything was time consuming, and it sapped her energy. I have such a vivid memory of her teaching me all those things which seemed so overwhelming to her. I just thought, "Why is this such a big deal?"

In other ways she was a classic housewife of that time, would get me off to school and then make lunch for me when I walked home in the middle of the day. Dinnertime was always a strain because of my father. He was like a bull in a china shop—always angry about something, yelling at my mother, making a scene. And she would just sit and cry the whole time he was yelling. And she cried during the day because he spent so much time out of the house. She was just chronically depressed and passive. I had the feeling I was supposed to take care of her, not the other way around.

Eleanor: I just remember her mostly lying down on the couch, smoking and reading. Any interaction with her was tinged with her suspiciousness about what was "really" going on under the surface, no matter what was going on. She had this tone of voice, like, "What do you mean by that?" all the time. She had many times of being psychotic and paranoid, but during this time, up until I was thirteen or fourteen, she just seemed not to be able to manage things. Her memory was awful, and she wrote everything down in little notebooks, so you never felt you were talking to her, you were talking to the notebook. She was very slow moving, like under water. Even talking about it right now, I feel antsy and fidgety and like I want to just get up and walk around or make something happen. It was very oppressive.

The word that described her the best was "furtive." She always seemed tentative, hesitant, moving around the house as though she was kind of sneaking around, like it wasn't even her house. The feeling was always that she was looking for clues or evidence about something. Nothing was easy or straightforward. Everything had more than one meaning, and she was going to find out what it was. Every question she asked was, like, "What are you hiding?" I thought she could read my mind, because she would stare at me in this intense way. I learned to appear very innocent, as though I didn't even realize that she was trying to look under the surface.

I'm amazingly lucky that my father kind of kept things together, and had someone come in and take care of things in the house. I had a strong relationship with this person, and that carried me through. My father made sure we had structure at home. If it had all been up to my mother, I don't know where we would have ended up.

There are bipolar mothers who can, at times, be good enough mothers and at other times be dominated by the intensity of their own moods. Alice's mother became overtly psychotic when Alice was an adolescent, but up until then seemed mostly to have been absent and negligent, minimally involved in the lives of her many children. Sandy's mother was clearly very unstable in her moods, swinging between manic, rageful states, as seen below, and states in which she was unable to function at all, as will be seen in later chapters.

Alice: When I was a kid, I was pretty much in charge of my younger brothers and sisters. By the time I was ten, when those two last kids were born, I mean, they were mine, they weren't hers. I would go with her when she was in labor. I remember writing the times of every contraction. There were times when I was really young that she could be fun—like, during Lent, she would get an empty string that was like a rosary, and whenever we did something good, we could put a bead on the string. That was fun. That was the only time I really felt a connection to her, not that she was giving something, but I felt that I could be with her and it was okay.

When she was manic, her activities were away from us, away from the house. She would often get into church, big time. I remember her saying, at one point, "I am so lucky I have finally found Jesus Christ." I thought at that moment, "Yeah, you found Jesus, but you lost us." Before her first psychotic break, she was still running around everywhere and doing everything except take care of us.

She left the house and the younger kids more or less completely up to me. When I was nine years old, my parents might leave at seven in the morning and leave me in charge of all four of my siblings. They would put our clothes on the bed and just say, "Just make sure all the kids get where they have to go." We used to have babysitters when they went out, but once I called them because two of the kids had stomach bugs and were throwing up all over the place. The sitter was kind of clueless and just stood there while I was changing sheets and stuff. Then my parents came home and saw me in charge of everything, and from then on they didn't get babysitters; I was it.

I would be really afraid at night, being in charge of them and being scared something would happen. It would be a relief when I heard their car on the gravel driveway.

There wasn't much structure at home. And we never knew what we would find when we came home, so that was the question when you would open the door. Will she be planning a party? Will she be going to church? Will she be in bed?

My aunt used to be horrified about how chaotic our house was, and how dirty. It was just always a big mess. Sometimes my father would crack the whip and all of us kids would try to pick up, but my friends' mothers would have some routine of cleaning up and vacuuming and dusting, and all that. We never did any of that. There was just shit all over the place.

She didn't even have any sense about feeding us kids. Everybody would get the same portion—whether you were two or ten. Then there wouldn't be enough food, not because there wasn't enough money but because she just didn't notice. My brother and I would sometimes go buy stuff like potatoes, which was really embarrassing when we were little.

Sandy: Starting at age seven, and then up to eleven or twelve, there was a lot of screaming and shouting, and my mother would come into my room at three a.m. and start putting away laundry and yelling at me about everything I had done wrong, in her eyes. She would just get on a roll. My parents had horrible fights—sometimes they got physical, but they were always emotionally abusive to each other, and then she would turn it on us.

The mothers with schizophrenia or other unclear psychotic illnesses could be unpredictable and often bizarre in their behavior, or seem remote and unreachable. June's mother was clearly struggling with dissociation when June was young, but became more overtly disturbed and impaired after her first hospitalization, when June was ten. It was around this time that she was given two diagnoses: schizophrenia and multiple personality disorder. Her relationship with her daughters deteriorated over the course of several years.

June: Before I was ten, she was better. She would be at the bus stop when I came home from school, and she would make my lunch to take to school. I remember feeling like I could rely on her for those things. She would ask me what happened at school, that kind of thing. And she might play with me, put shaving cream on the table and draw pictures in it, stuff like that. That was fun. Holidays were okay; she would decorate the house. Those were the better memories.

Even during those years, there would be a lot of times she just checked out. She would be sitting there looking at her nails and she'd just be gone. She'd just act like you weren't even there. The thing with the nails didn't change when she got sicker. No matter what, her nails were always manicured and beautiful, and they were her thing. But she got hospitalized when I was ten, I don't remember exactly how it happened, and then I just stopped trusting her, she got so unpredictable and crazy. She got much more angry after that. And she just basically stopped functioning as our mother. We would be dirty and smelly and wouldn't bathe for days on end, but her nails were always done. She would sit at the table and look at her nails and smoke cigarettes.

Once I told her I wanted to take a bath, and she asked me why, like it never occurred to her anybody should take a bath. When she was better, before that first hospitalization, she would go to the store with us, and afterwards she wouldn't. She had always been afraid they would lock her up, and they finally did. She got so much worse after that. And she would ask me to stay home from school and keep her company a lot. Sometimes I did. I had to kind of figure out for myself what I should do. Before she went to the hospital that first time, she would just go to bed if she was depressed. Afterwards she was just so dissociated so much of the time.

She just wasn't there. That's what I realize now. She wasn't anxious or upset, just not there. Then she would just change, and I couldn't figure out what was going on. Sometimes I would come home and she would say, "Who are you? Get out of my house," and she'd threaten to call the cops. She had no idea who I was. I was always afraid she was going to call the police, and they would come and see that she's insane, and they would take me away from my sister.

After she was in the hospital the first time, she would just sleep in the morning and stopped getting us up in the morning, and we had to do that for ourselves. My older sister started being away from the house a lot more, and me and my other sister were on our own. My hair was long and tangled, and I would just shove it in some kind of big clip.

A friend of mine at school kept saying to wear my hair down, and I would always say, "Oh, I forgot this morning," but it was just a rat's nest, and finally my sister had to chop it off.

When we came home after school there was no structure at all. There wasn't any dinnertime or any rules about homework, or whatever. My dinner would be Cap'n Crunch cereal out of the box while I watched TV. Sometimes I would do homework, and sometimes I wouldn't. I just did whatever I wanted. Once my oldest sister was on the front stoop drinking wine out of a bottle, and my mother got mad at her, not because of what she was doing but because the neighbors might object to it.

Tess's mother was periodically overtly psychotic and paranoid, acting very strangely in public. She did seem to try to follow some household structure, but was barely able to do that. In a later section, Tess describes her mother's bizarre paranoid behavior in public—at church, in the grocery store, and so forth. At home, this was the picture:

Tess: She would get us up in the morning and get us off to school. Looking back, that was amazing that she could even do it. We had uniforms, so that made things easier. And she would do the dishes, but she couldn't do a lot of the other household chores. She cried a lot, and you could also hear her whispering to herself. But she absolutely could not take care of herself. She wouldn't bathe, she wouldn't change her own clothes, she'd have the same clothes on for days and days. She was always disheveled, her face was always dirty. I remember dust balls hanging from her hair. That's how I remember my mother.

We couldn't go to the relatives for the holidays, or if we did we'd have to rush, because we always knew Mommy was home alone, crying and sad. So, how could you be happy to be out of the house? She wouldn't come, no matter what anybody said, and then sometimes we just had to stay home. Nobody could ever come to our house, because she didn't trust anyone at all.

When we were at school, the only thing she did was listen to Italian radio—no TV. She didn't trust anybody, so she didn't have any friends, never went out by herself. My father could sometimes persuade her to go out with us to the supermarket on a Friday night. He'd have to beg, though: "Maria, Maria, let's all go out, please. People aren't looking at you. Come on." Sometimes she'd pick up the phone and just start screaming at whoever had called. And then she'd hang up, and she'd just be crying and crying and crying. If one of us kids were there, we'd be trying to talk her out of it, talk her down. Then, and I don't know where this came from, she'd go through periods where she was just obsessive about stuff—washing her hands all the time, checking the lights and the stove, checking over and over again to make sure things were turned off. And checking the door to make sure it was locked. Open, close, lock, unlock, open, close, lock—that would go on forever. And those are memories of my mother, growing up.

The last group of mothers may not seem to be mentally ill at all. These are mothers who function well in the world and seem to be exemplary mothers—if one looks only at their public performance. At home, however, they act in cruel, unreasonable, and vindictive ways toward some or all of their children. These mothers go way beyond being strict or critical or perfectionistic. In *Wednesday's Child*,[1] the authors spent twenty years studying the long-term effects of abusive and neglectful parents on the development of adult depression. One category of abuse is labeled "antipathy," and its markers are parental hostility, persistent criticism, verbal and nonverbal rejecting behavior, and telling the child he is bad, a nuisance, and a burden. Favoring one of the child's siblings is very common in these families. Humiliation, both public and private, is common as well.

Antipathy to the child can also be shown through critical, harsh overinvolvement in the child's activities, typically with harsh punishment and demeaning responses when the child fails to live up to impossible standards. These researchers found that children raised by such parents are four times more likely to attempt suicide, and eight times more likely to engage in self-harming behavior, than children raised in functional homes.

The researchers characterize the behavior of parents who show antipathy, and two of the women here describe their mothers as having behaved in those ways. If we want to go a step further and venture to diagnose these mothers, both clearly have a serious personality disorder. Clinically, they would be seen as having narcissistic personality disorder with borderline features,[2] a diagnosis that describes people who show excessive self-absorption, extreme need for admiration and attention from others, inability to see others as more than two-dimensional bit players in one's own drama, and a need to control and humiliate others in a deliberate and psychologically sadistic way. The "borderline" feature of this diagnosis refers to mood instability, an intense focus on relationships with others, and the possibility of near-psychotic thinking at some time.

This is the *Mommie Dearest* kind of mother: publicly impressive in her mothering ability, but lethal behind closed doors.[3] *Mommie Dearest* (1981) has a reputation as a very campy film; however, the 1978 book by the same name was one of the first about a "bad" mother—especially a bad mother who looked good on the outside. Several women I interviewed said that reading this book was the first time they realized that maybe they weren't the only "bad" daughters in the world.

Both Rachel's and Juliana's mothers fall into this category. Clearly they were not psychotic, but their relationships with their daughters (although not their sons) was malevolent.

Rachel: I don't think there was a day I can remember when I wasn't just constantly criticized by my mom. From the time I was really young, I had to make my bed, clean my room, and vacuum the house and polish everything—in every room. Every single thing had to be taken off the furniture and polished every day. Then she would go around and make sure everything had been done. God forbid I missed one thing. I got chastised for anything that wasn't perfect. I washed the dishes at night, and she would come and inspect everything in the drainer. If there was one thing wrong she would dump all the dishes back in the sink and yell at me to do it right. She would say, "What's wrong with you? They think you're so smart at school. Well, what do they know? You can't do anything right." She just looked for things I didn't do perfectly so she could criticize me. She seemed to enjoy it.

She was anorexic for a while and then bulimic. We couldn't make any decision about our own food. Everything was put onto my plate and I had to eat it, even if I was sick and didn't want anything to eat. She would decide whether you ate, what you ate, and when you ate it. She would make herself throw up in the bathroom and then explain to me why she had to do it, because she thought she was fat. She would chew up food and then spit it out. She weighed herself all the time, and she must have thrown a dozen scales down the stairs when she didn't like how much she weighed. She went on every weird diet there was and had all kinds of special food in the fridge, just for her.

She was on medication for a while, and then she went off it. Then she would yell nonstop, and in the summer the windows would be open, and neighbors would say, "What the hell is going on at your house?"

Juliana: It was hard to anticipate what kind of mood my mother would be in when she came home from work. I spent most of my time walking on eggshells around her. She had a very short fuse and was violent a lot, physically, and emotionally demeaning most of the time. From about age nine I would get up in the morning and make her a cup of tea and bring it to her in bed. Then I would fix myself some cereal and then get dressed. My mother had total control over what I wore and would lay it out on my bed. And she would get up in time to comb my hair, which usually meant getting hit on the head with the wooden brush and yelled at. When I got home from school, she was working, so I would make her bed, clean up the house, and then I could do what I wanted if there was any time left. She seemed to care about how I looked, but it was more about how it reflected on her.

Christina Crawford, author of *Mommie Dearest*, writes something that Juliana and Rachel could relate to about her mother's profound sense of emptiness, characteristic of people with personality disorders: "The image was the bottomless pit into which you could pour years of loving, kindness, and attempts at reconciliation without visible results. It failed to erase the one mistake.... There just wasn't enough love in the whole world to fill her need.... She demanded such constant reassurance of devotion that she left no room for love. It was impossible to satisfy her."[4]

MOM AND ME

For some of the women, there were good times together with their mother—at least some of the time—cooking together, playing games, getting ready for holidays or other events. Some of the mothers had only intermittent periods of illness and at other times could be good and competent mothers. Others were chronically disturbed, with very few good periods, and still others seemed driven to mistreat their daughters, with little relief. June's mother, who had both schizophrenia and multiple personality disorder, could be very frightening.

> **June:** One of the most horrifying things for me—and it took a long time for me to even say this to myself or anyone else—was a time when my mother was just looking right through me. She wasn't looking at her nails or anything else, she was looking right at me, but right through me like she didn't even see me. I started to yell, which I never, ever did: "Am I dead? Am I dead?" And I realize now that everything that was real about me was in the other person's reaction to me. So if she didn't react to me, I didn't exist. That was absolutely terrifying.

Of course that would be terrifying to a young child; it takes a lot of "being seen" to have an internal sense of a core self. And as June says, if there's no mirroring reaction "out there"—or not enough—then that sense of core self is shaky. That's the wordless kind of feeling that was stirred up by her mother's looking through her. This feeling probably resonated so strongly for June because it stirred up implicit infant memories of seeing that same look in her mother's face.

June was also one of the women I interviewed who was sexually molested by her mother, although in a strange way.

> **June:** My mother, my sister, and I all slept in the same room, but my sister wet the bed, so I had to sleep with my mother. It was sexual abuse, but there was no sexual energy to it. I would feel her breasts against my back. And she would be rageful toward my father and toward me. She kind of knew about his sexually abusing me from a very young age, and it was like she was angry that I was "having sex" with him and not with her. I would get worms a lot because we were so dirty, and she would scrape the worms off my vagina with her nails and tell me what a slut I was, and that she would tell the doctor. She would be in a rage at me, like another personality. I remember lying there in so much pain, and I could see through the glass doors into the kitchen, and her washing my blood off her manicured fingernails. That was my blood. So it was more

like physical assault but it was sexual, but she didn't get off on it sexually at all. Was it incest if she didn't get off on it? My father got off on it. She didn't. It was invasive. But it's hard to figure out what to call it—a physical assault that was sexual? I don't know.

She had a complete absence of boundaries. She would have her breasts against my back and her hands on my vagina, and it was ongoing. It was like an ongoing sexual relationship.

June's experience of her mother's anger was quite different from that of other women I interviewed. When we talked about it at length, it became clear that June wasn't enough of a separate person, in her own mind, to feel upset or rejected if her mother was angry. There wasn't much of an internal, personal reaction at all. Her reactions had to do with an assessment of how dangerous her mother might be to the whole family if she was angry at June.

June: If she got angry at me, she would just wipe me out. She wouldn't yell, she would just act like I wasn't there. It was so much worse than her saying anything. I felt so much more able to control her when she was not mad at me, but if she was mad I couldn't control her—we weren't on the same team anymore, I wasn't her confidante anymore, there was this divide. It was the most dangerous place to be. She wasn't using me then, she was on her own—and I couldn't help her anymore. If I'm the only frontline defense in the world, then where is she when she's angry with me? She's on her own.

Danielle, whose mother was chronically depressed and abused alcohol, ran what sounds like a chaotic household, with her own ability to function at a low ebb, and her relationships with all three of her daughters seems to have been chaotic and negative. Danielle's experience alternated between escaping from her mother and feeling responsible for helping her emotionally, despite the lack of any close relationship or positive interactions.

Danielle: I wasn't ever close to her. I got in trouble a lot. I never knew what I did, but I did get in a lot of trouble. I got locked in my room, I would hide in my room, I was beaten, things like that. I used to jump out my window if she locked me in my room. But other times she treated me as the person who was responsible and in control. She would kind of collapse onto me, and I thought it was my duty to change things and make her feel better. I had a feeling of power in a way, because I could run faster than she could, and when she did beat me, I would try as hard as I could not to cry, so that she wouldn't know it hurt. I remember more a feeling of animation than of fear. But on the other hand, me and my sisters were absolutely powerless to change anything. I was always doing something wrong in her eyes.

Helen's mother didn't behave in any bizarre way during this period of Helen's life, although her kids already treated her as though she were supersensitive and they couldn't rely on her for anything since she might get upset. The problem here was that Helen's mother identified her daughter as being like her—too sensitive to do things—just at the age when Helen needed to be mastering school and friendships and developing physical strength and stamina as well as emotional resilience. This became a lifelong issue and matter of concern for Helen, who for years worried that she was too weak to cope with things.

> **Helen:** She actually treated me, in elementary school, as though I were just like her. I came home for lunch, and then she had me stay home and not go back for the afternoon session because I was supposedly too weak to go for a whole day. I started to think the way she did, that I wasn't capable of doing a lot, and she agreed with me about that.

Sometimes a mother's behavior was just a little strange and scary. Sandy describes an incident that wasn't traumatic or earth-shattering, but just one in a series of strange interactions that confused her and made her uncertain whether her mother was the safe figure she could go to when frightened or would instead become the source of the fright.

> **Sandy:** I used to be scared of spiders, and every night I would ask her to check for spiders before I went to bed. Then one day I went into my bedroom and there was a spider on the wall—she had put it there, it was fake—and she said, "It's time you get over this fear of spiders." So she took my hand and made me touch it, and then I started yelling and she started chasing me around the house holding the spider. It was very weird. Then there were other times she would get really hyped up in a scary kind of way—she was really wild. And she would get angry and just stop talking to you for days at a time. I felt compelled to keep trying to make her talk to me. I'm still like that in my relationship, and I'm in my forties.

Rachel's and Juliana's mothers both continued to be critical and demeaning, seeming to put obstacles in their daughters' paths deliberately. Some of the mothers we've heard about weren't very supportive or present, but these two mothers, in particular, seemed bent on making things more difficult, undermining their daughters' abilities and self-confidence. Notice in both the following accounts that when other adults showed positive interest in these young girls, their mothers disparaged it and undermined the relationships. This is in contrast to some mothers who seemed to realize they could not be supportive or present, and who seemed to let their daughters go without interference. This is extremely important, since one of the central factors in psychological resilience is the availability of at least one adult who is interested and supportive.

Rachel: In sixth grade I was in this program for the gifted and talented, and we were making these models of buildings. We had to do the graphic design and everything and then actually construct the building. My teacher was very supportive of my taking on a big project like this, and I won an award for it. But when my parents and I went to the award evening, I just went in my regular boy's school clothes—she always made me dress in boy's clothes because she said they were less expensive. She got furious because I was supposed to be dressed up. So I had to go home and change, but the only dress I had was this gift from the people who lived next door, who really liked me—I didn't have any others. And she had been furious when I accepted the dress as a gift, so I had just stuck it in the closet. So I put it on and went to the award ceremony. And she cut all the kids' hair, so my hair was just chopped off. I must have looked awful, with this wrinkled dress and chopped-off hair. So though I won an award, it's a bad memory. My mother had nothing good to say—just anger about my not being dressed right.

Juliana: In terms of the violence, it was just so prevalent, it was just always there. It wasn't enough for it to be violent, it had to be demeaning and humiliating. You got beatings bent over the bed with your pants down around your ankles with a belt.

My mother was the kind of person that if you showed that you loved someone, you never told her, because she would start attacking that person. There was an older woman that I used to go and visit all the time, and my mother just hated her for no particular reason except that she befriended me. So I learned very early that you don't divulge that information. If I went to see Mrs. Wallace on my bicycle, I would not tell my mother!

One of the things my mother always made very clear was that she was our only lifeboat. She told us that my father didn't want us and wasn't interested in us, and then if she was angry she would say, "If you don't like it here, just get out. And if you're out, you're out—there's no coming back." So the threat of being abandoned was always there. Every argument, every fight, every time we did anything wrong—"If you don't like it, go live with your father," she would say, but you knew that wasn't a choice, because she already told us he didn't want us. Later on, we learned that wasn't really true, but at the time we believed her.

She took total control of what I wore, up to the time I was fourteen or fifteen. She would lay stuff out on the bed, and that's what you wore. I would take stuff in my schoolbag and change at school sometimes. Or I would come home and my mother—the funny part of my mother—I would come home and there would be a bag of new clothing on the bed, a gift. "I was thinking about you. Look at the things I do for you. I think about you all the time." There was always a price tag with all the gifts.

First of all, you had to like them and you had to wear them, whether you liked them or not, and you had to be grateful that she got them for you.

Once a week, on Wednesday, she would go through my closet and throw out stuff she didn't like. On the way home from school on Wednesdays, I would go in the rubbish and pick out the stuff I wanted and hide it somewhere.

I actually remember in school in the 1950s we had "cover drills" where you would have to hit the floor and cover your head with your hands to protect you from the atomic bomb explosion. That's what it was like. I always considered life with Mom to be one continual cover drill.

Sarah's father died unexpectedly, in an accident, when Sarah was quite young. Her mother simply couldn't cope, and they ended up living with the maternal grandmother. This is Sarah's memory of how that all came to be.

Sarah: I was seven or eight, and I don't remember what I was doing, but all of a sudden my mother took off all her clothes, put on a bedsheet, and made me take off all my clothes and put an afghan on me, and we went over to a neighbor's house. The neighbor called the cops, and they took her away, and I found out later she went to the psych hospital. I remember cops being at the house a lot after we lived with my maternal grandmother, because my grandmother would beat the crap out of my mother, and my mother would be crazy, and maybe drunk, too, and get hauled off to the hospital.

Some of what these women experienced as children was simply neglect. Ironically, as Antonia Bifulco and Patricia Moran, the authors of *Wednesday's Child*, point out, this topic has been neglected in the literature. Bifulco and Moran refer to it as invisible abuse,[5] since there's also research showing that long-term neglect has consequences similar to those of outright abuse. Parental neglect obviously impairs secure attachment, and we know that insecure attachment compromises healthy brain/mind development. Neglect goes beyond a feeling of being unimportant or invisible; when it occurs early in life, it affects the development of a secure core self and becomes part of one's self-definition in an implicit way that one later has little access to. Sarah expresses this succinctly.

Sarah: My own well-being was never taken into consideration by any of my mother's caretakers at all. I was just an object that existed to meet her needs, nothing more.

Neglect also appears as nonprotection, as can be seen in June's description of heedlessly roaming into dangerous places without her mother's knowing—or, apparently, caring—where she was. Alice provides a similar description.

June: I think of places I went and neighborhoods I went into—there was so much danger I had no idea of at all. Train tracks, the back way to places that were creepy, having no sense of safety at all and no sense of needing to watch out or protect myself at all. I wasn't putting myself in danger for some psychological reason or anything—I was completely clueless, like a two-year-old walking in front of a car.

Alice: I was left to fend for myself from the age of four or five. We lived not far from a four-lane street that ran through the center of town, which had a lot of traffic. Here I would be trying to cross with my three younger brothers and sister, and we would be just running like hell so we could get across in time. We were just little kids, and people would look at us when they realized there weren't any adults with us. I used to be petrified, running across that street, and I knew it was wrong, I knew I wasn't old enough. I look at that road now and I'm appalled. But my mother was just doing her own thing, whatever that would be, and she didn't have the faintest idea where we were, as long as she didn't have to be bothered with us.

EXPLANATIONS

In *Growing Up with a Schizophrenic Mother*, one woman says something that every woman in my study would affirm, and in fact almost all of them said explicitly: "If someone had come and talked to us as children, and said, 'This is the illness your mother has, this is what you can expect,' my life would have been changed forever."[6]

Cecily's experience in having her mother's illness explained is as close to ideal as can be imagined.

Cecily: I was ten or eleven when my father told me what was going on when my mother had to be away. She wasn't floridly psychotic. She wasn't banging around and doing anything. When she got ill, she became overprotective, and there were paranoid qualities to it, like "Don't pull out anything from the electrical socket" or "Be very, very careful crossing the street"—just more a sense that the world was extremely dangerous.

He explained that my mother had a biological disorder: "It can happen to anyone, and as a result, she needs treatment. She's in a special hospital where they treat people with like illnesses. It's a mental illness," and that was it. It was much more biological, rather than "Your mother is a nut." Because of her kind of illness, she was diagnosed as simple schizophrenia at that time, and it was the advent also of Thorazine. This was the early 1950s. Nobody in the family ever used a euphemism, or whatever—nobody ever said she was "sensitive"—they would say she was sick. There was never any shit about it, honestly. It was never a criticism. It was never a "poor, poor, children."

There was no shame. It's not a secret, and it's not a main event. It's not something that we need to shine the light on and say, "Okay, how's Martha doing?" It was never in the spotlight and it wasn't in the closet. It was just a fact—"Martha is sick right now"—and it was referred to as her being sick.

There are so many good aspects to this that it's hard to know where to start articulating them. First, Cecily's father conveyed to her that he knew what was happening, that he wasn't afraid or ashamed of it, and that he was handling it competently, with professional help. She took her cue from him in not reacting with fear or shame. Second, he didn't offer any false hopes about a permanent recovery and didn't caution Cecily about behaving in any particular way, so she didn't come away with the sense that her behavior determined her mother's well-being. She also didn't have unrealistic expectations, which would have set her up for many disappointments. A patient of mine whose mother was seriously physically ill with a chronic illness talked about the nuns' instructions to her as a young child: "Pray for your mother to get well." She devoted much time and effort, every day, to praying that her mother would get well. Every day, she was disappointed, and every day she felt she had failed and should try harder. There's a wide gap between being realistically hopeful and feeling that it's up to you to make someone get well.

The explanation Cecily's father gave her made sense and was congruent with her own experience of her mother, and therefore confirmed her own reading of reality. Even as adults we find it hard not to blame ourselves or others unless we have a plausible alternative explanation for what has gone wrong. Thus, being given information about the illness, in neutral terms, was extremely helpful to Cecily. She was explicitly told that she didn't make this happen and it wasn't about her, and that it was an illness with a name and a treatment.

I was interested not only in how kids were told, overtly, about their mother's illness or difficulty but also what they picked up from other people about what was wrong with their mother, and why.

> **Tess:** She was sick. Everybody said she was sick. They didn't ever say "crazy," but they would just say, "We gotta help her." When she went to the hospital, my father told us, "Mommy's gonna go away for a little while. We're gonna help so she'll be back." I was very embarrassed—we all were. We didn't explain it to anyone else or at school or anything. My father's sisters came over like the maid brigade and just cleaned up everything and put everything in order.

Alice got the message from some other adults, like the school nurse, that things in her house were "not normal." But she was also told, indirectly, that her mother's problems were the kids' responsibility and that she should be more understanding and sympathetic. Juliana was also told that her mother was angry and impatient because of being saddled with two kids, and from there it was a short step to Juliana's feeling it was her fault that her mother was the way she was.

Alice: At home, I don't ever recall my father saying, "Your mother is sick." I remember him saying things like "We need to work together, we need to do our chores," and that was the way he conveyed that we had to pick up the slack.

My father wasn't direct. He would use excuses and make it seem it was our responsibility because she was sick. My mother actually was more direct. She would say, "I can't help it because I am sick. If I had a broken leg, you would be understanding. If I had cancer, you would be understanding." Again, whenever she didn't get whatever she wanted from us, she would say that. It wasn't an explanation, it was a manipulation. There was no message saying, "Your mother has a problem and it's not your fault." That would have been great.

Juliana: My mother explained any problems she had as being because she was a single mother, and divorced, and had a mind of her own. She would say people wanted to attack her or put her down because of those things. I believed her for a long time, because I didn't know any other single mothers, but eventually I spent enough time with other families that I could see how mean and undermining my mother was by comparison. And her other explanation was that she would have been fine if it hadn't been for us kids, that she was left with us and it held her back, and that was why she was angry or impatient. It was never that she had a problem.

Her boyfriend [later Juliana's stepfather] would come in and lay across my bed and try and talk to me and say, "You know how your mother is, she'll get past it," and he would try and talk me down. Other people made comments; my friends would make comments to me. They would ask me why she was so mean.

Some of the girls were told indirectly that their mother's problems weren't their fault, but it was done in a pretty dismissive way, as in Sandy's case. Jerri heard an "explanation" from a friend.

Sandy: I was about six or seven, and my father was going to take me out to dinner as a treat. My mother was angry with him about something, and she said to me, "Well, I won't be here when you get back." It sounded very final. I don't think I knew what suicide was, but I know later on she used to threaten that all the time. I just froze, thinking I would never see my mother again—she was going away, or something horrible was about to happen. I told my father, and he just said, "She just says things like that; don't worry about it," and we did go out to dinner. I couldn't eat anything. He acted like it was no big deal.

Jerri: Nobody told me anything at all. It was all a big secret. That was very difficult for me, because nobody else in the family wanted to talk about it. We had a routine—if I came home and my father would say to me, "Go over to Aunt so and so," then I would know she was going back in the hospital.

The main thing I remember feeling was that my mother gained a lot of weight when she got sick, and after a while she really didn't look like herself anymore. I hated it because I was physically losing my mother, and now I was losing the memory that I had of her at a very young age, and that bothered me tremendously. She couldn't button her coats. That sticks in my head.

I never even knew that she was mentally ill until I was about twelve years old. Nobody ever told me. I was playing with some friends of mine in the neighborhood, and one girl I wasn't too friendly with just up and says, "Oh, yeah, your mother was in the nuthouse with my mother." This was the first that I had ever heard that my mother was in a mental institution.

At first I was hurt so much to hear that she would use the term "nuthouse." I remember saying, "That's for insane people." To me that's what it was. My measure of insanity was people who are nonfunctioning. My mother can cook, she can clean house. To have this girl tell me that—until this day, I can see her face, I can hear those words. I know this girl's mother, and she seemed liked a nice woman. But after that, I started to think of my mother being insane. It made her seem like a different person and not anybody I wanted to be associated with.

Helen: Everyone thought of my mother as "sensitive." It meant that you had to be really careful and quiet, never ask her anything or go to her for anything. She had to rest, and she was weak and couldn't handle things. She would say she was anxious and would ask other people to do things for her. She was just not capable of doing much.

Pat: People said my mother was "doctoring," meaning always going to doctors. Nobody knew what was wrong with her. She had this facial pain and would walk around all the time with a rag on her face and obviously in a lot of physical pain. That became, over the years, the central thing about her, this facial pain. People would also kind of blame her depression on my father, since everyone knew how impossible he was. They would just say, eventually, "That's the way your mother is," like "That's it, don't ask any questions and don't expect any answers." Nobody actually really knew what was wrong with her, anyway.

Sarah got an "explanation" from her mother's family about why her mother was psychotic, and it managed to both blame Sarah and also undermine a potential positive escape for her.

Sarah: The explanation given to me when I was a kid, was that she was too smart and she had a very high IQ and went to college, and that's what made her crazy. She had her first breakdown then, I found out later. Luckily, even when I was a kid, I knew this explanation was crap, so I kept doing really well in school, read, studied, all that. They also said if she had problems, it was because I was spoiled and made things harder for her.

In this obviously bad "explanation," one negative is piled on another. If a child takes in the message very young that she is "bad" in some fundamental way, and then in this developmental period she is also blamed for having the destructive power to make her mother sick, this is a kid at serious risk for problems in adolescence and adulthood. Children in reality have very little power, and part of normal development is to be secure that you as a child have a lot less power (and, therefore, responsibility) than the adults who are supposed to be in charge of things. As much as children want power, good parents know that children are also relieved when they know they don't have too much. Furthermore, during this period children are developing and testing who they are and what they can and can't do. It's problematic when the child feels she has the power to make her parent sick or well, but it's also a problem when the child feels she has no impact whatsoever on the parent.

> **Danielle:** As a younger kid, I was scared. I didn't know what was going on, and I would try to talk to them about the situation, and I would try not to cry. I thought there was something wrong in that I couldn't impact it. What was wrong with me that they won't listen? That's been one of the hardest things to get over, to really understand that it wasn't me, it was her.

In both cases, this early distortion of a sense of efficacy in the world becomes part of the implicit "working model" for what will come later in interpersonal relationships. A fair amount of therapy, with many patients, is helping them discern what power they do and don't have in relation to other people. There's often huge relief as well as disappointment when it becomes clear that although we can influence others, we cannot really change or control them to any great degree.

> **Pat:** I always had the feeling that what I could do could make her worse. My mother got really bad about the time I became sexual—it would have been around my adolescence. Somehow in my mind, I associated my mother getting really sick with my budding sexuality, that it was somehow a factor in her getting really sick.

Childhood is the best time to learn how to balance attention to oneself and attention to others, as children interact with their siblings and also with parents. This is when it's most destructive to be getting the message either that your very existence has a huge negative influence on a parent and you alone are responsible for how your parent fares in the world or, on the other hand, that you aren't even on the radar screen of what's important in their lives.

WHO AM I?

In *Growing Up with a Schizophrenic Mother*, one woman, who also speaks for many women in this book, says, "I am my mother's daughter. That is the single most important and the most devastating fact of my life."[7]

> **Tess:** I was so sad growing up. You could see it in pictures. And I've even cut myself out of pictures because the picture that was there wasn't the image I hoped for. I was just devastated that I felt so awful and I knew she felt so awful. I was scared that what I felt was going to show and people were going to react to me that way. They'd react to me like I was weird—and basically, I did feel weird.

It often happens in dysfunctional families that roles are reversed or otherwise distorted. Alice was expected to switch back and forth between being a respectful daughter and, when her mother couldn't function, a take-charge adult. She talks here about her frustration at her father's expectations.

> **Alice:** My father would be mad if I didn't take care of her, like I was her mother instead of the other way around. And he was rarely home anyway.
> So my dilemma was: I was her mother, which was fine. Then, once in a while she would act like the adult and I could be a kid. But that was very rare. So if he was around, mostly what he saw was me acting like the adult, but if I *sounded* like I was treating her like a child, he would ream me out. I think it took me until maybe I was in high school to kind of yell back at him, you know, "I'm acting like the mother here, what do you *want* me to do?" To me, it wasn't disrespect, it was trying to keep her in line with the other kids. But he would defend her to the end!

Danielle's mother seemed to want her daughter's forgiveness or understanding in the following incident, but without considering Danielle's age or all the intervening chaos and violence that was part of their family life. Again, the understanding that should rightly be extended first to the child, is expected *from* the child, without reciprocity.

> **Danielle:** Once she told me, when I was ten or eleven, that I had been in an incubator and she had felt awful because she couldn't touch me. I just thought, "Are you kidding? Why are you telling me this?" She had never comforted me about anything, and now I'm supposed to agree with her how awful it was she couldn't touch me ten years ago when I was a

baby? She had all those years to make up for it, and she never did. I was just furious. I was mad at her most of the time.

Pat describes a life-changing experience for her as an eleven-year-old child. Although she felt responsible for her mother in some ways, she also felt rather invisible in her family. School was a place to shine, a place to excel and hear well-deserved praise for her abilities, not a place to worry about her mother's feelings, which here overshadow everything else.

> **Pat:** I think I was in the sixth grade. I loved school, and my memory of my grammar school is really happy. My favorite teacher was in history, because I did so well in that class. I thought I was just the cat's meow, and she was pretty encouraging of me in class. My mother and I went in for a student conference, and this teacher said that I was a show-off and that I spoke out of turn. My mother just sort of fell apart in front of me. It was like all of the air went out of her. We walked home, and I can remember walking across those railroad tracks and my mother being so upset and saying she never, never thought that anybody would say such bad things about her daughter. It was all about her. I both felt upset but furious and enraged. I remember thinking, "I'm never, never going to let you in my world again." I had let her in my private world, somehow, or my space, and it wasn't safe to have her there somehow. I never did—that was my last year in that school. There used to be open houses at high school also, but I don't think she ever went. I don't think I ever let her know about them.
>
> In some ways I suppose every child has what they could call the moment that's the end of innocence. In some ways that was my end of innocence. I don't know if I was ever the same after that. Nothing was the same after that.

Kids this age are still vulnerable to taking on a sense of internal responsibility or blame for whatever is wrong in the family. When they do, they try all kinds of things to make the situation better. Rachel prayed every night to be perfect so her mother would be happy with her, and Helen tried to figure out how to fix her depressed and silent mother. Even Cecily, knowing the facts of her mother's illness and being told explicitly that she had nothing to do with it, had a few moments of uncertainty. Pat was convinced that she was the cause of her parents' problems, and in an interesting internal role reversal, thought for years that the problem was that she didn't love her parents unconditionally.

> **Rachel:** I never thought I was a terrible bad kid who does bad things. I just kept thinking, "I didn't try hard enough. I need to try harder." But I didn't think of home at school—I just separated them in my mind.

It wasn't too long before I stopped knowing how I felt about things because of keeping everything inside.

I would go to bed at night and pray. I would pray to Santa Claus and the tooth fairy, when I still believed in them, because they were some sort of supreme beings who knew everything. My parents laughed at any religion or anybody who went to church, so I guess I was left with Santa and the tooth fairy. I would pray, "Please, please just let me get through the day without making a mistake. Just for tomorrow let me be perfect."

Helen: I think I liked my mother okay. I was much closer to my sister, though. She protected me, and we talked about things. With my mother, I didn't want to upset her, and I also didn't want the trouble there would be if I upset her. If I did try to talk to her about anything important to me, somehow it always backfired. I just stopped talking to her—she was just kind of at a distance. My sister really protected me, very much so. But I spent a lot of time trying to figure out how to fix her, what to do. I thought if I knew the right things to say, that would make her better.

Cecily: I remember one time my dad drove us down to Tennessee when she was ill, and we stayed there for the summer. He came down, and when she was well, she came down. So things like that. It wasn't a big deal. There was just one incident with my favorite aunt, who got upset about something I did and said, "Cecily, dammit, you're enough to drive anybody crazy," referring to the exasperation of it. If she had known what that had meant to me, she would have never gone there.

Pat: Every weekend I went to the apartment across town where my aunt and my grandmother lived. I loved it over there—I was special, we did fun things, they were really happy to be with me. I remember this one time I called her on the phone while I was there, and she just said, "Oh, you don't miss me," and she was crying, and I kind of went numb when she said that. I remember the sense that I was supposed to say something, but nothing would come out of my throat; I remained silent. But the fact was, I didn't miss her, and I didn't miss being at home, and she was right and she knew it. There must have been this relief for me not to be at home. But what's interesting is, it was about what she needed from me, not what I needed.

I always felt the argument was about me, somehow that I was the cause of it. (I found out years later that my mother refused to have sex with my father after I was born, and that went on for years, so in a way the arguments *were* about me.) I had the feeling I would do something wrong, then my father would get mad and yell and storm around, and my mother would get upset. I felt like I was the one that lit the fuse, and then whatever happened must be my fault. I thought I was supposed to love them more.

Cynthia also assumed that her mother's unhappiness must be her fault and was preoccupied with criticizing herself and pushing herself to do more to try to help or heal her mother. She not only kept a journal but also made tapes of her thoughts and feelings, so her recollections here are unusually specific.

Cynthia: I was the one that was wrong. When I look back in my journals and see these tapes, I was always writing or saying into the tape recorder, "Mom's so sad," and "Why can't I either love her enough or be better, get better grades?" so it was really just Mom being really sad, and because she was so sad, she drank, and then it just made her more sad. She made me crazy! I wrote more than once, "I'm just such a bad kid. It's my fault."

We all walked on eggshells, in our own way. My brother just disappeared. I liked crafts, so I would make stuff all the time. I remember once for her birthday, I think I was probably ten or eleven, I found a place out in the woods and I cleared it out, and it was just this beautiful bed of moss, and it was just a real quiet, peaceful place. So I made this into a sitting place for her, so Mom could come out and just sit and have some peace and quiet and get away from whatever it was that was bothering her. She loved it and she loved the thought, but she never used it, and so in my young mind, there was another time that I blew it. I just couldn't get it right.

Guilt, preoccupation, and worry are only some of the feelings these women experienced. Most of the women I interviewed talked about their anger at their mothers, fathers, other relatives, and mental health professionals, but much of this is in hindsight. Being angry at a parent is easier to acknowledge when a child is old enough to have some self-sufficiency, especially when the attachment is already insecure. Jerri, who seemed to have made primary attachments apart from her mother, was the freest in showing her anger as a child and recalls here how she reacted.

Jerri: I remember being about eight or nine years old when my mother wanted my hair in a pageboy. She came home from the hospital one weekend and she was going to do my hair. She started fussing with it, and I kicked her in the shins. I yelled at her, and I think I said something about wanting to go back and live with my grandmother. It was the only time I can honestly remember being angry about all of that. I felt bad, but at the same time I didn't feel as if I had a mother. I could count on my grandmother being there, and I couldn't count on my mother being there for any length of time. I got angry other times when she would tell me to do things I thought were just stupid. When I got my period, I didn't know what was going on, and she told me "Your blood is changing and your body is changing," and I thought it was all about my blood changing. When I found out the real explanation I was so mad at her— she just didn't know anything, she couldn't help me with the things I needed help with.

I can remember her buying a dress for me once. I came home from school and she showed me the dress that she bought for me. I absolutely hated it. I think I was just very angry because this was so disruptive to my life and I already didn't have a stable place to live. I'd be at my grandmother's house, and then I'd be at my mother's house, and back and forth, and I didn't have any say about it. Somebody—usually my father—would just say, "Okay, get your stuff. We're going here now" or "We're going back home now." I really hated not being told what was going on. And I blamed her, sometimes, for all that.

June had trouble for a long time knowing what she felt, since her primary focus was her mother's feelings and behavior. But as she got a little older, she recalls more angry feelings toward her mother. She said several times that for her whole life, it's been okay to hate her father and see him as bad, because he was known to have sexually abused her and probably her sisters. Her mother, though, has been a different story.

June: I felt extremely loyal to her and to the secrets we were supposed to keep. It was just a given. As far as specific memories of things that I remember emotionally, there aren't that many. Feeling worried and concerned all the time, I remember that. But if you're on "red alert" all the time, you're not feeling a lot, you're just on red alert! I didn't pay any attention to how I felt, I just focused on handling her. I knew pretty early that the goal of listening to my mother was to calm her down, make her feel better, keep her from killing herself. So I wasn't listening to get information or taking what she said seriously, I was listening to take care of her.

After a long time of that, I would be really angry when she said she was going to kill herself. On the inside I would be thinking, "What a fucking trump card. I can't say anything to that, can I?"

My father was sexually abusive, and it was known and labeled and acknowledged. People couldn't really prevent it from happening, they couldn't stop him, but it was known as wrong. He had been bad. It's been okay my whole life to hate him. But about her, it's always been so complicated.

Tara Elgin Holley speaks for many of the women in this book when she writes, "I was constantly trying to piece together the puzzle. I was obsessed with this woman who, to me, was more than just my mother.... At some point, I had begun to understand that she was not to be talked about. To other members of the family, she was a symbol of darkness, of something forbidden."[8]

MOM GOES TO THE HOSPITAL

As with any chronic illness, there are signs and symptoms that alert the family of someone with psychiatric problems that things are deteriorating. The interviewees in middle childhood knew and understood somewhat more than they had as younger kids and were sometimes given more responsibility by other family members or even by mental health professionals. Some of these women's mothers were never hospitalized but were diagnosed or treated as outpatients, and ironically, some of the most destructive mothers were never treated at all or even seen as having psychiatric problems.

Treatments, especially in the 1960s and 1970s, were often almost as bad as the illness. Insulin shock treatment, as seen in the movie *A Beautiful Mind* (2001), was used infrequently by this time, but ECT (electroconvulsive treatment) was in favor, and many women in this book report that their mothers had one or more series of ECT. It's still used today, but almost exclusively for intractable depression, and the way it's administered is much improved. In these earlier decades, though, ECT seems to have been used somewhat indiscriminately. Then and now, it causes memory loss, to varying degrees. It's quite common that when children, even today, visit their mothers in a psychiatric hospital after ECT, their mothers don't recognize them.

Medications are also an important part of psychiatric treatment and, again, have changed pretty dramatically in the past couple of decades. For most of the mothers we're discussing, given the time period involved, medication had significant side effects, including lethargy, weight gain, a feeling of mental fog, and so forth. The medications for psychosis sometimes caused a condition called tardive dyskinesia, a disorder causing very unattractive and strange-looking facial movements. The antipsychotic medications available today generally have fewer side effects, and therefore a somewhat higher rate of compliance. Given some of the extreme side effects of the older medications, it's hard to blame patients for not wanting to take them.

Some of the stories that follow are about these women's visits to their mothers in the hospital, and some are about the attempts of other relatives, neighbors, or friends to help out in these circumstances.

June: When my mother went to the hospital the first time, when I was ten, me and my sister stayed with a friend of my mother's. And she took us to see the psychologist once, because she was concerned. She said, "Their mother is gone, and the children don't cry. Something is wrong—shouldn't they be crying and missing her?" And my sister and I still laugh about that. But the truth is, she had the right idea—she knew there was something really wrong if we didn't even miss our mother.

It was very strange to be at her house. You'd think we would like it, but I didn't know what to do, I didn't know how to do it. By that time, things were just chaotic at home, so I didn't know how to sit at the table and have a regular dinner or follow certain rules or whatever. I was clueless. I didn't know the rules. So it wasn't a refuge at all.

Alice: I was eleven when she went in the hospital the first time. I was relieved—I felt I could breathe. The house was much quieter, much more organized with just me and my father and the kids. When she was out of the house, there were certain things that we knew were going to happen day to day.

This became a typical pattern when she started going in the hospital more often: A neighbor would meet us at school and would say, "Your mom had to go to the hospital." My dad never really talked about it, he just focused on getting the house in order. Like he could be in control of something if he just ran a tight ship. But my feeling was, "What a break from the craziness."

I was in therapy then, when I was about eleven. [The therapist] invited the whole family up, and we had a family session. It was a kind of therapy where I got to have people act out the family picture, who was doing what. I got to set up the family picture, and at one point I had my mother—I will never forget this—I had her facing the door, she was leaving, and I said, "Mom, put your hand on the door and open it about a foot and act like you are leaving," so her back was to everybody else. Everybody was supposed to freeze in their roles so we could get a feeling of what it was like. Well, she freaked, she started sobbing, and then it was just all about her and her being upset, from then on. But at least I got to say something about how it was for us.

Jerri: There was a stigma about the state mental hospital, and kids would joke about it—"You're going to [the hospital] if you don't straighten up." So of course, every time I heard that, I would just cringe, because my mother had been in there. I would never want them to know. It was a big joke.

I knew that it was weird to go there to see her, that it wasn't a normal hospital. I still remember going up the big, long driveway and seeing all of the trees and going in the door. The lobby was beautiful. I didn't know the word then, but it seemed so sterile. It didn't look like a place where people would get better. That's the way it looked to me, like everybody was acting out a role. It's funny, because I can just remember Mom never seemed to ever be getting better, so I couldn't figure out what was going on. I didn't see hospital beds, like you do in a regular hospital, so I couldn't figure out where people were and what they were doing.

I felt like I was going through the motions. My father would be there, and I knew I was supposed to hug my mother and act glad to see her, so I did it, but not because I felt like it. I was nervous because I didn't know what she would do. She was pretty out of it. I think by that time I didn't feel very connected to her anymore.

It got to be a routine that if I came home and my dad told me I had to stay at my aunt's for a while, I knew she was going into the hospital again. But he really didn't explain it at all.

Tess: God, there were so many times she had to go to the hospital. She might go for months sometimes. I remember most of this starting when I was nine or ten. She had electroshock treatment, but I think she had it twice, because it failed the first time. She said she knew what they were going to do and she didn't want her thoughts erased, or to forget what she was thinking. So she wrote everything down so she could remember later. She lied to the nurses—she told them she wanted to write a letter home to her mother in Italy. Meanwhile, she wrote everything that she wanted to remember, which were all these thoughts about a conspiracy against her. And of course, it was all in Italian, so the nurses had no idea! She believed for years that my father's family had a conspiracy against her and plotted about her behind her back.

One striking element of these stories is how little these women, even at this young age, were told or understood about what the hospital, or various treatments would do, so that they could understand what was happening. During those decades, though, physical illnesses were handled the same way. Nowadays we're much more likely to explain things to children, although this applies more to physical illnesses than to mental ones.

Danielle: When we were in Connecticut, I know she was taking pills, and my sister thinks they were Valium. And so, did she ever go to a psychiatrist? No, I don't think so. A psychologist or a therapist? No. But I think her GP, or whatever, gave her psychiatric medications.

Pat: Her primary symptom was facial pain. She used to walk around with a rag on her face or lie down with something on her face. It was like there was this open wound of some sort. I don't know if my sister could put a time on that or not, but the crisis around her medical care evolved into the focus on the pain, the facial pain. Although she was clearly very depressed and unable to do much, she and my father always defined it as this physical problem.

Rachel: My mom had anorexia and bulimia. She would make herself throw up in the bathroom and explain to me why she needed to do it. She would chew the food and spit it out. She also did something a psychiatrist told me is called rumination—she would chew up food, like brownies, and then spit it up. From the time I was really young I remember her weighing herself all the time. She threw so many scales down the living room stairs to smash them, it was just a routine thing. She would go on every weird diet there was and had all kinds of special foods in the house just for herself.

But according to her, it was everyone else that had the problem. She was perfectly fine—in fact, she was the best mother anybody could have. So—treatment? Diagnosis? Going to a hospital? No way.

Barbara: It's easy to identify my mother's illness—she's been hospitalized many, many times. The first was when I was about ten. She was brought to a place in Massachusetts. I have no memories before that, but my sister said she had torn up my sister's homework and done other weird stuff. I have images but no real memories of what happened. I wasn't told what happened and had to figure it out later.

> **Cecily:** I remember sitting in the kitchen once, and she had on an apron, and I remember her being worried about fire in the house, saying something like electrical outlets were not safe because there was electricity flowing through them. I remember thinking "That's a little strange," so I called my dad. I said, "Something's up, Dad, I don't know." In a second he was there, because he had that kind of job. He came home, and she went to the hospital ... but I never felt like I told on her and she had to go. It was more like "I think your mother is getting sick." And he took care of it.

One of the most striking things about Cecily's family and her mother's illness was that her mother and father consulted with an extremely enlightened psychiatrist, who took care of Cecily's mother for many years. She provided accurate information about schizophrenia and was ahead of her time in saying that Cecily and her brothers should be told in simple terms what the illness was and what to expect in the future. It would be hard to overestimate the importance of this extraordinary person in the life of this family. Even now, in 2007, this is an enlightened approach, and one would be lucky to find a mental health professional who is as helpful.

MOM IN PUBLIC

Here we look at experiences with a "mad" mother outside the family—either in a social gathering or out in public. Sometimes there was a dramatic difference in public versus private behavior, and although, of course, we all behave somewhat differently around "outsiders," the differences reported here are more like 180-degree turns. This was most characteristic of the personality-disordered mothers. Since their reality testing isn't impaired and they are often very charming and pleasant, they frequently create the impression that their families are Disney productions, and children in these families are repeatedly told how lucky they are to have such a wonderful/kind/loving/cool mother.

> **Juliana:** She put a whole different persona out to the public. People thought she was very kind and nurturing, and she would save that for the office. She gave people gifts and she would be really sweet, and people fell for it. But there were times we would be out somewhere and she would be that way and act nice to me in public—and then we'd get in the car and she'd crawl over the seat to get at me and scream at me about how bad I had been and how much she was fed up with me.

Needless to say, this makes it much harder for a child or adolescent to confide in others about what's going on behind closed doors, and

Juliana reported that when she confided in a friend, the friend just said, "That can't possibly be true," and walked away. Children of personality-disordered mothers have a much harder time believing that their own perceptions are valid, as their mothers routinely deny this validity, and the fact that the destructive behavior is visible only to them makes it that much harder. Recall that it's Juliana who said she still struggles with feeling that "maybe it was all me, I made her behave that way."

It's a rare parent who doesn't sometimes act relaxed when they're out with their kids in public, but will take any available private moment to hiss furiously at a misbehaving child. And it's a rare parent who wouldn't be embarrassed to be caught in one of these "bad parent" moments. But here we're talking about a much more calculated kind of interchange.

Rachel saw early on that her mother was full of rage and often out of control and used that memory to clarify any confusion she might otherwise have felt when her mother was gracious and friendly in public. Helen and her sister also saw the warm "outside" mother and contrasted it with the mother they knew at home, but Helen's mother was not personality disordered, nor did her public-private difference seem calculated to discredit the children's experience. It also helped that Helen and her sister had each other, as it's much easier to hold onto one's perceptions if even one other person agrees with it.

> **Helen:** She was warm towards other people. It was only us—my sister and myself, who lived in the house—who saw the other way she was. We always felt like we didn't dare say anything, because everybody was crazy about my mother. We sort of had to keep it to ourselves, just the two of us. Luckily we had each other, and we were honest with each other. We could talk to each other.

Sometimes mothers were cutting or nasty to their daughters in front of others, not only calling attention to the particular incident but making it easy for others to see how bad the relationship was. There were also many instances of daughters overhearing their mothers, especially when the mothers were "high" or beginning a manic state, and being deeply embarrassed by their inappropriate talk or behavior. And sometimes mothers were conspicuous by their absence.

> **Cynthia:** Mom wouldn't start yelling—she didn't yell with neighbors around—but she would get this tone in her voice that is really harsh and very cutting. It just wakes you up in a second, and it would be horrible for me and really uncomfortable for whoever else was there, like kids I was playing with.

Alice: I just remember my bedroom window was above the patio, and I would hear these things she would be saying, and even at age eight I knew you just don't say those things in mixed company. I remember just shrinking in bed thinking, "Oh my god, shut up, don't say these things."

She just didn't want anything to do with us kids, really. My friends in school, their mothers would come and bring cupcakes to the school, they would go on field trips, and they would be the ones in the classroom. She didn't do shit. Whether she couldn't or wouldn't or it was too much, who knows? She always had an excuse.

The worst of having a mad mother in a public place is something like what these two women experienced. In *Wishing for Snow*, Minrose Gwin says:

By the time she had gotten crazier and begun to do things like walk up and down the street in her bathrobe with stockings drooping and blooming at her ankles, she had become a town legend. But even as a child I could see people shrink from her. She was known for her temper, for the way she had of lashing out. While she fed us and [took care of us at home], she would scream at us and hit us with vigor and determination, as if this were part of her job.[9]

Tess: She was sure that people were tape-recording her. You didn't know when you went out if she would spot somebody in church or in the supermarket and just start in on them. She would just wait for the Mass to end, and right when we got outside, or once we got in the supermarket, she'd have these outbursts. She'd start screaming and making a scene, and we knew what was coming. It was, like, "Please, Mommy, please, don't, don't, don't. We're little kids. Let's go home, let's go home." We'd drag her out. It was so embarrassing, even for the person she was suspicious of, and it was always, like, "Please don't say that. You don't know what you're saying. You don't know what you're saying." And *to* them: "You've been hurting me, and I know what you're doing"—all in Italian, and all these curses. Oh my God, and it was just as heart-wrenching as it was embarrassing, and you felt bad for the person, and you felt bad for her and for us. You just never knew what was going to happen.

DAUGHTERS GO OUT INTO THE WORLD

Given the way things felt at home, it should come as no surprise that the women I talked to had clear recollections of visiting other kids' families and seeing what life was like on the inside with them. These days, the chance to see other families is readily available on TV and in children's movies, so kids growing up with mentally ill parents may not experience the difference so profoundly. (As well, people actually talk about mental illness openly today, both on TV and in real life.) Most of the women interviewed here grew up at a time when there were some ideal families on TV programs, but they didn't come up much in the interviews as being very influential. What seemed to pack the wallop was actually being in the midst of another kid's family and feeling the difference.

> **Eleanor:** Our next-door neighbors had kids our age, and when we all started playing together, I really liked it at their house. It was lively, and the mother seemed to really like her kids—she smiled at them and at us. And the kids acted like they liked her back. They seemed relaxed and happy. There wasn't any of the tension of my house, the feeling of always being on the lookout for something bad to happen. Being at home felt even more oppressive and heavy after I would hang out at other houses, and most other kids around seemed to have moms more like their mom, and I started to see how different my mother was.

Helen, whose mother was chronically depressed, felt more freedom at other kids' houses, and she talks about a difference between her own home and "over there."

> **Helen:** I couldn't wait to finish my dinner and run over there, because all the action was over there. Our place was pretty dead, it wasn't fun or exciting. At home I had to walk on eggshells all the time, not do anything that would upset Mom and cause a problem. There I felt like I could relax and play.
>
> **Alice:** When I went to elementary school, I remember going to kids' houses to play and just seeing this clean house, mothers who would give us snacks, having a playroom where the toys were organized, and, you know, doing fun things and having interactions with the parents. I just would want to go there all the time after school.

That phrase of Alice's, "having interactions with the parents," seems rather poignant and says it all. Just seeing a child and mother interact was a noticeable event for her.

> **June:** In a friend of mine's house, everybody was yelling all the time—about everything: "Hey, get the pizza out of the oven," or whatever. I felt so much relief there because people were saying stuff and talking to each other. I felt so calm at her house, it was amazing. And if my friend ever came to my house, *she* felt calm because nobody was yelling, it was nice and quiet! To me it was deadly; to her it was calm.

As kids grow up and spend even more time away from their homes and families, the contrasts become even more stark. Yet some of these women felt they never got a clear sense of how different their home life was until they were adults. Some felt that it was normal for parents and children to be hostile to each other, as a matter of course, and were surprised that there were families with genuine warmth and regard for one another despite tensions and conflicts. Others idealized "normal" families and had to get a more realistic view, but even then they could see a vast difference between many other families and their own. This is common among people who grew up in dysfunctional families of all kinds. Because Jerri spent time away from her mother, living at relatives' houses when her mother was in the hospital, she knew what she was missing when her mother isolated herself from others. Jerri's longing to be part of normal family activities is poignantly related in this story.

Jerri: I remember one Christmas Eve my dad went down to his mother's house for an hour or so to have a drink. Now, my mother couldn't go to other people's houses, or have people over, anything like that. And I was just wanting to be with people all the time. My mother said, "Let's go take a walk." When I think of how far we walked that night, we must have gone three miles. We walked by my grandmother's house, where they were having Christmas Eve, and I could see in the window, and I remember thinking, "I hope Mom stops. I hope we're going to go visit." I was just praying that we were going to stop there, but we just kept walking in the dark. I remember getting so excited looking at our Christmas tree and always praying that somebody was going to stop by. That's why my Christmases now have got to be filled with people.

I felt very alienated from her. She was my mother and I respected her, but I always felt I was so completely different from her. I never worried about getting sick like her, because I never thought I was like her at all.

KEEPING FAMILY SECRETS

When kids start to spend substantial amounts of time in school, not under their parents' direct supervision, the issue of enforced secrecy rears its ugly head. None of the women in this book voluntarily told anyone what was going on at home, at least not without pressure.

Tess: I wouldn't bring friends home—it would be totally embarrassing. I would have been embarrassed if they were to see my mother. She was scary, even to look at. You didn't know what the heck was going on inside of her.

Danielle: Nothing I would do on the outside would betray what went on in the house at all when I was older.

Eleanor: I would never dream of telling anybody that my mother was mentally ill or in a hospital. It was just overwhelmingly obvious that it was a shameful secret and something you'd make sure nobody ever knew about. That meant nobody coming over to be at my house, first off. And just not talking about anything personal.

Jerri: After I was about ten, she started getting better, I think, because she didn't go back to the hospital after that. We still had to walk on eggshells all the time, but she wasn't as bad. When she came home from the hospital, it always seemed like she was zonked out on medication. She would be really slow. But she would talk about her electric shock treatments in front of people, even my girlfriends if they were there. She'd say, "Oh yeah, I had treatments and they put all these wires on my head." That was really embarrassing, and I remember my friends staring at her. She just seemed oblivious to how they were reacting to her and what she was saying.

I never, ever told anybody, because I always got the impression that it was very wrong to talk about anything that was private. So therefore, I was always afraid to talk about anything, not just my mother but anything at all that was private or in the family. It felt like I would be breaching some kind of a trust or it was a sin. Of course, that followed me into marriage later on.

Several of the women expressed their sense that there was "shame by association" with a mother who was mentally ill or had been in a psychiatric hospital. Laura Love, author of *You Ain't Got No Easter Clothes*, describes the feeling she had when taunted by a schoolmate ridiculing her family and her shabby clothes at Easter: "Consuming, overpowering shame. Shame and rage. Absolute, all-encompassing, overarching hatred overwhelmed me."[10] She then jumped on the schoolmate and beat her up, which under the circumstances seemed justified and very satisfying to the author (not to mention the reader).

There are other reasons for secrecy, too. Some families explicitly tell kids not to talk to outsiders, not to trust anybody outside the family. Others threaten that if kids say anything, they'll be taken away or something awful will happen to them or their siblings. Love writes that she and her sister "were threatened with bodily harm and abandonment if we ever discussed our mother's past with anyone. Specifically we were never to tell a soul, be it child or adult, that our mother had tried to hang herself, nor were we to entertain questions about our dead father. She told us she could not forgive us if we ever revealed our family secrets, and that we would have to fend for ourselves if we did, because she would be called home to be with God in the event of our betrayal."[11] This was not an idle threat, as their mother frequently made suicide attempts and threatened suicide.

Rachel: My mother told me that if I ever told anybody at school what happened at home that my brothers and I would be taken from the home, be split up, and each be put in separate foster homes, and it would be my fault. I believed her, and it scared me to death.

June: I sometimes would tell friends she was mentally ill, since it seemed in a way like everybody knew anyway. I did say that, but I still didn't let anyone come to my house, or whatever. When I look back at my friends then, they were all from alcoholic homes, so they all had secrets, too. We just gravitated together. We didn't really talk, but they got it. My friend whose mother was a pothead and whose father was an alcoholic, at two in the afternoon we'd move the bureau in front of her bedroom door, because pretty soon her father would be coming home and he would be drunk, and we didn't want him in there when he was drunk. We didn't talk about it; it was just, "Help me move the bureau."

Pat, on the other hand, was in on her mother's secret. She was sent to the pharmacy by her mother to pick up pills (she now thinks they may have been phenobarbital) and was cautioned not to talk to anyone except one particular pharmacist.

> **Pat:** I knew that whatever he was giving her, he wasn't supposed to give her. It was in the days before you had to sign for medications. It was kind of a secret, and she definitely didn't want me talking to anybody else about it.

In Alice's family, marked primarily by neglect, there were no secrets, and in fact no privacy. Everyone from outside seemed to know everything that was going on. There was an advantage in that she didn't have to cover for her mother, but she also had no choice about what to keep to herself.

> **Alice:** When her friends would call, I would have to say, "She's in bed, she can't answer the phone." And they knew what I meant, so it was like everybody knew what was going on but nobody ever did anything about it.

Although June was supposed to keep family secrets, she paradoxically had a feeling of transparency especially in relation to her neighbors. It seemed to her that everyone knew more than she did, in fact. The family lived on a major road through town and was visible to neighbors and passersby. Neighbors at times brought priests to the house to try exorcism on June's mother, and once on June herself, and people in the local shops knew all about the "crazy woman" down the street. There was no sense of boundaries. Still, there was the prohibition against talking to anyone who might take action.

> **June:** She would tell me, "Look, you're going to meet with the social worker today, and be sure you don't say anything, because they might take you away." She told us you couldn't trust anybody, not to talk to anybody. So it was trying to learn how to ask for enough help from the outside without getting so much help that they'd want to take us away!
>
> **Sarah:** After my father died when I was eight, my mother got a widow's pension from Social Security because she had an underage

child—me. So I was her only source of income. Her whole family—her abusive mother and all the other relatives—knew that would be in jeopardy if anyone found out what was going on at home, so I was told very explicitly to keep quiet, period. One of my aunts was also concerned that if I told what was going on and was taken out of there and put in foster care, that she might not be able to see me. So at least there was a little caring there. So when the neighbors called DCFS [the Department of Child and Family Services] to report crazy stuff at our house, my aunt would run over and explain that I was just a bad kid, nothing was wrong, all that, and they would eventually leave. She really believed she'd never see me again if I got taken away. Also, she was a devout Catholic, and at that time it seemed it was okay to beat kids all the time, to discipline them. So my grandmother did it to my mother, and it just went on from there. Once someone on my father's side of the family said I could come live with them, but I didn't know them well, and they lived a long way away, and I was also scared about leaving my mother alone and being the cause of her having no money. I was twelve then.

When something feels like the most important thing in your life, keeping it secret exacts a high price. There's significant evidence that when a person is traumatized, how others handle the situation is almost as important as the trauma itself. Being able to talk about what happened with others who are supportive and being able to integrate it into your life in a way that makes sense to you are two of the key elements in healing from trauma. Bad secrets tend to fester, making children feel isolated, and protecting a shameful secret requires a lot of work, a lot of avoidance, and a lot of distance from other people who might find out. Real intimacy and trust can be compromised permanently.

Secrets are troublesome in another way: if you have a shameful secret from when you were ten, your understanding of it is pretty much limited by your ten-year-old understanding. Actually telling it out loud, in words, to another person, can feel like opening a time capsule. I've sat with patients who finally reveal something they've kept guarded for decades, and it's almost as though we're opening a vault filled with old, stale air. Hearing the secret spoken aloud is powerful and is often enough, just in itself, to put it in a more realistic perspective. Once the secret is spoken, I may only have to ask, "How old were you when this happened?" for us both to see with amazing clarity how young they were, how vulnerable, how limited in their power to act and even to understand.

Secrets can also be hidden in plain sight, as June found out, to her amusement.

June: When my mother called up my friend's mother to see why the kids weren't in school, my mother introduced herself as "Ed," because I guess that was one of her personalities and happened to be male. I was freaking out about how I would ever explain that to my friend. But it turned out her mother was so stoned that she thought it must be *her* being stoned and imagining the whole thing. So one craziness covered another, and there was nothing to explain. That was pretty funny.

FATHERS AND SIBLINGS

Where were the fathers in these families? And what happened to sisters and brothers? Most of the books about mental illness in the family focus on spouses and parents of mentally ill people, so much so that in some "family" books, the children of mentally ill parents are barely mentioned. Here we'll try to understand the role of fathers, brothers, sisters, and extended family members, but in relation to the *daughters* of mentally ill mothers. Often it's the daughter, especially an older daughter, who is expected to take on the mother's role in the house when she's not able to, running the household and taking care of younger siblings. She often becomes the father's confidante, as well. When things go extremely badly, daughters can also be sexually abused by fathers if mothers are absent or impaired. When elderly parents need care, hospital charts have a space to fill in for "primary caregiver," and the "joke" among hospital social workers is that this is just a euphemism for "daughter." Daughters are on the front line to pick up the slack when their mothers are ill, whether physically or mentally, and this expectation can begin in childhood.

The authors of *Growing Up with a Schizophrenic Mother* found that almost half of the adults they interviewed had fathers who left the family in one way or another.[12] When the mother was seen as the automatic custodial parent, almost all schizophrenic mothers retained custody of their children, even when fathers or other family members made strenuous efforts to remove the children from an unsafe or chaotic environment.

When fathers stayed in the family, they cited a number of reasons for doing so: they felt loyalty or a sense of duty, or they took their marriage vows seriously and didn't consider leaving. Some described their wife as "the love of my life" and took care of her for decades. Some felt religious prohibition, some felt they didn't deserve a more fulfilling marriage, and some said they were "not a quitter." Some seemed simply to be disengaged and uncaring, not bothering to go to the trouble of getting a divorce or leaving, whereas others persisted in hoping that their wife would recover. In still other families, there were periods of relative quiet and calm, when life went on as normal, and this seemed a good buffer against the bad times.

Cynthia: My dad would try to be calm, he tried to tough it out and find out what it was he could do. What does Mom need now? How can he help? He tried to give nice gifts; he was quite conscious of trying to be helpful and show his love to this person who just—I mean, there was nothing any of us could do, she just felt so unlovable. I hear all of our voices pleading, "What is it that we can do?" But he would also get very angry and frustrated. I remember his frustration, and there was a lot of yelling.

Alice: As far as my father, there was no privacy in the house at all. Nobody was allowed to close any doors, and he would shower and walk around naked. Once, when I was seven or eight, he ended up lying on top of me on the bed, and he had his underwear on, but I remember thinking, "What is he doing?" He was hugging me. So I had nothing at all from my mother, and this smothering, inappropriate stuff from him. When she finally went in the hospital for a longer time, when I was ten, then I was more his confidante, more like a husband-and-wife kind of thing. He and I would go food shopping, then we would clean on Sundays after Sunday's dinner—music on the hi-fi, dishtowel over the shoulder. He would wash, I would dry, whatever.

When my mother was home, he would never really cross her. He wouldn't say to her, "This isn't appropriate," even once. When she had us kneeling on the floor every night saying the rosary, he would never challenge it or say, "This is a bit much." We weren't supposed to do anything to upset her. So there was no protection from him.

Pat: My father was obviously a huge factor here, being so aggressive, verbally abusive, and just impossible. But she had incredible loyalty to him. She never exposed him, she never complained about him. She would cry about him, and I saw that, and I saw how he treated her, but she never blamed him for anything. I'm sure she felt she had no choice but to stay with him. My younger sister was like a nonperson to me. I was just trying to survive in that house, and she was so much younger. Some kids bond, I guess, but we just went our separate ways.

Rose: In my house you were supposed to be very stoic. But I realized at some point that my father saw my mother as very fragile. My cousin once made me hold a plate of gunpowder and lit it, and it blew up right in my face, burned my eyebrows, my hair, my face. My father came running out, then my mother came out, saw me, passed out, and my father goes to take care of my mother. I was standing there smelling flesh burning and wondering, "Did I lose my face?" But he was obviously very nervous about how well she could cope. After he died [when Rose was a teenager], she just fell apart. I saw what he had been nervous about.

Eleanor: My mother was riveted on my father. He was the one she felt was controlling her, and everything was a hidden war between them. He was very controlling in many ways, some direct and some subtle, so in a way she was right. He needed to dominate everything. You could just tell from the tones of voice—he would be very polite in telling her what to do, and she would try to find holes in his logic. Then he would be even more polite and condescending, but you knew he was seething. He never hit her, but if we were at all questioning his authority, he would lash out and hit us kids. You were just not ever supposed to question anything. I know some of that was fury at my mother. She was pretty powerless in trying to get him to stop beating us up if it happened in front of her. So even though I know he was the one that provided the structure and normalcy in our lives, there wasn't much feeling of safety around him, because he was wound so tight.

Helen: In some ways my father made my sister take the role of the wife. She spoke English better than they did, so part of it was that. But also, it was just accepted that my mother was incapable of doing things, so my father just turned to my sister as though she were an adult. And I turned to her, too—she was more like a mother than my mother was.

Jerri: My father really ruled the roost. It was just "Never, ever do anything to upset your mother." She needed all this protection, I guess, and he was very domineering and controlling, so it came naturally to him.

Some of the women had extended families that played a role in one way or another. Some relatives turned a blind eye, or were in denial, as Danielle relates.

Danielle: My grandparents were in denial that there was any kind of problem—in fact, *I* was the problem, because I was being "mean" to my mother. They didn't see the mistreatment directly. I told them my mother needed help, but they just couldn't accept it at all.

Tess's relatives, all on her father's side, tried to help in various ways, but Tess's mother was too suspicious to make any connection with them. They could have been more a source of relief and comfort for Tess and her siblings, except for her mother's hatred of them and refusal to spend time at their houses.

Tess: We couldn't go to the relatives for holidays, or if we did, we'd have to rush, because we always knew Mommy was home alone, crying and sad. So how could you be happy there? She wouldn't come and she wouldn't come, and then sometimes we just couldn't go, either. Nobody could come to our house because she hated everyone. She didn't trust anybody.

She hated my father. She used to wish for his death. She said, "You ruined my life. You and your horrible family." He had married her in Italy and brought her here, and she just never forgave him for that. And he'd beg her to understand that she was wrong, that everybody loved her and we're trying to help her. And other people, the relatives, God they really tried. They took a lot of put-downs from her.

My father was an absolute saint. He did everything. He took care of us; he worked long hours and then would come home and cook for us;

play with us, when he could; make sure there were special occasions for us. People in town all knew what a great guy he was—they'd see him doing the shopping, taking us to church. They knew what was going on even when we didn't say anything. They loved him and would say to us, "Your dad is such a great guy." He had kind of raised his younger sisters, and they would do anything for him, so they would come in and clean the house when my mother was in the hospital.

Tess's brother also became psychotic as an adolescent, and Alice's and Sandy's brothers developed significant emotional problems and drug problems in adolescence. This isn't surprising, as boys tend to act out and abuse substances to help them manage emotional pain, whereas girls are somewhat more likely to become depressed, develop eating disorders, or self-mutilate.

Tess: My brother also got sick, just like my mother. He got very paranoid and violent and would beat me up. And he would lock himself in his room. He's still very strange—he's in the air force and lives on base and has never married or had a girlfriend. Just very rigid and obsessive and angry. My sisters kind of clung to each other, and they're still close. I'm the one that doesn't fit in.

    Alice: In this family therapy psychodrama, I put my brother Robert as a dog because of his coping mechanism. When my brother came home from seeing Mom in the hospital, it was two weeks before he would talk. He would drink water and milk out of a bowl, and he acted like a dog. I just felt so sad. I was ten or eleven, and they were younger, and they were really groping for some kind of love or comfort. My grandfather helped some, and my sister was close to a neighbor and spent time over there, but my sister ended up acting out with drinking and sexual behavior, and my brother got into drugs by the time he was twelve. They did what they had to do.

    Sandy: My older brother had some significant emotional problems, and then started using drugs a lot, and then selling, so we had police at the house, and he was carted off a number of times. This just kept happening. He was a casualty of their war.

This following story from Rachel is one of the strangest I've ever heard and shows how little the extended family can intervene or help, even when the home situation is obviously out of control.

Rachel: I was very close to my mother's parents. I think they were better grandparents than they had been parents, because my mom would constantly say, "Your grandparents only love you because they're trying to get back at me" or "They're trying to show you the love that they never gave me." They were very loving and paid attention to me and enjoyed playing with me. They were a refuge for me.

My mother and her mother had very strong, controlling personalities, and both my father and my mother's father were the "stand by your woman" kind of men, and they would never cross their wives. When I was seven, my parents were adopting their second son, who was black. My mother was trying to inflame her parents, because my grandparents are very prejudiced. To take it a step further, my mother renamed him after my grandfather! As soon as the adoption went through, my mother said to her parents, "That's enough. I've had enough with the two of you; you've been a bother to me all of my life. I don't want to have anything to do with you." Then the rest of her family said, "This isn't fair, what you are doing to your parents. You should at least allow your kids to see their grandparents, and vice versa." So my mom said, "Well that's it, then *you* can all go to hell, too." So I lost all my great-aunts and -uncles, my cousins. She disowned her entire family.

I tried to take care of my stepbrothers. None of us were getting what we needed. My mother would yell at them and criticize, and she would actually tell them she hated them. And after they went to bed, she would be screaming at my father how much she hated them, and of course they heard every word.

No one should hear that, especially a child who has been adopted. I would go downstairs in the evening and I would tuck them both in and read to them. I would tell them, "Listen, Mom's just not right. You can't listen to what she says. You're a great person. I love you to death, and you need to know that you're special. I really love you, you're a wonderful kid." I just kept repeating those things to them every night. When they were taken away, I felt that it was my fault, that if I had done more to let them know how special they were, they wouldn't have needed to act out in the ways that they did.

When Jackie got back in touch with me, he told me that being taken out of our home was the best thing that could have happened to him, because he dug his way out of hell. He said I was the one who had raised them, and that I was the one that allowed him to be the person he is today, and that I'm the most important person in his life. Joey said the same thing to me, that getting out was the best thing that could have happened to him, that he'd been through hell and nothing could be worse, and he was prepared for life after that. He was grateful for everything that I had done. It eased the guilt that I had lived with for all those years.

SUICIDE THREATS AND MORE

At the extreme end of the continuum of neglect, making the child feel invisible and unimportant, is a parent's threat of suicide. It's well known that children who witness suicidal behavior or whose parent actually commits suicide feel that they were not enough to make the parent want to stay alive. When the parent is a mother, whose love and devotion is supposed to be unquestioned, the message goes even deeper. It is the ultimate disconfirmation of the child's existence and worth.

Often, others in the family will not acknowledge either the suicidal intention or the actual suicide, redefining it as something else. In these stories, however, there was no doubt or lack of confirmation about what happened.

Sandy: I was seven years old, and my parents and I were all supposed to go out to dinner. But my mother got angry and sat down and said in this cold voice, "You're going out to dinner with your father, and when you come home, I won't be here." And I felt this chill go down my spine. I was sitting in this little black Hitchcock chair in the living room, and she was telling me, basically, I would never see her again. That was the first of probably one hundred suicide threats. My father just kind of dismissed it.

June: My mother was always suicidal, it seemed like. She would talk about it or play with her pills or whatever. It was like it was always a possibility, and my job was to distract her or make sure she didn't do it. It was just part of what we kids did to make sure things didn't get any crazier.

Laura Love had a harrowing experience as a young child, which she describes in her biography:

I do remember my mother's eyes and voice as she paced unseeing through the basement, constantly retracing her steps as if she were on a track. She kept saying, "I'm going to kill myself, I'm going to kill myself, I gotta get out, I'm going to kill myself," while looking periodically to the left and right for the yellow plastic braided laundry rope she knew was stashed somewhere in that house. She didn't seem to be aware of our presence, she was so engrossed and focused on the task before her. We tugged on her hands and her arms, imploring her not to do it. "Please, Mommy . . . Please don't. Pleeeeeease." I have never felt so invisible in my life as in those minutes of that day. She did eventually find the yellow rope and she tied it onto an exposed pipe. She pushed a kitchen chair up under that rope, climbed onto the chair, slipped her head through the knot and walked forward as if simply stepping off a curb . . . she was swinging from a yellow braided laundry rope right in front of our faces. [Both kids working together managed to hold her up while one of them untied the rope. Neighbors came, and then the girls were taken to a picnic to distract them.] My arms were heavy, my legs were heavy, my head was heavy, my hair was heavy.[13]

Children of very disturbed parents have a dual duty: first, to be invisible so as not to cause trouble and attract attention, and second, to be right there, on hand, when help is needed. In *Growing Up with a*

Schizophrenic Mother, the authors interviewed adult children who spoke often of feeling invisible.[14] Sometimes it was a good escape, but other times, as Love illustrates, it meant complete powerlessness to affect the mother's behavior, or even to be enough of a presence in the mother's own mind to prevent her from abandoning the child through suicide.

RESILIENCE

Certain children seem to fare well in adversity, so much so that we shake our heads and wonder how in the world they came out of chaos, abuse, or neglect in one piece. Researchers originally thought that some kids were "invulnerable" to early stress, but this has been shown not to be the case. Resilient kids, as they are called, *do* suffer damage from early family dysfunction. Puzzling out the "how" of this has been the work of many researchers, and the answers still aren't complete. What we do know is that, because of some children's inborn qualities or certain factors in the environment, they're able to make strong connections with people and/or find a meaningful focus for their positive energies. At this middle-childhood stage, kids now spend substantial amounts of time in school and possibly other places away from home. School, church, sports, scouting, jobs—all can be places of refuge where kids can thrive, do well, and lose themselves in something nurturing. These may be the places where kids get love, attention, and encouragement.

Resilient kids describe living in two worlds, taking pains that the two worlds don't collide. They learn to compartmentalize things so that their good experiences remain uncontaminated by their toxic home environment. It's a powerful coping ability, and part of what we see in the most resilient kids. When kids in very dysfunctional families can't find some other place to thrive, for whatever reason, they may just sink out of sight.

> **Pat:** I did really well in school. When I was in the third grade, I made a double promotion. I was called in and I skipped a grade. They told me I had a very high IQ. I was proud of that and loved school.
>
> **Rachel:** School was my safety net away from home. It was my one place to be something, somebody. I could excel. I could be a great student. I could be liked by the teachers. I learned in kindergarten that I was good and that I could get positive attention for being smart and for being a good student. I don't think anyone had a clue that things were so bad at home. Once a teacher told me, "Rachel, when you laugh, the walls start shaking." I was known throughout the school for my laugh. I was just totally out of my shell at school. I was a different person, so there was no clue to the life I had at home when I was at school.
>
> My next-door neighbors, who didn't have kids, kind of took me under their wing and gave me a Christmas gift, and my mother was mad and

tried to make me feel awful about it. They gave me a dress one time because I was always dressed in boy's clothes—and I had to just stick it in a closet.

Having at least one positive adult is extremely important and often cited as the primary protective factor in kids surviving abusive or neglectful childhoods. Some of these women had that experience—for example, Pat, with her aunt and grandmother.

Pat: I had an enormous closeness to my aunt Maureen. I loved my grandmother and my aunt Maureen more than anybody. I just have nothing but happy memories of being out there and being with both of them. My grandmother used to pack me a lunch, and we would go to the park a few blocks away and have a little picnic. I thought that was the greatest thing in the world. I was the center of attention there, and I had friends over in their neighborhood. I went over quite often and have so many good memories of those times.

 Danielle: Outside of the house, I did okay because I had friends and I did well at school. I was a good student, and I also did extracurricular activities like sports. Nobody knew what was going on at my house, so it was an escape. Nobody would have guessed.

 June: Church was a refuge from fourth grade to ninth grade. I went with a friend, the one whose mother smoked pot. There was a puppet show at the church, and we went, and afterwards the minister said, "Who wants to be saved?" and "Who wants to go to heaven?" And I thought that was a good deal, so I went for it. Then he told me he didn't mean I could go to heaven right then. But I ended up going to church two times or three times during the week for choir practice and youth group, and also on the weekend. It was a kind environment, and there were clear rules. I knew what to do—I could memorize the Bible verses and get rewards for that. It was the same every single time that I went, I knew what to expect. If I did certain things, people always thought it was really cool, and they liked me for it. If I did stuff at home, my mother might not even know it's me from one day to the next. At home, one day might be she's comforting or nice, and the next day yelling at me for the same thing.

These kids sought and clung to positive responses they got from people and built on good experiences. Less fortunate kids seem to feel they don't deserve anything good and will actually avoid environments where they are likely to be well received or praised for anything. For some other kids, like Sandy and Eleanor, their inner world was their refuge. And Jerri, whose imagination was so vivid in her earlier years, continued to play with her dolls and write secret notes about her feelings.

Sandy: I spent a lot of time outdoors, in the woods, by myself. I had a whole little life out there. That was where I would find calm and peace and be away from all the craziness at home. I had special places I would go, where it was private and nobody could see me from the house. I made friends with the animals and tried to just lose myself.

Eleanor: I did well in school but didn't make special connections with any teachers, partly because I was very good at being invisible there, just like at home. What I remember most was how much I read. I just read constantly—stories, biographies, adventures, everything and anything. And when I was reading, I was totally absorbed and in another world. That's where I would go when I felt bad. I always had a book in my hand wherever I went, with my finger stuck in it so I wouldn't lose my place.

Chapter 4

Adolescence

Adolescents have to build on whatever foundation they have as they move more fully out into the world. Some have families who support and nurture their success; others make it despite their families. All the women in this book, growing up in the 1960s, 1970s, and a few in the 1980s, successfully completed high school, and many went on to college for at least a year. The teenagers who fell by the wayside at this critical point therefore have no voice here, and we can only guess at what happened to them. Some, I'm sure, ran away from home and ended up on the streets, some probably killed themselves, and some no doubt developed severe emotional problems. A small percentage would have developed the same illness as their mothers. Most have just muddled along quietly, not unlike many of the women in this book. So keeping in mind that these interviews represent only a fraction of the women growing up with a mentally ill mother, let's look at adolescence and its challenges.

If parents and teenagers can agree on one thing, it's that this is a difficult time. As kids try to make stronger attachments with their friends and loosen the bond with their parents, they're in a precarious position. Problems in adolescence can reflect long-standing problems in attachment and in managing feelings, but these are also normal adolescent problems. Working with adolescents in a clinical setting always challenges the clinician to make the call: Is this a kid who's got serious problems that warrant serious interventions? Or is this one who, with some support and containment, can get through these stormy years and into smoother waters in their twenties?

Teenagers typically struggle to become more emotionally independent and to rely more on their own skills and judgment. Ideally they will have internalized ways of managing their intense feelings, and not in a self-destructive way. For kids from troubled homes, adolescence can be a second chance, or it can be so difficult that destructive patterns take hold. Some of the women here were able to break away from their families in a good way and to listen to the positive feedback they got from friends, employers, or teachers. Most found themselves living two lives: one on the surface, where they might appear carefree or confident, and another at home, where they felt guilty, angry, bad, and helpless. In few of these stories do we hear about mothers being actively supportive of their daughters' activities, or taking pride in their accomplishments. Many times, mothers got sicker during this time (as the mothers' menopausal years coincided with their daughters' adolescence), and their daughters, being older, were expected to be more involved in their care and supervision and in running the household, when necessary. Like many kids in dysfunctional families, they all seemed to have to grow up too fast, take on responsibilities too early, and figure the world out with little constructive guidance. In this kind of family, there's often simply not enough energy to go around. The neediest person gets the available attention, and the others make do. In these families, the mother was the neediest person most of the time, although at times siblings acted out or developed serious enough problems to put an extra load on everyone.

There are also rites of passage for adolescent girls and (usually) their mothers: their first menstrual period and their first bra. Both events stood out in the memories of most of the women here.

MOM AT HOME

For Maggie, life at home took a sharp turn when she was thirteen or fourteen, as her mother suddenly developed obsessive-compulsive disorder (OCD). Up until that time, life at home had seemed pretty normal, with the usual ups and downs of family life. Since Maggie wasn't a child when her mother developed OCD, she had some perspective and knew that she hadn't caused the problem, but she did get hooked into thinking it was up to her to find a solution. The impossibility of her mother's demands drove Maggie to develop higher and higher levels of persistence to try to calm things down, despite the fact that she was never successful.

> **Maggie:** She just suddenly got extreme OCD, and it was focused on particular things. Suddenly, when we went grocery shopping she was fixated on different things contaminating each other. The meat couldn't

touch certain things. The cleansers were dangerous. Then she'd just go around and around on whether stuff was contaminated, and it made no sense whatever. But she would hook you into the conversation, and there was no way out.

She would just keep repeating it, no matter what you did: "Do you think the detergent touched the meat?" "Do you think it's safe to cook the meat and eat it for dinner?" She would start to make dinner, and I would go do homework. But then she'd start obsessing: "I'm afraid the meat defrosted too long" or that the meat went bad. "Okay," I'd say, "why would you think the meat went bad?" "Well, because I defrosted it and it's been sitting out." "Did you smell the meat?" "I'm not sure. Would you smell the meat?" "Okay, I'll go smell the meat," and the meat would smell fine. "Well, but smell it again, because maybe you're not smelling it right. I really do smell something. Can you smell the meat again?" "Okay, I'll smell the meat again." Then she'd say, "I really don't think we should eat this, because I just don't think it'll be okay." "Well, what do you want me to do?" "Well, I don't know, maybe I should make something else." "Well, then the meat will be wasted, and we won't have anything to eat." You couldn't get out of the conversation; she'd just keep it going— anything that had to do with food preparation, germs in the house, and not wanting to touch any cleaners at all. She couldn't do that, because they were bad, and if you touched them you'd get sick. I ended up being the one who cleaned the house, because she wouldn't touch any cleaner at all.

Did you ever see that movie with Dustin Hoffman, *Marathon Man*? The one where the Germans captured him and interrogated him. First he would say he didn't know anything about what they were asking, then they kept torturing him and he'd say, "Okay, the answer is yes." And that wasn't good enough, and they'd keep torturing him, and he'd say, "Okay, the answer is no." And then that wasn't good enough, either. He just tried every possible way to escape the torture. I remember seeing that movie twenty years ago thinking, "That's it." There is no right answer, and you are not allowed to walk away from the conversation.

I never knew what she would be like. Is it safe to go home this afternoon? Maybe it is, maybe it isn't. You never knew. The anxiety of it was really awful. There were a couple of times my father would come home and I'd say, "We have to go out. Just get me out of here for an hour or so." Or he would come home from work and he might ask me, "How was your day? and I'd say, "Okay, we've thrown out the meat, we've started the spaghetti. It's your turn now." Then during dinner it could keep going—she would be impossible, and he would start raising his voice. She would run from the table crying, and then we all felt crappy. We felt angry, too, but that wasn't allowed. If I cried, she'd get upset and run into her room and say, "Why can't you understand that I'm sick?" The consequence of that would be me going, "Oh, my God, I made my mother cry. I shouldn't have had this feeling. I shouldn't have said anything about it." I always thought if I could just figure out a way to handle it right, I could make it stop. I just kept trying, even though it was impossible, once she got going. This went on for years.

Without exception, these women said they could not rely on their mothers or go to them for help or support in any area. Their mothers, by and large, didn't provide the elements of a safe attachment, as they were struggling with their own problems.

> **Helen:** I remember friends saying, "I'm going to talk to my mother about this." I never had that sense that I could do that. I couldn't go home and talk to my mother about things.
>
> **Lee:** I think I would just get into taking care of the house and my brother because she was fairly out of it. I remember bits and pieces of things—like putting too much detergent in the machine and it flooded, and my father being extremely kind about it. Or trying to cook, needing help with that. Watching out for my brother. She just wasn't all there.
>
> **Sandy:** I stopped thinking of her as my mother a really long time ago. She would make me feel so goddamn bad and wrong and guilty for not doing what she wanted me to do. I just tried to do whatever it would take to keep her level.

When a parent has been physically abusive, the tide often turns in adolescence. Once the teenager is tall enough and strong enough to challenge a violent parent, a physical confrontation in which the teenager prevails often stops the abuse permanently. This is a very common phenomenon in alcoholics' families and abusive families with all kinds of dysfunction other than mental illness. Juliana was very intimidated by her personality-disordered mother for many years, but less in this instance.

> **Juliana:** When I was about fifteen, she backed me up in the kitchen against the stove and was getting ready to slap me in the face, and I grabbed her by the wrist and I just looked her in the eye and said, "Not ever again, ever," and I dug my fingers in her arm, and I just flung her away from me, and she went in her room and closed the door. The next time she was really angry at me, my brother was still home, and she had him beat me. But at least she stopped, when I stood up to her. I was tall enough and had some confidence in myself. I felt good for doing it.

On the other hand, there was an oasis for Juliana after her brother went off to college. Whether in the long run it turned out to be more confusing or more reassuring is hard to know.

> **Juliana:** Things changed dramatically when my brother moved out to go to school. By then I also had a car and could drive myself to school and to work. I was sixteen or seventeen, and my mother and I actually got along that year. She would come home after work and we would have dinner together or go out to get dinner. She just kind of laid off me.

Barbara also had a powerful and intimidating mother, but needed her friends to confirm her view that it was her mother who was troubled, not her.

Barbara: My friends in high school used to say to me, "Your mother is scary" or "Christ, your mother is weird. She is so mean to you. What a bitch." She was very controlling, would go through all my stuff. I considered her a force to be reckoned with. My friends confirmed it—it wasn't just me. She's just very powerful, and not in a good way.

One tactic used by very controlling mothers is to search through their daughters' possessions in a violent and intrusive way. Many parents surreptitiously take a peek at their kids' journals or go through their backpacks at times—usually when they're worried about specific problems like drugs or sexual behavior—but at least they seem to feel guilty about it. Most parents recognize that their teenage kids need some privacy, but some of the mothers of these women seemed intent on undermining that privacy, and doing so in a demeaning way. Sometimes the intrusion wasn't even in the service of checking up on the child, but simply seems to have been an abusive outburst directed against the daughter's possessions rather than her person. The mothers who acted this way inevitably were the personality-disordered ones, who seemed to function well in the outside world.

Juliana: But I think when I really, really knew that she was out of it was when I was a teenager, and she didn't feel like she could control me as much physically anymore, so she would terrorize my room. If my room wasn't clean enough, she would take everything out of my closet and dump it in a pile in the center of the floor, and she would take the drawers out of the dresser, and she would dump them in the pile, and then she would strip the bed and dump that in the pile, and she would sweep everything off the dresser. I would be standing there backed up against the corner of the room with her verbally berating me. There never seemed to be any specific reason for it, but she acted like she had a perfect right to destroy my room and I had no right to object. She would tell me to clean it up, and I would have to spend hours and hours picking it all up and putting it back together. I realized that wasn't normal.

Rachel: She would go through my room and tear into everything, and I never knew if she had found something she might misconstrue as being wrong. She wouldn't tell me what she found or was looking for, but whatever it was, she'd let me know how bad I was and how angry she was. Her way of expressing her anger was that if I was in the room that she was in, for a two-week period she would slam all the cabinets, not speak to me, and not acknowledge that she was angry with me. After about two weeks she would tell me what it was that I had done. It was a living nightmare.

I could never figure out what I could have done wrong. I was a straight-A student, I tried my best at everything. I never knew what she was thinking was so bad about me. She also had this ritual when it came to pimples. She would pick at mine and my brother's all the time, sometimes with a needle, and it hurt a lot and made a big mess on my face. Her own face was scarred, and I really didn't want to look like her or be like her in any way. I got it in my head that she was getting the evil out of me or something, that this was all bad pus and dirty stuff, and that she had to get the bad out of me. I couldn't figure out anything else—nothing else made any sense. I felt dirty.

There were times my dad would get so frustrated that he would yell at her. Then she would get into the car and say, "That's it, I'm going to kill myself. That's the last you're going to see of me." Sometimes she would just drive around the block; sometimes she would be gone for an hour. The funny thing is, it never scared me. I would be relieved, actually, but I knew she would be back. Of course, that would stop my dad in his tracks. It would be a long time before he got mad again.

She had weird habits, just off the wall. If she was on the phone and had to go to the bathroom, she would take a bowl from the cabinet and go in there and empty it in the sink, so she could stay on the phone. And when we went on a car trip, she'd make us use a coffee can instead of stopping to use a restroom. We didn't stop for anybody who had to go to the bathroom.

Dating proved to be problematic for the girls who tried it. Again, the personality-disordered mothers made things a lot harder, seemingly on purpose.

Juliana: At first when I started to date, I would go through the interrogation routine with my mother. It was very detailed: who their family was, where they lived—a barrage of questions. And she always found something bad about them so she could say I couldn't go out with them. One really nice guy showed up, and she was grilling him and she asked him if his health insurance was paid up. I just about crawled out of the room. We had an okay time, but needless to say, he never asked me out again.

My mother told me all men were shit, they were all assholes, they just want sex, and they'll screw up your life.

For daughters of depressed mothers, the picture was very different. Their mothers just seemed to be absent from the scene. Pat can't remember many details, but does describe her own depression and poor school performance during this time.

Pat: My mother, instead of getting better, seemed to get worse. She was really not well at all. I remember coming home from school, and the house would be totally silent and totally dark, and she would be up in bed. I look back now, and clearly she was extremely depressed, but I don't remember what I did or what I thought at the time.

My relatives would just say, "That's the way she is." I remember going out to my grandmother's house, and my mother would sit in the chair and never speak to anybody. She would go long hours and not say anything. She would eventually go upstairs, and everyone knew she was either going to take pills or going to lie down.

Cynthia: There was a long period where she was, like, "manic-y," and the house had to be spotless every second. She was just in constant motion. Then all of a sudden she went into depression and got slowed down and started to gain weight, then the perfect house didn't matter anymore. You really never knew what would be going on with her and what you could say or do. No matter what, she was always self-critical. There wasn't a time when she was just okay and relaxed and not raging against herself.

Rose's father died suddenly and at home when she was in her middle teens, and the family pretty much fell apart at that point. Although relatives came in from time to time to help, her mother couldn't really function well and was eventually hospitalized while Rose was in high school.

Rose: She couldn't manage the house or figure out how to handle the money. My father had done everything financial, and he had protected her in a lot of ways, and it started to be clear she was really having some kind of major problem, much more than losing her husband. He had always been critical of how she took care of the house and the kids, and I personally thought after he died that things were going to be easier and more relaxed without him being there. I was shocked. She lost the house, couldn't handle it. She wasn't paying the mortgage. Suddenly something snapped and she would pay the phone bill of $2,500 instead of $25. She was making checks out that were kind of wild and crazy.

She kept a BB gun under her bed, and I think she was afraid to be there. I remember her coming to wake me up from a sound sleep and bringing me in bed with her. I thought it was weird and felt like "whoever sleeps with her will die," and I didn't want to be in the bed where my father died. Once she put her arms around me and caressed me, and I hated it! I remember getting the BB gun, and I pointed it at her, and saying, "You touch me again, I will kill you, and don't you ever wake me up in the middle of the night again!" I went back in my room, and she never did come and get me again!

I remember coming home from school one day and I was playing basketball outside, and my mother had a butcher knife in her hands, and she came running downstairs with this knife and pinned me up against the wall with the blade. I remember thinking, "I'm going to kill this bitch, and I'm strong enough to do it!" Then she got me down and she grabbed my neck and was really going to strangle me, and my grandmother ran over and took the knife away from her and made her stop. I think that was the first time she ended up in the hospital.

June's mother's difficulties escalated from the time of the first hospitalization, when June was about ten. She became increasingly delusional about people wanting to kill her and continued to switch from one personality to another. She was repeatedly hospitalized, often for suicide gestures or threats.

June: I was her guardian when I was twelve or thirteen years old. Sometimes I would see her lying on the floor with her head in her hands, just watching cartoons like a kid. Once when I came home she was making paper snowflakes out of something, and I realized it was my journal! She had always kept a journal, and I take after her that way, I always keep a journal. So she's making paper snowflakes out of my journal, and I thought I was going to explode. I knew she was in a different personality, she was a little girl named Trudy, but it was my writing! After that, any writing I did about her I burned, because I knew I needed to get it out, to write it down, but then I just burned it.

This next incident was life-changing for both June and her mother.

June: The last night I lived with her, when I was fifteen, she came into my room with the idea that both of us were going to overdose because her father was coming to kill both of us. So she brought in pills for both of us to take. That was the first time I really thought, "My mother is crazy." Before that, I had been defending the mentally ill, like, "My mother is mentally ill." This time I thought, "My mother is fucking nuts! She is off her rocker." I put the pills under my tongue and drank the water, and later I spit out the pills and I thought, "If we both live through this night, I'm never going to live with her again." And we did live through that night, and I never did live with her again.

Before that I thought, "I have to keep her from dying," but this time I realized I could die, too. My sister had left, gone to college, and my mother and I were living alone for about six months, and things just fell apart. I just I couldn't do it. I couldn't do it the way my sister and I had done it together. I can hear myself even right now, twenty years later—I'm kind of apologizing. My sister and I did it together, but I'm a failure because I can't do it by myself.

So she went to the hospital then, and after a couple of weeks they wanted to discharge her again, and they assumed that I would take care of her, and I said I didn't want to live with her anymore. They asked me where I wanted to live and I said, "I don't know." They didn't ask if they could help, but they didn't oppose it either. My mother asked me if she could come home and we could live in the apartment. I said no.

When I said that, I thought I had killed her. That was probably one of the hardest things I've ever done. She was always terrified that she would get locked up for a really long time, and it was like I was dooming her to that. That was when she asked them to tell me her diagnosis. I think she thought that if I knew how sick she was, I would say yes. So they did tell me, but it didn't make me change my mind.

Two weeks before that happened, my mother said to me, "You don't even need me," and this is when she had been in and out of the hospital every other week. And I said, "I do need you," and I had never said anything like that to her before—never before—and I meant it, in a way. I mean, I needed a *mother*, but I'm not sure I meant I needed her the way she was. And then a couple of weeks later she wanted us to take pills together. I know she was psychotic, but still—she kind of tried to kill me.

Part of the power of the interviews, both for me as interviewer and for the women talking about their experience, was the catharsis of simply "telling the story" from beginning to end. Because June ended her first interview with this last vignette, she had several weeks between interviews to ponder not only this incident, which she had recounted many times in therapy, but also where it fit into the whole story. June realized for the first time that she was not responsible for what happened, but that her mother had made a series of choices, for many years, that led her to that point in her own adult life. She had refused or resisted help, had been hospitalized against her will, and never used help to make changes she could have made. She had never even told her children what her diagnosis was, nor had she allowed professionals to do so. All her efforts had been to hide or deny her problems and to ignore the impact on her children. Therefore, when this "moment of truth" came, June saw that she was not the one who had "doomed" her mother to years in the hospital. Her decision not to live with her mother was the end point of many decisions her mother had made, not simply the one June had made.

MOM IN PUBLIC

Adolescents are notoriously sensitive about how they and their parents appear out in the world. Even the hippest, coolest parents can seem hopelessly out of it when they appear in the teen's world. Teens are trying to make new connections in their own world and to have some control over how others see them, and parents who might make the kid seem uncool by association are to be avoided at all costs. For teens with impaired parents, whether substance-abusing, mentally ill, or otherwise "different," this can be excruciating. These adolescents have usually invested a lot in creating a world apart from their family, and they often avoid any reference to their family inside this bubble. Other kids' comments or reactions have a huge impact, and although at times the reactions might be validating, in other situations having a friend or acquaintance witness the worst, out in public, puts the teen in an impossible situation.

Many of these women experienced a kind of chronic anxiety or dread that their mothers would show up at school or at other activities, and usually tried to discourage them from coming, even to important events.

> **Sandy:** I had a kind of a system of keeping her out of my life, I hate to say. When she came to my high school graduation, she was about thirty minutes late—it was a huge graduation—and I had said to her, "Don't come, it's not that important to me," knowing that she couldn't come in a way that was less than conspicuous. It made me sick to my stomach waiting for her. She'd wear this bright clothing, these capes and hats— you didn't lose my mother in a crowd! And she created a spectacle. She always made me feel very embarrassed, because people would be looking at her like she was weird, and then, of course, looking at me, like, "That's your mother?"

The situation might also involve other adults seeing something that gave away the secret, to everyone's embarrassment.

> **Helen:** I was sixteen when my sister got married, and my mother became very depressed, and it was obvious to everyone there. I remember getting dressed in the room, just beforehand, and my sister's new mother-in-law was trying to fill in the gap. That mask just came over my mother. She looked grim—couldn't smile or talk at all. She was very detached, and just "there." She barely got through the day. She went in the hospital very soon after that, for the first time but not for the last. So that was how my sister's new family got introduced to the family secret.

The worst incidents involved mothers who were, literally, out on the streets and flagrantly psychotic or dissociated. Tara Elgin Holley, in her memoir, wrote about walking with one of her high school friends in Greenwich Village as they shopped for clothes, when she saw her mother on the street.

> Mommy was alone, and as she shuffled slowly down the middle of the sidewalk, she mumbled to herself. She was wearing a wrinkled dress ... mis-buttoned so that you could see her bra. She had slipped into a pair of dingy old house slippers, the heels bent down beneath her feet. She occasionally looked to the side as if carrying on a conversation with an invisible companion. She had scraps of paper pinned to her dress, and as she walked she scattered rolled-up balls of the newspaper she was carrying. I noticed how people eddied around her, how they glanced back at her as they passed. It wasn't unusual for us to run into each other in the Village, but I had always been alone when we met. I knew what would happen if she spotted me. "Oh, honey! Oh darling!" she would exclaim, taking me

into her arms.... I panicked. If Hallie found out, she would know the truth about me. Hallie wouldn't like me anymore and I wouldn't have a friend. "I've got to go home!" I muttered.... Before Hallie could say a word, I turned my back on my mother and on my friend, and I fled.

I was embarrassed about deserting Hallie, but most of all I was ashamed of running from the person I cared about most in the world, the person who so desperately needed my love.

I wanted to love her—I did love her—but I was tired of carrying around this burden. I just wanted life to be normal. I wanted a mother and a father I could watch and know and love. I also wanted a glimpse of future possibility.... To imagine my mother as my future was almost more than I could bear.[1]

June had very similar experiences with her mother, and handled them pretty much the same way.

June: Sometimes I'd see her out on the street, on an outdoor phone, crying and all upset. She would have had some dissociative episode and forgot who she was or where she was and would call someone to ask who she was, and she'd be really upset. And once a friend of mine and I were walking home from school and my mother was across the street on the phone and crying, and I was afraid my friend would see her and say, "Isn't that your mother?" And I didn't want to go over and try to help her, because she might have forgotten who I was, and she'd be scared or mad if I tried to take her arm. And of course, I didn't want my friend to know anything about it. We just walked by and I distracted my friend, and luckily my mother didn't see us.

Other experiences were not nearly so extreme, but embarrassing nonetheless. Shame is an emotion with a long half-life, and it sticks to such memories for a very long time.

Eleanor: When I was about thirteen, my father took me and my mother to Chicago for a few days while he went to a conference. When we got there, she was—for her, anyway—kind of manic. We went shopping, and she was buying all kinds of stuff and talking really loud, and just attracting a lot of attention. In one store, an office supply place, she bought a huge amount of stuff, and they put it all in bags that I had to carry. She was just going a mile a minute, and they were all looking at her and at me. I couldn't have been more mortified. She didn't have a clue. I just wanted her to shut up and stop attracting all this attention.

PSYCHIATRIC TREATMENT AND HOSPITALS

With some exceptions, kids in these families became increasingly involved in their mother's treatments and hospitalizations as they became adolescents. They were made to assume the role of the parent in many ways: being left to take care of their sick mother or reporting on her behavior, or taking over the parental role with younger kids, without questions, when their mother was hospitalized. In most of these cases, the mothers were coerced into going to the hospital and were sometimes taken away by ambulance while their daughters looked on. Still, the explanations about what was wrong don't seem to have improved markedly. Mothers seemed to feel freer to blame their daughters for problems, at times, and others in the extended family did so as well. And as we see in a couple of instances, mental health professionals sometimes blamed these kids for not making sure that their mothers took their medications, didn't make suicide attempts, and so forth.

As anyone who has worked with seriously ill patients knows, they're often very resistant to treatment in any form. Considering some of the treatments and medications available, especially before the 1990s, such resistance sometimes made a lot of sense. However, when these mothers resisted and were hauled off in restraints, it left their children very vulnerable. It's hard to judge them, given the stigma of their illnesses and the paucity of adequate treatment. In the last chapter we'll look at what we can learn from all this and how to provide more support and help for those affected; for now, the focus is on the daughters' experience.

Having an adolescent child help with the care of a sick parent is not, in itself, a bad thing. In fact, having some responsibility and a sense of being needed can help kids mature and develop a sense of compassion, understanding, and mutuality. It can strengthen family bonds in a way that little else can. But there are healthy ways to have kids help and destructive ways. It works best when adults acknowledge that the child is helping, and in what way, and when the adults make it clear that they are ultimately in charge and responsible and that the illness is not the child's fault. It also helps to acknowledge that the child is being asked to do something unusual. Children and adolescents are almost unfailingly eager to help when adults can present their needs in this way. And it helps when the child is given a clear, age-appropriate explanation for what's going on and her input is valued and sought.

A group of researchers studying families of mentally ill parents asked kids and teens about their reactions to their parent's illness and how things could go better for them.[2] Across the board, the children wanted information about the illness and what to expect, and they wanted the professionals to take them into account. They said that because they lived with the sick parent, they knew better than anyone what the symptoms were and often were the best at figuring out how to manage as well as possible. They wanted to be consulted about what they knew and to be respected as people who were in the role of care-taker, rather than being dismissed as kids who happened to live in the same space. And of course, they wanted professionals to be aware of what was happening in their family and their home and to provide help and protection when necessary.

For several of the women interviewed for this book, the impact of their mother's hospitalizations was softened somewhat by the fact that many of the older psychiatric hospitals in this country were designed around the theory that patients needed rest and a supportive environment. Many of them are quite beautiful, with sweeping grounds and huge old shade trees, providing an estate-like feeling. This was often in contrast to what was inside, of course. Here's Cecily's description of what it was like to visit her mother in the hospital, with her father managing to arrange some things behind the scenes to soften the impact of the reality without denying it.

> **Cecily:** We would go visit her in the hospital when she was there. I can see now how carefully my dad must have orchestrated it. It's a beautiful place, and the grounds have big trees that give a lot of shade and make it just seem like such a peaceful place. They usually had Mom outside wait-ing for us, so we didn't have to go in. We would have lunch there and go for a drive, and we would just visit with Mother. Then she would go back. She seemed quieter. She wouldn't have any makeup on. She had perfectly straight hair, and she was very fair. We would always see her outdoors, and she was always nicely dressed. The grounds were nice, so it was kind of a picnic atmosphere. But of course he couldn't control everything, so I would see other patients, and they would be walking around and they were smoking and looking spaced out. I did some student volunteer work at that hospital, but it didn't last long—it seemed like there were really ill people there, and I had never, ever seen my mother like that.
>
> She always responded well to medication—Thorazine, it was then. But when she got cancer, later on, I visited her when she was having cancer treatment, and she was starting to get very withdrawn and I could see she was having trouble mentally. They had stopped giving her the Thorazine. I was only eighteen, but I reamed them out for that—she was dying, and on top of that she had to be suffering with symptoms of schizophrenia? That wasn't going to happen.

Contrast this with June's experience of visiting her mother in the hospital. Both Cecily's and June's mothers were at very large hospitals, so this difference isn't due to a difference between a small, expensive private institution and a big public hospital.

> **June:** At this hospital, there weren't a lot of visitors, and there were a lot of locked doors and you were escorted through the door. One time when I went, they had a fire drill or something while I was there. This big

group of crazy people walked through a door into a wide hallway, then waited for someone to unlock the next door, then the same thing through all these locked doors. It was horrible. My sister and I were mixed in with all these patients who were panicked about the fire drill and heavily medicated. If I look back, they were just probably very depressed, but I thought they were dangerous. At school, kids always talked about how there were ax murderers in the loony bin. I had nightmares about that fire drill—being stuck, waiting for someone to go find a key to unlock a door, being trapped. I think the attendants were just trying to get the fire drill over with; they didn't have any time to deal with us.

A lot of times when we'd visit my mother, she would just be sitting in this big room, smoking, with all these other patients around. There was one lady who would come up right in your face and scream at you. Her hair was all crazy—it was terrifying. Nobody told us what to expect or tried to find us a room to visit in, anything like that. We were on our own. I would have been thirteen or fourteen then.

There was only one good thing I remember, and it's kind of funny. At home I was responsible for everything from taking care of money and paying the bills to watching her mood and making sure she didn't kill herself. My sister and I would hide money. We didn't have money for toilet paper, for example. But we couldn't tell anybody, because it would be, "What's wrong with your mother that you don't have toilet paper?" I remember when I visited her at the hospital, in their bathroom they had like a hundred rolls of toilet paper! It was great! I used to load up my backpack every time I went! I was scared they'd catch me—I must have looked pretty strange walking out the door with this enormous backpack—but they never did. Even now I think it was pretty smart!

Maggie was involved in a positive way with her mother's treatment. In her case it was very clear that her mother had a serious problem—her mother would acknowledge it herself, albeit in a manipulative way. She was never hospitalized, although she came close.

Maggie: We went to family therapy, which was completely useless. [The therapist] told us to laugh at her when she did the obsessional stuff with the food and the cleansers and all that. How helpful is that? Then somebody else my father consulted wanted her to have ECT [electroconvulsive therapy], but we decided against that. Somebody finally found this really amazing psychiatrist who did behavioral therapy and also used Anafranil before it was approved as a medication for OCD. It helped enormously, and by the time I went off to college, she was much better.

Like Maggie, Eleanor had input about her mother's behavior, but for her it backfired, and Eleanor ended up feeling that she had somehow betrayed her mother. When adults decide not to talk about unpleasant things, there's seldom a good outcome. When children or teens are parentified—treated like adults or like parents in a role reversal—they often seem to take to it. After all, being treated like a grown-up is usually a good thing and offers the kid a special place in the parent's eyes. When the parentification comes about by neglect, as in Alice's case, it doesn't have this flavor. But when one parent turns to a child and asks her opinion or treats her as an equal, it's hard to resist. Kids hardly ever complain about this emotional parentification. They may complain about having chores to do that are burdensome (more than age-appropriate) or being given too much child care, but rarely will they complain about emotional parentification. It's invisible, and children don't quite understand the exploitive nature of it. Indeed, the parent who's doing the leaning isn't always overtly or consciously exploitive. But they're turning to a child who by definition almost always will be loyal to them, see things their way, and bolster their self-confidence.

> **Eleanor:** I told you about the trip my parents and I took, where my father was off giving some lectures and my mother went on a manic buying binge while I was with her. Well, when we got back home I told my father she was acting pretty strange, and as I found out later, he called her psychiatrist, and the psychiatrist had her come in and told her she had to go in the hospital. His decision would have been based on my "report" more than anything else, because she was good at denying stuff. When she came home from that appointment, she just glared at me like I had turned her in, which, of course, I had. I just froze. My father acted completely innocent, like the psychiatrist had just happened to call on the phone—not that he had called behind her back. Since she was paranoid, this didn't go over very well. Now I can see, *of course* she was paranoid—not just because of her illness, but because my father was, in fact, plotting things behind her back! She was in the hospital for a few weeks. They gave her shock therapy and she kind of forgot everything for a while and didn't recognize me when I went to visit once. She had a private room, and it wasn't scary to be there. But she sure wasn't manic after that. I thought it was kind of a punishment for her. Nobody talked to me about it or explained anything.

Helen's father took charge of getting her mother into the hospital. The worst part of this experience, unlike that of some other women in this book, was not the hospital itself or witnessing frightening behavior. It was simply that no matter what happened, nothing ever helped her mother.

> **Helen:** When I was sixteen, she just got—I wouldn't say catatonic, but she just stopped doing everything, and my father brought her to the hospital. She was just sitting in a chair. She went in there for a good month or more. By then I was old enough to understand what was going on. We just felt terrible that she wasn't herself, and it was very scary in some ways for me. After that, we never wanted her to go through that again,

so we were even more careful around her. But she went in and out of the hospital many times. Nothing ever helped her. It didn't seem to make any difference.

Lee's experience was much worse, just as her mother's illness was worse. Lee was aware that her mother was sick, although there weren't any real explanations, but what she had to go through in the critical phases of her mother's illness, and the subsequent hospitalizations, is almost the stuff of fiction.

Lee: The shit would hit the fan when she would have florid manic episodes. One of the worst ones was when I was thirteen, when she was about forty, and she got very, very crazy. She started out getting pretty manic—not sleeping, doing all these crafts projects, buying tons of things, getting very irritable—then ended up being psychotic. That was really horrible, because she was refusing to get any help, and as she got more crazy and paranoid, she began to think I was being possessed by my father's oldest sister, who had died about five years before. She had a very bad relationship with this aunt of mine, who was also my godmother. She was very competent, and I think my mother was jealous. Anyway, she got paranoid about that and started making me do stuff like ripping up pictures that had my aunt in them. Of course, that included a lot of pictures of me, too, but I had to rip them all up. There aren't many family photos with my aunt, I can tell you that! There's a picture of me in a communion dress—there's just me, and the rest of the picture got ripped up.

All this just got worse and worse over a period of a couple of weeks, and she ended up holding a knife up to me and my brother. He was only eight. My father talked to the family doctor, and he came to the house, then somebody called the ambulance and they took her to the hospital. She was screaming at me the whole time—"You just want your father all to yourself" and all other kinds of crap. Can you imagine being thirteen and having your mother saying this kind of stuff to you? I knew she was crazy, but it still hurt me and made me furious, too. She was really bad.

This stands out: When the ambulance came, they brought the stretcher in, and they were going to restrain her. I said, "No, you don't have to do that, she'll walk out," and she did. I don't know how I knew that, but I was right. I wanted to protect her and protect her dignity.

I look back now and see how dangerous all that was—she would take these big ceramic ashtrays and put them on the stove and start fires in them. She would have the priest come out and do exorcisms, she would walk around the house with a cross and say things like "begone" to the evil spirits, stuff like that.

When she was in the hospital, she wouldn't write to us, but she'd write letters addressed to the dog, and she'd be ranting about how angry she was at all of us.

When she went to the hospital, that time and then later times, initially there was a lot of relief, then it was kind of "business as usual." There was some sense of loss, and I didn't know when I would ever see her again, and I remember being fearful that she wouldn't ever want to see us at all. Two months later she had improved to the point we could visit. The hospital she was in at that time was very posh: Jonathan Winters was there, Lana Turner's daughter—the one that killed her boyfriend—she was there, and what I remember is that she had chocolate chip cookies that she had baked there, and she gave them to us. She was clearly overmedicated, but recognized us and talked with us—but overmedicated. But it was scary to visit her there.

She never really got back in her role in the family after she had been in the hospital that first time. We all just worked around her. She was overmedicated, and on Thorazine, and I don't know why she wasn't on lithium. But she would take to her bed and sleep for long periods of time. She would get out of bed and get something to eat, then she'd just go back to bed. She was very slow. She was in day treatment for a while. She came home in a very invalid state, and everything went on around her the same way it had been when she was gone, and probably the same as when she was depressed.

I kept getting afraid that she would come in my room, and I remember locking my door, even though when she came home she was doing well. I remember it was the same fear I had before she went in the hospital, because she'd be up at night, just crashing around the house.

Barbara's mother would say it was up to Barbara to keep her out of the hospital. It's bad enough when relatives have this view, whether expressed up front or just implied, but it cuts deeper in situations like this.

Barbara: When I was younger, in my teens, my mother would always say to me, "If you would spend more time with me, I wouldn't have to go into the hospital." That's kind of a lot to put on a kid. So I would try, because I really partly believed it. I would do everything for her, get her everything she needed, all that. For years. No matter what else I was doing, I was always kind of mentally keeping an eye on her, waiting for when she would need me and I'd have to just run and be there and do whatever. But it didn't work, because she kept going in and out of the hospital.

Rose didn't get any help figuring out what was wrong with her mother and how to help her. Her mother was clearly psychotic at times, but the reason for the shock therapy was unclear, except that in the 1960s many women were given ECT as a matter of course. Rose as a teenager was pretty much left to her own devices.

Rose: Right after my father died so suddenly, my mother was medicated and she was like a zombie. And I don't mean for a few days, I mean kind of permanently. She ended up dying four years after my father died, but I feel like I lost them both at the same time. She couldn't make

decisions. She spent a lot of time just staring into space. And because she
was a nurse and my father had been a doctor, Lord knows what stuff
they had in the house, and she was medicating herself, too.

She was really psychotic on and off during that time. Once, I was
driving her somewhere, and she was looking up and saying, "See, Daddy
is there in the trees." I looked up and I ran right into something and
crashed the car. She was just crazy. My sister didn't want to hear it.

Then she had shock therapy and she literally didn't recognize me
afterwards. I remember I asked her about smoking and told her I had
decided to smoke, and then she said, "How old are you?" and I said seventeen. Then she said, "Well, where is your mother?" and I realized—
God, she doesn't even know that she's my mother. So I said, "You're my
mother." And she said, "Then I forbid you to smoke." I just couldn't
believe it.

Sarah's experience shows how kids can be abandoned by everyone
once a protector is gone. Her father died when she was young, and
things deteriorated rapidly after that. Her mother's family did the mini-
mum in caring for her, and in fact, blamed her for her mother's illness.

Sarah: I was always blamed for her problem by her side of the family,
and then by doctors, when she was in the hospital. They would be on my
case for not making sure she took her medication. Once she took an overdose of pills and drove to the grocery store and passed out. I was pulled
out of high school, and my guidance counselor drove me to the hospital.
When I was told she tried to kill herself and I said she'd made threats,
the ER doctor got in my face and screamed at me, "Why didn't you do
something to stop her?" I just cried. I was seventeen. Luckily, when I was
eighteen I had some legal rights, so I could get a writ of detention to get
the cops to take her in, but when I was seventeen I couldn't.

She would attack me when she was psychotic—I don't know who she
thought I was. And even though my family knew about it, and the cops
knew about it because they'd get called and she'd be hauled off to the
hospital, nobody ever seemed to think anything about it. Then, once she
was out of the house and went nuts and attacked someone, and *then* they
did something about it. She attacked a "real" person, so that mattered.
Attacking me wasn't important.

I was constantly told that I would end up just like my mother. They
said if I ever got married and had kids, they would be just the same. It
would be a complete waste. That would cut through me like a knife.

June's experience with the mental health profession is something out
of *Snake Pit* days, and as June is one of the youngest women I interviewed, this happened in the 1980s. It's difficult for me as a professional to think that colleagues whom I may have known professionally, or
even gone to school with, would create this kind of situation for anyone, much less an adolescent. For an adult, with resources and help

available, this would have been daunting. For an adolescent, it's beyond inexcusable.

> **June:** The psychiatrist who treated my mother only saw us kids when she needed to go in the hospital. This one time stands out the most vividly, when my older sister and I went to his office with my mother. It was just the three of us because my oldest sister had moved out by then, and the shit really hit the fan. My sister was fifteen and I was thirteen, and my mother was very psychotic, and we knew she needed to go to the hospital. So this psychiatrist gets us all in the office together, and he seems to think he has to convince us how crazy she is. So he says to my mother, "Tell me what you're seeing." Well, she says, "The walls are bleeding, and the room is going to fill up with blood! We're going to drown!" and she's flipping out. He kept this up and got her to say all this terrifying stuff that was going on in her mind. He was trying to prove she was sick, which we already knew. So then he makes a phone call to get her in, and oops—there's no bed available in the "good" hospital. (That meant the local hospital, where she'd gone before.)
>
> So we're sitting there wondering what's going to happen now, and he says we should take her home. I was only thirteen, but I said, "Um, this is a bad idea. Isn't there anything else?" and he said, "Well, the other alternative is to send her to the police station. Do you want me to do that?" Well, of course we didn't, and he wasn't really serious anyway, so we just took her home to wait for a bed in the good hospital, which was going to take a few days, according to him. He said to keep a watch on her, remove all the knives, put sheets over the mirrors so she can't see herself, because that would set her off. And of course, make sure she doesn't kill herself, or kill anybody else.
>
> You know, before we went in there we knew she was bad. And she would sometimes say this stuff to me about the "walls are bleeding." But hearing her say it like this, sitting in an office with this guy, and hearing him just ask her questions and make her answer, that was so much worse. It made it that much more real, and it also gave me some hope that since he was a grown-up and a doctor, that he would do something about it. To this day it's hard to believe this really happened. I know my mother has multiple personality disorder, but when I think about this kind of thing, *I* feel like a multiple—that it must have been somebody besides me sitting in that office with her.

WHAT TO THINK? WHAT TO FEEL?

The effect of their mother's illness not only caused psychological problems but also deeply affected the inner life and musings of these adolescents. Cecily was coping, at seventeen, with her mother's death from cancer, Jerri was trying to become independent, and June at fifteen had come to the very difficult decision not to be her mother's caretaker anymore. Rose went through the motions of her high school graduation without any joy or sense of accomplishment. All of these kids were dealing with things that would be difficult enough for adults, and all the more so for adolescents with shaky foundations.

> **Cecily:** But I can tell you what I was really worried about. I was worried about my father dying. When my mother died, the first thing I was worried about was my father. I was, of course, totally destroyed by her death. I was just a mess, but the thought of him going threw me into just a terrible place. I remember that very consciously.
>
> **Jerri:** It took my mother a long time to get back into the routine of being a wife and housewife, and then having this daughter she hadn't seen much growing up. There just wasn't much connection. I was growing away from the home, and my dad wanted to keep us together, at least for some time. Eventually my mother had to let go, and he had to let go, and I had to let go. I was ready for all of that, but how do we prepare Mom for this?
>
> I really didn't feel much connection. That's the real hard part, because there was not much that we really could share. I guess I liked her. I was certainly nice to her. I knew the things she was interested in around the house. But that was the extent of the relationship.

The statements "I guess I liked her" and "I was certainly nice to her" point to the detachment in Jerri's relationship to her mother. Although Jerri may have been securely attached to her mother before her mother first got sick (when Jerri was five or six), by this time Jerri had made other primary attachments, especially to her grandmother. The profound neutrality of the above statements isn't something one often hears in adolescents.

> **Rose:** I felt kind of ashamed about even having a graduation. In a way, nothing felt good anymore, and there I was in my cap and gown and pretending to be happy, and my father was dead and my mother was in the loony bin.

June's refusal to take care of her mother anymore, so that her mother was committed long-term to the hospital, has been detailed previously. It was a major turning point in her life, and here she talks about the immediate aftermath.

> **June:** After I told her she couldn't come home and I left the hospital, I remember when I left I lay down in the snow to make a snow angel, and I remember feeling the snow melting on my face, and I was surprised. I was alive. The snow was melting. Up to then, my sole purpose in life was to keep her alive, and now I didn't have to do that anymore. I was surprised to feel something.

Tess's mother continued to be psychotic throughout Tess's adolescence, and Tess vividly recalls her own distress.

> **Tess:** I didn't try to figure it out. I begged God. At that point I was much more religious than I am now. But I would pray that God would help her, make her get well. Other times I hated being part of this family. I wondered why I had to be born into a family that wasn't normal. But I didn't try to figure it out any more than that—I just thought she was crazy, most of the time.

And sometimes, there's insult added to injury, when an astute adult might have helped a struggling adolescent.

> **Eleanor:** I somehow endured feeling a kind of constant anger and feeling helpless to change anything, and mostly turned inward. To say anything out loud about what was going on was unthinkable, just taboo. I wrote poetry—pretty high-schoolish and dark, but it was something, and I showed it to my English teacher, who was very encouraging. Then I found out from a friend of mine, whose mother was the school nurse, that my English teacher was reading the poetry to other teachers in the teachers' lounge, and they were all getting a good laugh out of it. My friend's mother didn't want to hurt my feelings by telling me, but she didn't want me to be made a fool of, either. I kind of slunk away mentally. I wasn't even angry, just mortified. It didn't do a lot for my ability to trust people with what was going on internally. I look back now and see what an opportunity that would have been for that teacher to help me out.

The impact on Helen of her mother's illness was insidious rather than dramatic. Her mother saw herself as sensitive and weak, and Helen was in some danger of seeing herself that way, too. Her mother had kept her home from half a day of kindergarten, thinking she wasn't strong enough, and in adolescence the same theme emerges.

> **Helen:** It was my eighth-grade graduation, and I was being given an award that I didn't know about. My mother came to find me before we all sat down to let me know that I was getting the award, because she thought I couldn't handle it if I was surprised. The message was that I could not handle things, not that she couldn't handle things. The question was in the back of my mind for many years, decades even, about whether I was strong enough to do things.

RITES OF PASSAGE

There are two specific rites of passage for a young female adolescent in this culture, both having to do with physical development: getting her first period and getting her first bra. When most of these women grew up, such things were not talked about much, and boxes of Kotex were somewhat mysterious products that seemed to appear in closets and cause everyone embarrassment. Health classes in school might help a bit, but some older female relative—preferably an attentive mother—would be the first line of defense. And a mother might be expected to be the first one to notice her daughter's development and suggest getting a bra. The notice taken of these rites of passage was more muted a few decades ago, but still memorable.

> **Alice:** My father took me to get my first bra when I was twelve, and I was mortified. He was evidently watching my development. It was just so humiliating that he was the one standing there in the department store. We had gone there for years, so the ladies knew us, and they kind of took over. I have no idea where my mother was. She wasn't there for anything important, so it wasn't a big surprise, but it was just embarrassing.
>
> **Rachel:** I got my period the first day of high school. It was very heavy, and I got bad cramps and a fever. I remember I ended up making one of my friends go to the nurse's office and get me a pad because I was so embarrassed about the whole thing. It was never anything that was talked about in my house enough for me to have any kind of understanding or comfort with it. I came home that day and I was bleeding so hard that I just bled through everything that I had. My brother thought that it was funny and called me Bloody Mary. Here I'm embarrassed enough: It's my first day and my first day of high school. I was embarrassed all day. My mother wasn't home that evening and my brother sat through dinner going, "Bloody Mary, Bloody Mary." Everyone seemed to think it was funny. Nobody told him to be quiet.
>
> The other thing was that, because my mother had made me wear boy's clothes for so long, that I was really confused about my own body. I kind of felt like if I undressed in a room with any of my friends, somehow I would look different from them. I didn't get my period till I was fourteen, and since I didn't ask why and didn't understand why, it just made me feel more weird.
>
> In my house, the rule was nobody ever could shut the door to the bathroom. You could be in there and my mother would walk in and out. But after that, the rule was that when I had my period I could close the door. Then, when it was over, I'd have to leave the door open again. So even though I had some privacy, it was like a big announcement to everyone that I had my period. It was constantly embarrassing to have it be that way. It just seemed to be a cause for hilarity to everyone else.
>
> **Pat:** My aunt told me about my period, probably realizing that my mother wasn't going to do it. The feeling is just dark, sad, ugly, and empty. There was this dresser where I kept my clothes. The bottom two drawers were mine. I remember I used to put my soiled pants in the drawers. What she finally did was show them to my dad. I would have been fourteen or so at the time. That was so humiliating to me and so

upsetting to me. I felt so betrayed and enraged. I don't know why she did it, except that she seemed to think he was the big authority on everything.

My mother was pretty oblivious to what was going on with me. I was in junior high and wearing this big, baggy sweater and my cousin said, "You need a bra!" and told me to tell my mother. So I did, and we went shopping, and it's probably the best memory I have of being with her. She told the clerk at the store that "my daughter is developing, and it may be time for a bra"—and at the same time my mother bought me a coat. You have to understand that most of my clothes were hand-me-downs, so for me to get this brand-new coat was really something. After that, we went to a movie. I remember feeling so close to my mother at that point. I remember in the movie theater taking her hand and holding her hand, but that was not a feeling that I had very often. I can't ever remember another feeling like that. I think when I took my mother's hand I was looking for some kind of a physical closeness that I didn't feel. There was no such physical closeness in the family. I don't remember getting hugged. My mother was thin and bony, she didn't exude warmth in that sense. But I felt a strong connection that one time.

FATHERS AND SIBLINGS

A few of these women had fathers who really came through for them. They didn't avoid or run away from the problems with their wives, and they saw or anticipated the impact of these problems on their kids. This provided a critical buffer and support. A downside, though, is that when either parent fills the role of both parents, any shift in that relationship causes a strong sense of insecurity. When only one parent is reliable, the child tends to idealize that parent long beyond the time it's appropriate.

> **Cecily:** My father was a very strong, highly educated professional man who had a lot of political and civic responsibilities. We were firmly middle class to upper middle class, and as a result he had a housekeeper come in. He had a person come in to cook. He had resources that other families might not have, and he also had a sensitivity about it.
>
> He would protect my mother from going out and handling something at my school, for example. He'd just say, "I'll do that, honey." It was never, "Oh, you can't do that. I'll do that." And I don't think there was any resentment on her part. I just think if I were to look at my father squarely without as much idealism as I had, I would have to say he's a pretty controlling guy. But he was also right so much of the time, and he just was so giving, and he just knew what you needed, so it didn't lead to resentment or rebelliousness. He would give you the shirt off his back and then tell you why you needed to be careful about your shirts. So the control was there, but it wasn't something he got off on. He saw what

needed to be done, and he had the strength to do it well and to oversee things.

Tess also idealized her warm and loving father, whom she called "both a father and a mother in one." He stopped being very affectionate with her when she reached puberty, which isn't unusual; however, for Tess it was devastating, because he was virtually her only parent.

> **Tess:** My father would give us big bear hugs and kisses. And I remember him calling me "my rose"—"You're my little rose"—and then, when that stopped, I remember feeling bad. I was very paranoid and insecure for many, many years. I thought I wasn't good enough anymore.

Eleanor's father put difficult things into mental compartments, which evidently worked well for him, as he was able to keep the family structure intact and maintain a happy front. Despite his lashing out angrily at the kids and his tightly controlled anger at home, he also had a fantasy of what a happy family was like, and he went to some pains to try to produce it. The family he grew up in was chaotic and unsupportive, so his ideas of a happy family came from books and movies, not experience. Despite the negatives, his ability to maintain some stability and control was a significant help.

> **Eleanor:** My mother was hospitalized during the summer when I was thirteen. I didn't have anything to do—my brothers were away for the summer, and my father was working. He decided to take me on a trip— to cheer me up, I guess—and we never once talked about my mother, who was still in the hospital while we were away. It was very important to him that I be cheered up, so I tried to act cheerful. It was very weird to be pretending to have this great time when my mother was back in the hospital getting shock therapy. My father could completely put it out of his mind, but I couldn't.

In other cases, fathers, even though present, added to the problem or—in Pat's eyes—made the mothers' problems worse. For her, neither parent was available.

> **Pat:** I don't remember what the argument was about, but he was berating her in some way, which is what he would tend to do. I ran upstairs and screamed for him to stop it and for them to stop arguing. That's when I turned to him said, "I hate you. I've always hated you. I'll hate you the rest of my life and I'll never speak to you again," and I ran out of the house. I didn't speak to my father for at least a year after that. It would have been within a year of that my mother would have gone in for shock treatments.

For more than one of these women, exploitive or abusive fathers took advantage of their wife's illness or absence to get access to the children.

> **June:** My father continued to sexually abuse me and my sister even after my mother divorced him. He could only have visitation during the day, and of course everyone knows that sexual abuse only happens at night, right? Anyway, he tried to get custody when I was thirteen and my sister was living somewhere else. My father goes into court and says, "My wife is in an insane asylum, and my thirteen-year-old daughter is living with her boyfriend. Can I have custody?" And of course they said yes, and then my father showed up at my school, and the school calls my mother, who was in the fucking hospital. They knew she wasn't an employee of the hospital, they knew she was a patient. But they didn't know what to do. I remember screaming at the secretary, "You called my *mother?*" So I called the lawyer, and the lawyer called the judge, and the judge called DCF [the Department of Children and Families], and they called the school, and I just hid out until they could revoke this piece of paper that my father had.
>
> **Alice:** There was a lot of covert abuse from my father, lots of intrusive stuff, I think partly because my mother wasn't there doing the normal mom things, and he just tried to take that over, but he had his own motives. He washed my hair in the bathtub until I was fourteen. It was strange. I finally made him stop, but we never talked about it. You couldn't say anything—it was disrespectful. I did feel I could push him away to some extent, but it was very yucky.
>
> My mother wasn't there at all to make him act more appropriate. She was very strange with sexual stuff, too. She must have told me a thousand times, "I was a virgin when I got married," and I used to wonder, "Why is she telling me this?" My bedroom was over the patio where they would have parties sometimes, and I could hear her telling inappropriate jokes about her and my father's sex life.

Relationships with siblings are often more intense, either in a good or a bad way, when parents are less available or difficult to deal with. Both Helen and Maggie were very close to their siblings, Helen being very attached to and dependent on her older sister, and Maggie very protective of her younger brother. It's clear from this and other statements of Helen's that her primary attachment figure was her sister, and this was enormously helpful for her. It may not have been so good for her older sister, who shouldered way too much responsibility and was not able to change that pattern as an adult. Maggie was protective of her brother during adolescence, but was not able to protect him later on. Tess's brother was probably in the early stages of schizophrenia when she was a teenager, which made life at home almost unbearable.

> **Helen:** I was devastated when my sister left, I really was. I really cried, I remember that. I really thought I was going to miss her terribly. I did

okay after a while, and it was actually liberating because I made more friends and got more active in school, came into my own. My mother wasn't really a factor—it was my sister I missed.

Maggie: My brother always had unbelievable energy levels. We would get pretty wild when we went out. He would be on a roll, and I didn't recognize at the time that he was really manic. He was probably bipolar at that point. He also had bad OCD, and it was clear that he got it from our mother; there's a strong genetic component. But eventually he couldn't deal with it. Whatever was happening at home, I was very protective of him.

Tess: My brother got sicker and sicker. I think it's because nobody would admit that he was sick, and this was a double whammy that we got. He got so controlling, and I think it was because he was trying to replace our mother. He would tell us how to sit on the couch, how to clean things, how to cook things. I started to assert my own personality and I made friends, but I had a lot of suffering going on inside of me and my own paranoia going on inside of me that he couldn't see. He was very scary, and as he got sicker, would have that same crazy look in his eyes that my mother had.

Rachel's story stretches one's imagination. Recall that her parents had adopted two boys, one African American, and then her mother had cut off her relationship with her own parents and siblings. A few years later, however, the boys were so "disturbed" that she gave them back to foster care. Later, these boys said the atmosphere was so toxic that removal was the best thing that could have happened to them.

Rachel: By that time, my mother had already given away my stepbrothers. They went to court to turn them over, and the judge said either my parents had to go into counseling themselves or they would have to pay for the foster care, because they had legally adopted the boys. My mother chose to pay for the foster care. It was clear that she had really messed these kids up. I was having serious problems, these kids were acting out, but she kept thinking she was the best parent in the world.

SHAME AND SECRETS

Shame is usually a constant companion for children growing up in dysfunctional families, and so also for these young women. It's pervasive: there's shame that your family is different, that you don't know basic things that other kids know. There's shame that your family is so visibly flawed, and shame by association. All the women in this book grew up before *Oprah*, which is now code for telling people about things that have been shameful secrets. Despite our laughing at some of the excesses on the *Oprah* show, there's been an openness to the interiors of different families that was absent during the 1960s, 1970s, and 1980s. During that period, people didn't talk about family problems and didn't have any way to relate to other people who might be struggling with the same things. The Adult Children of Alcoholics movement certainly helped a lot of people identify and name that phenomenon, despite the oversimplifications. Mental illness has been coming out of the closet in the past few years, but for the women here, this was the last thing they would have wanted.

Juliana: I was so busy protecting the family secret that I don't think I really realized that other people had a normal existence. I spent as much time out of the house as I could, and I withheld information and tried to present myself as a normal kid. At some point during this time, I started to realize that life was different for other people. First I thought, "Well, my mother is a single mom and she works, so that's what's different. But my friends would say, "What's wrong with your mother?" or "Christ, your mother is so weird." They said she was mean. I never really talked to anybody about it. I didn't expect anyone to understand. If she was pissed off at me she would embarrass me in front of them. She didn't care. She would yell or scream at me and demean me in front of them. She wouldn't hit me in front of them, though.

Lee: I have a lot of shame generally, just left over from growing up. I started to talk more when I got older, but everybody else's mother looked fine to me. I didn't know anybody else whose mother had this kind of problem. I never had anybody come to the house—I would go to their house. I feel guilty now for feeling that way, and I understand why I felt that way as a kid, but I do feel guilty. I never explained it to anyone.

Sandy: When I was an adolescent, I really did keep people away from her, but this one girl in particular—she caught on that I wasn't ever bringing anyone over to my house, and I remember being devastated by it. I was just shaken, because she noticed, and she said something, and she was kind of a mean-spirited kid. She came to my house once, and I didn't let her in. She came unannounced, and I just didn't let her come in.

Rose: We just wouldn't respond to questions, wouldn't talk about it at all. That's the way the family was—just don't respond, talk about something else. Change the subject.

Danielle: I was ashamed of them. The feeling was that your family is this way, and you're included in that. Like, if they're out of control, then so are you. I tried to have friends far away, and it was hard because I had to get rides from them, since nothing was in walking distance. Then there was a teacher I had confided in, and in the middle of some meeting she stood up and asked me to confront the fact that my family was dysfunctional. I was shocked, because it was a teacher I had confided in. It changed everything. There were people who treated me differently after that, at least it seemed that way to me.

Rachel: I was dressed in boy's clothes up until the age of about eighth grade. Obviously, by sixth and seventh grade other kids could tell that

I wasn't wearing girl's clothing. In seventh grade I started pushing my mom to try to buy me girl's clothing, but it was more expensive than boy's clothing, so then I would only get things on the clearance rack.

Whatever fit and was cheap was what I had to wear. It was quite embarrassing. They always told us that we were extremely poor and we couldn't afford girl's clothes. But my mom would buy special food for herself that we weren't allowed to have. I realized later that we weren't poor at all.

My mother did all of our haircuts. My brothers got teased because their hair looked so goofy. She didn't care and thought she was saving money, and she always thought she was a good hair cutter. Her whole idea was, she's a good mother, and if anybody says different, it's their problem. Whatever she did, it was what she wanted, and never what you might want. I wore the dress she told me to wear and had the haircut she wanted to give me—that was it. She was an excellent mother, in her own eyes—and she told us that plenty of times—because she cooked dinner every night and didn't take her kids to McDonald's. So be it!

Teachers were very kind to me and always said, "If you need to talk, I'm here." I didn't say anything, but I guess they realized things weren't good at home. I had a friend that lived two houses down. Her father said that to me, and I could just cry, wishing he could see on my face how much I needed to talk, but I couldn't initiate it. If he had just asked me some questions, I probably would have spilled my guts. I wasn't really supposed to talk to anyone outside the family.

Eleanor: I was terribly ashamed of her and angry at her all the time. Other mothers seemed energetic and seemed to know what they were doing and took care of their kids. We would all wait outside after school to be picked up, if we didn't take the bus. Everyone's mother would show up on time and seem happy to see their kids. My mother was always late, one of the last ones to pick her kids up. She always drove about ten miles an hour, and of course people stared at her. It was obvious something was really wrong with her. She looked like she barely knew where she was or who we were.

Helen: I felt the usual stigma about somebody being crazy. If somebody is different in any way, you don't want to advertise it. They would see me differently, because your home is your image and your parents are your image.

Sandy: We lived on Doctors Row, where there were all these professionals and their offices, and we were the ones that had the police and the ambulances, and the cars parked up on the lawn. The house started to look like hell, and I remember there were plaster walls and there were big chunks of wall with paint missing. When they would fight, things would get thrown and smashed, and they didn't care about fixing it up. In that kind of suburb, I never had kids over. I went over to other kids' houses, and their houses were really the huge, perfect houses in this very affluent neighborhood. I would have been horrified if they had wanted to come to my house—it would be like slumming.

PSYCHOLOGICAL FALLOUT

By junior high and high school, many of these women had developed serious psychological problems. Going back to the discussion of attachment and neurological development in chapter 1, we anticipated that these kids would have trouble feeling secure in their relationships with others and would not have developed sufficient means of tempering their own emotions. The storms of adolescence are bad enough even with the best "equipment," and without that, the problems multiply. These daughters, first of all, did not have an adult to guide them and care about what was going on during their teenage years, and they didn't have much "felt" history of having had such assurance as children. Many of them felt they were bad in some way—either just plain bad or guilty of having caused their mothers' problems, and thus responsible for fixing them. Going back even earlier, their attachment relationships with their mothers were often compromised, and now we can begin to see more serious fallout from that deficit. As adolescents, they were likely to bring the same difficult attachment style to their relationships.

They didn't have a secure base, a home to go home to, when they were bruised by the world, emotionally or physically, and they didn't have the internal equipment to modulate feelings.

When attachment is compromised, internal regulation systems don't develop well enough to keep a good sense of emotional balance. Strong negative emotions feel overwhelming and swamp what resources there are, and people grab the first thing they can find that helps them hang on. Alcohol or drugs, food or food restriction, sex, self-mutilation—all provide very predictable and rapid short-term relief. Overwhelming feelings, like anger or sadness, aren't necessarily the ones that can easily be labeled. For someone without much internal regulation, any strong negative emotion quickly becomes an unbearable total-body experience. A well-regulated person feeling strong anger might clench her fists, scowl, and feel like hitting someone; however, an underregulated person might feel blinding rage, off-the-charts physiological arousal, short-circuiting of the "thinking" parts of the brain, and an urge to attack. What normally feels like anxiety and butterflies in the stomach might feel like terror or panic. Without the ability to regulate or temper emotions, people are easily tipped over into emergency reactions—their ability to stop and think is at a low ebb, and immediate action seems essential for psychological survival.

Serious substance abuse that begins during adolescence is likely to be a problem for a long time, especially when it provides immediate relief of painful feelings. Researchers studying the kinds of problems adolescents have when they have insecure attachments have found that girls with dismissive attachments (seeming indifferent to their rejecting mothers; see chapter 1) are more likely to develop eating disorders of some kind and to focus their energies on controlling internal emotional states by controlling food intake.[3] There's some good evidence that the food restriction typical of anorexia causes the brain to release endorphins, since starvation signals "emergency" to the brain. Endorphins cause a "high" feeling and relief of anxiety, quickly and reliably, and can be as addictive as drugs that are ingested. It may be the addiction component that makes eating disorders so difficult to resolve.

Anxiously attached adolescents often focus too much on their peer relationships, reacting strongly to the slightest changes in friendships. Since adolescence is a rocky time for relationships anyway, this additional anxiety makes for a high state of crisis and drama on a regular basis. These are kids who are very vulnerable to peer pressure, feeling that they must please others in order to have any security at all. Drugs, alcohol, self-injury, sexual acting out, and attention-seeking behaviors are real risks.

However, adolescence also offers a second or third chance to make healthy attachments and find new ways to cope. In the last section of the chapter, Resilience, we'll take a look at some of the positive solutions these daughters found. But for now, the destructive coping strategies are the focus.

As we saw, Rachel had already begun some self-destructive ways to cope with unbearable feelings in childhood (cutting, burning, clenching her muscles until she was exhausted). Her self-injurious behavior continued into adolescence, accompanied by a preoccupation with suicide.

We understand much more about self-injury now than we did even ten years ago, but the behavior has been around for a very long time. Cutting, burning, hitting oneself, and other such self-harm may, first and foremost, provide relief from intolerable internal feelings by causing a distraction and by flooding the brain with chemicals that cause temporary relief. It also expresses the feeling of being bad and deserving to be hurt, it takes painful feelings and puts them in a more visible form, and it may help the person who's injuring herself feel more in her body if she's been feeling numb or dissociated. Some kids who appear to be doing very well and seem happy and upbeat will slip into the school bathroom and cut themselves or hit themselves or do something else self-destructive. Their public persona is extremely important to them, but it makes them feel two-dimensional and "fake." The self-injury makes them feel more real, is a private expression of their "real" self, and allows them to carry on without missing a beat. It's also a reminder to themselves that they are carrying a secret.

Rachel explains some of the many elements that went into her self-harming actions.

Rachel: By the time I was thirteen or fourteen, I was sniffing Wite-Out, because I was kind of hoping it would kill me. There was a danger warning on the back of it. I thought about different ways of killing or hurting myself.

I was also burning myself with candles, not leaving scars at that point. By sixteen or seventeen I was cutting with razors. It was a relief, but also I was trying to see how deeply I could cut. I was trying to make sure that if I felt I had to kill myself, I would be able to do it, I would be able to cut my wrist. I wanted to make sure I knew where the artery was, so I went to a medical manual at school to see exactly where it was. I didn't want to cut just a ligament and survive and not be able to use my hands. I cut and burned myself on my arms, and my dad saw the marks once, and I just made up an excuse and he dropped it.

There was a cemetery we used to ride around as kids on our bicycles, and it was right on the edge of a sort of cliff that was very steep and rocky, and there were rocks down below. I used to stand on top of it, and I thought if I threw myself off of it and landed down on the rock I could break my spine, I could break my head open, snap my neck. I would stand there and think about throwing myself off, but I just didn't have the courage to do it. I think back and remember I just wanted not to be alive any more. I always thought I was just too chicken to do it, and that made me hate myself even more.

In high school a teacher took notice that I seemed really depressed and had bad headaches every day, it seemed, and she suggested that I go and talk to a teacher that I was close to. Right away, as soon as I saw that teacher, I was all smiles, and I seemed as happy as anything. It wasn't going to happen that I talked to anyone about what was going on and why.

On top of everything else, I developed bulimia. When I had to babysit for my brothers I'd wait until they were asleep and I would go around the house and eat a little bit of all of the different foods that I wasn't allowed to have that were only my mother's. Then I would throw up. I figured if my mom could do it, I could do it. Why not?

I didn't think I'd graduate from high school, because I just couldn't imagine it. I thought I'd either take my life or be killed in a car crash or something. I was very depressed the last two years of high school. I had a harder time faking it, harder time keeping a smile up. In fact, there were days and weeks I couldn't smile. I would dream about going to jail, because I thought that living in jail would be better than my life.

While Rachel's home life was dominated by criticism and undermining, Rose describes the trauma of her father's unexpected death and her mother's emotional collapse and makes reference to her own beginning use of drugs. Tess also began smoking pot. In both instances, this was not the casual social experimentation or use that's common among adolescents, but rather the beginning of some real difficulties with substance abuse.

Rose: My father died in the middle of the night from a heart attack when I was fourteen, and I had to do mouth-to-mouth resuscitation. My mother was completely hysterical. The paramedics finally got there and took him to the hospital, and he died. After that she fell apart, and I was living in the house by myself a lot while she went back and forth to the hospital. A friend of mine came over the house and saw a complete mess. I was just trying to survive—you know, I was trying to get to school, and that kind of thing. And so she and her mother came over to clean the house, and she was just muttering, "You rich kids don't even know how to clean a house." I didn't ask her to help me, she just barged in. It didn't matter to me at all.

And also I recall just going to school, sometimes sleeping in my clothes, being that I was at the house by myself, and so just sleeping in my clothes and getting up and going to school and not really washing. I just didn't pay any attention to what I was doing; it didn't matter. I was just trying to make it through. The gym teacher told me I had to take a shower and made sure I did. And I would spend a fair amount of time in the nurse's office. I would say I had a headache, even though I didn't, to get down there. I would just go to sleep for a couple of hours. I couldn't sleep at home at all. If my mother was home, I didn't know what she would do in the middle of the night. And then she was in the psych hospital at the same time my grandmother was in the hospital with a heart attack, and I couldn't sleep then. That persisted for me— seventh and eighth grade were really difficult years for me. Nobody really had the whole story of what was going on because my grandmother was supposed to be looking after me. I did okay in school, but unfortunately I got into drugs. I think I was bright, and so I could pass. I did not miss much school, but I just couldn't really read at home or study.

Tess: I would do the same thing as my mother used to do, with staring into the mirror for hours. I would want to be somebody else, like somebody on TV, and I'd really want people to react to me as though I were that person. I didn't want to be who I was. And when I was a teenager, my brother became mentally ill, too. I mean, we had two shocks, one after the other, with them. You're torn between pitying them to death or hating them. I would think, "Come on, you can do things, you have two hands, you can wash the dishes." I was in high school then. I just wanted to be normal and have a normal family but I knew I was far from normal. I smoked a lot of pot, I did my own thing, I just tried not to feel how sad and crazy it all seemed.

Alice used sex as a way to punish her parents and as a distraction from her own distress. She also got into drugs and alcohol in a very serious way and needed inpatient treatment as a young adult.

Alice: I used sex as a way to stab her in the back, and as I acted out sexually and started to have sex, we went to Planned Parenthood. I had sex starting in my senior year in high school and through college. I just knew that if she knew, I could use it against her, so that was my way of turn-ing the knife. There was a huge amount of anger in me.

By the time I was a teenager I was doing anything I wanted to, and my parents had no clue whatever. I had, like, two separate lives. I was drinking and doing drugs and having sex with all these different guys. I could just tell my parents some bullshit and they'd buy it. My grades were fine then. I worked second shift at my job, so they were used to me coming home late anyway.

Pat's mother was more emotionally neglectful, not seeming to notice what was going on with her. These were the years when her mother was preoccupied with facial pain and was barely functioning at home. Here Pat talks about her own depression in high school and how invis-ible that was at home.

Pat: I was still wearing dresses with tiebacks when everybody else was wearing skirts, sweaters, and saddle shoes. That's when I picked up that navy blue sweater that I wore over everything, partly to hide my devel-oping breasts. It was that year that my homeroom teacher called me in and asked me, "How are things at home?" I just stood there speechless. She was the one that told me I had an IQ of 140 yet I was failing all of my classes. I was getting Cs and Ds. I just don't remember what hap-pened after that, but I remember taking report cards home with Cs and Ds and no one saying anything. I had been an A student up to that point.

If we wished that these kids had more healthy solutions to their troubles, we would be disappointed to find that even "doing the right thing"—going to a therapist—didn't always do any good, and in fact, it could do harm.

Danielle: I did go to see a psychiatrist when I was in high school—I don't even remember how I got there. I told him the stuff going on at home, and he said I was making it all up to get attention. That was that. It didn't even make any sense to me at the time, because he was the only person I had told, so where was I getting attention?

EARLY EXITS

As we've seen previously, some of the women whose stories are told here essentially left home, in one way or another, before graduating from high school. Here are some other examples of kids capitalizing on their growing independence to leave a toxic environment and make their way in the world. Sometimes there were feelings of liberation and expansiveness, and sometimes just a sense of barely escaping intact.

Leaving home early, although a good choice for these adolescents, inevitably added to their sense of having to go it alone, without support or guidance, when they were already struggling with big cracks in their foundations. Leaving home early in this way can mean that kids move to some kind of premature adulthoood, but they typically continue to struggle with managing and understanding their feelings and family relationships.

> **Sandy:** I moved out just before I was sixteen and stayed in different friends' houses. This was in high school. The last straw for me was when she and I had an argument downstairs in the laundry room. She used to hit me, or slap me in the face, when she got mad. She hit me and I hit her back, and I slapped her on one arm and then the other arm, and I felt myself losing control. It's the only time I ever felt that. I took her body and I pushed her into the playroom, behind the laundry room, and I took the dryer and pushed it against the door so she couldn't get out. I went upstairs and packed, and that was it. I knew that if I stayed there, something terrible was going to happen. I thought if I stayed there I would kill her.
>
> **Pat:** I graduated in June and turned seventeen in August, then left home for social work school. I got out of there as soon as I could, and I just blossomed once I left. That last year of school was when I would come home and the house would be dark and lights out, although she did continue to function.
>
> **Eleanor:** My older brother had graduated high school a year early, and so did I. Where we lived was very isolated, and I was depressed during the whole time I was in high school. I took classes by mail to make up a year in high school and graduated when I was sixteen. I was anxious about going far away to college, but I did it. I only went back one summer, after my freshman year, and things were even worse at home. Then my parents moved again, so there wasn't even a home to go home to if I had wanted. I was just out of there.

RESILIENCE

Teenagers have even more opportunity than younger kids to see other families from the inside, and with their more mature ability to make judgments and abstract information, it doesn't take long to figure out that other families can be very different from their own.

> **Sandy:** And I had been out and about, had seen other families, had been babysitting. I saw that the things that were happening in my family were not normal! In other families, people don't yell and scream, and they care about each other. The other thing that helped was that my aunt and uncle lived a couple of hours away, and I was able to spend some time with them when I was a teenager. My aunt would refer to the

"craziness" in my family. They really encouraged me to get good grades and get into a good college, and kind of told me, not in so many words, that that was the way out for me. They couldn't have been more different from my parents.

If a child grows up in with a conviction that she is bad, that feeling certainly doesn't dissolve by itself, even with new feedback from other people. But layered over that bedrock feeling can be an awareness that a parent has serious problems of her own. This opens the door for new and more accurate positive feedback from teachers, friends, coaches, ministers, and others. It may seem, for years, that the person has really transcended a bad beginning and now has an accurate view of themselves. But as we've seen, the early self-view is "stored," so to speak, in a different way from later thoughts and feelings about the self and isn't easily modified by present-day experience. In her previous statements, Rachel is very clear about this—despite her popularity and resilience in college, she was still convinced that if she let her friends get close and they "really" knew her, they would see how bad she was. It allowed her to do well in the present (for a while, at least) but didn't undo the sense of being held hostage to feelings of badness that came from earlier times. These underlying feelings, these old implicit feelings, must be unearthed and faced head-on if even the most resilient person is ever to feel completely whole and integrated.

Resilience for teens in dysfunctional families is almost universally based on making a life apart for themselves, whether at school or a job, with sports, music, art, or drama—whatever takes them into a world that gives them more accurate feedback about themselves.

So let's see what our daughters experienced in the way of constructing parallel lives.

Juliana: I worked in an import shop when I was seventeen, and the guy who owned it went away and put me in charge. So every day after school, I would go and open the store, and at the end of the day I would do the books and close up the shop. It gave me a very good sense of myself.

I also went away for a summer, and that was what helped change my sense of myself, at least for then. I went to work for a summer at an amusement park out of state, where they hired a lot of kids every summer to come and work and live there. It was great. I made a lot of money and took total care of myself. When I came home, I started hanging around with some people a few years older, who were working and living on their own. For the most part, they were very good for me. I just couldn't relate to kids my own age; I didn't have anything in common with them.

Rachel: My best friend lived nearby, and his mother said, once, "You know you are always welcome here, you're welcome to any food that we have. You're welcome to anything you ever want here. You can come over anytime you want to, no questions asked. You are just plain old welcome here." From that point on, I would spend a lot of my holidays there. The Fourth of July I was always at their house. For once, and luckily for me, my mother didn't object.

At school my mom wouldn't let me go out for sports, because she didn't want to come late to pick me up. But some teachers got me involved in different activities, and they would drive me home. The more time I had away from home, the happier I was. Later on, I had a job and did really well. I had the respect of all of my managers because I counted the safe at night, and they couldn't leave until we had it balanced. I thrived in environments where I could show leadership and gain acceptance for that. My mother never had anything good to say about it.

My senior year I took a trip to France. I was working thirty hours a week during my senior year of high school, but I was also taking college credit classes: calculus, biology, physics. My mother was really jealous that I got to go, and said she never did when she was in high school. One of my teachers gave me some pocket money because she saw how hard I was working, and my mom was angry about that, too. It was like, anything I did on my own, where I did well or was recognized by anybody else, just made her angry and more negative toward me.

Jerri: I didn't want to be talking about my mother, but when I made close friends, I did end up connecting with girls who knew about her and were pretty accepting of it, so that helped me accept it and not feel it was something I had to keep so secret. I was always looking for close friends.

Jerri also figured out, and implemented, a way to have friends in her life without making her mother too anxious. Since both her parents emphasized her staying at home and being part of their small family, it wasn't possible for her to "escape" to the outside world. The way she found, fortunately, seemed to work well. If her mother had been deliberately undermining and hostile, it wouldn't have worked.

Jerri: I figured out a way so my mother would be more okay with my growing up and having friends. I would carefully bring them in the house. They would sit down and talk to her. Then later I would say, "Ma, these are my friends. They're good people—get to know them." I tried to find as many eastern European links as I possibly could. If they were eastern European, that made it much easier. She trusted them more. Eventually she got more comfortable with my growing up and with more people being around.

June gravitated to the church that was so welcoming and affirming to her, but the "working model" she had learned earlier in her life kicked in when there was a problem there. So although her resilience shines through, it's also possible to see where she could get stuck in old patterns that she wasn't even aware of.

June: Church was wonderful. I loved it, and it was a lifesaver up until I was thirteen. But I was thirteen, and I was dating a boy who wasn't a Christian, and they told me I shouldn't do that. So that was the end of it, and I stopped going to the church. It wasn't that I was angry or anything—I felt like I wasn't doing it right anymore, so I couldn't stay.

Once, when I was late getting there, it never occurred to me to tell somebody if I was going to be late, or to even think that they would notice or anything. There were no trustworthy, reliable adults in my life, so it never occurred to me that someone would notice if you were late, or that they would expect you to tell them what you were doing. The lady at church really scolded me, so I figured I had to leave. I thought I heard, "I'm mad at you. You did it wrong, so you have to leave."

Resilience doesn't always have to be active and doesn't always involve other people. Some adolescents turned inward, relying on books for escape or using their imaginations to create an oasis for themselves.

Eleanor: I read a huge amount. Partly it was to escape things at home that were awful and oppressive, and partly to get away from my own anger. Just walking into the house was enough to make me angry, by that time. We had moved to a very isolated small town, where my mother got worse and we all felt trapped, with nowhere to go. I got the hell out of there as soon as I possibly could, took high school courses by correspondence during the summer and graduated a year early. My seventeenth birthday was the first day of college for me.

After I got home from school, almost every day I would take books and go outside, a couple of miles from the house. We lived in a very rural area near rice paddies that would periodically be flooded so the rice would grow. There were these wooden platforms, with sides, that were on stilts above the waterline. I would climb up onto one of these platforms and read for hours. It was like being in my own little room, where nobody knew where I was and nobody bothered me. I read everything Dostoyevsky wrote, and Sinclair Lewis, and John Steinbeck. I got into Thomas Wolfe and loved his novels. I just picked things at random from the library shelves, and this is what I ended up with. Lots of times I picked things by how thick they were—the thicker the better. I could get lost in them and live another life.

Sandy: I had a couple of good friends, and apart from them the most significant way I coped was that I had a really strong relationship with nature. I would go down to the pond and just sit there and breathe and think that pleasant things were happening. I guess I was meditating, but I didn't know what that was.

And my uncle and aunt were a very good influence. They both said, "If you're smart enough, you can go to college," and that became a driving force. In high school I found some things I was good at and escaped into those things. I got a lot of good support at school, although they didn't recognize what was going on.

Rose found a spiritual connection through nature, which helped her feel better emotionally and gave her perspective on her situation.

Rose: Growing up on a lake, I frequently would think of Mother Nature as my real parent. I swam a lot—underwater swimming, above water, on the boat, watching the lake. I actually have that recollection of looking into the lake and seeing myself and having a sense of myself. I would watch my hand move in the water, or make ripples in the sand. It was very spiritual, but I wouldn't have thought that at the time. It just made me feel calm and that there was something else out there that wasn't crazy and painful.

Cynthia: The most important thing was that I had some amazing adult mentors: a coach, who I was madly in love with; an English teacher—a couple of teachers, actually. My journal teacher was great. She let me unload, and she responded beautifully.

Tess: My escape was my jobs, after I started working when I was pretty young. There was one point I was holding three jobs. One was babysitting when I thirteen and fourteen. Once I had a job in a therapist's office, which was the best thing that I ended up there, because there was one woman there who I could kind of talk to. I worked in food service at a local women's college, and I ended up going there for a couple of years. And then I went to Europe for a year and loved it, and I've traveled in Europe a lot. I visited relatives there, and it was really great for me. I was very independent in all this, and I knew I could handle things and be on my own.

Chapter 5

Young Adulthood

The trajectory in young adulthood should be out and away, with the family as a stable base from which those in their late teens fly to the near or far corners of their world. There's been some change in the past decade, as witnessed by the number of magazine articles expressing dismay over young adults who either don't leave home or return like a boomerang after leaving in their late teens or early twenties.

At the time these women grew up, though, the norm was to leave home, both emotionally and physically, after high school and either go to college, marry, or live independently and find a job. Ideally, the energy of young adults is focused on mastery and self-definition, on forming new, more serious relationships, and on testing themselves and their capabilities.

Being launched from the family home usually means giving up being taken care of, protected, and guided, but the women telling their stories here had found protection, guidance, and care in short supply for most of their lives. The challenge for them was to strike a balance between their growth and development and their ongoing obligations to the family. Although different ethnicities seek different balances of these two forces, the main thrust initially is, at least to some extent, away from the family identity and toward an individual identity, then toward making a new family of one's own. College provides some cushioning and gives kids permission to try new ways of being or to abandon adolescent personas that may no longer fit. When eighteen- or nineteen-year-olds move directly from high school into the world of work, they forgo this cushioning and shoulder more responsibility, often being faced pretty quickly with adult decisions and consequences.

Dysfunctional families seem to produce two variants on the theme of leaving home. One is the early exit, as late adolescents graduate early or forgo graduating altogether and seek refuge outside the family. We saw some examples of this in the last chapter: Sandy left at sixteen to live with friends' families after a physical fight with her mother; Eleanor crammed high school into three years and started college at seventeen; Pat left home at seventeen and moved right into social work school; and June no longer lived with her mother after age fifteen. The other variant is to leave home physically but not emotionally, staying tuned to the "home channel" long after kids from healthier families do. Sometimes this is in the service of parents who still need help, and sometimes it's in the service of younger brothers and sisters who are left behind without the care and protection of their older sibling.

Another important task in this period, which extends through adulthood, is establishing appropriate boundaries. It can mean learning one's own physical or emotional limits or learning to separate oneself from others when one doesn't want to follow along. It can also mean sorting out appropriate from inappropriate demands coming from others, whether friends, family, or employers. It can be a difficult decision to put a lot of energy into a job that makes one unavailable to needy family members. Some people wonder if they should come home every weekend to help their parents and to hang out with their neglected younger brothers and sisters. Do you drop everything and run when your mother calls, threatening suicide—and if so, how many times? How can you feel okay going after what you want, maybe even being happy, when other people in the family may be so miserable and hopeless? If you escape and make a new life for yourself, aren't you a rat deserting the sinking ship?

Boundaries between the self and the family are important and can set the stage positively or negatively for boundaries with friends, bosses, and in intimate relationships. Even if one figures out how to do this well in young adulthood, boundary questions resurface in middle age, when caring for aging parents may become a new priority.

GOING OUT INTO THE WORLD

For these daughters of mentally ill mothers, the transition to independence often offered new possibilities and a chance for a resilient response to old problems.

> **Pat:** Escape was everything to me, at that point. I moved into my own life and was very happy. My social work job went really well, people liked me and thought I did a great job, and I felt completely myself and

alive for the first time ever. That was probably one of the best times of my entire life! But it was all apart from my family. They weren't part of it at all. I did try to get treatment for my mother, so some people knew about her problems, but otherwise I didn't want to be associated with them, really. And that was as much my father as it was my mother.

Juliana: My mother offered me junior college and wanted me to be a nurse. That was it. So I put together a portfolio and went around to some places and got accepted at an art school, which is where I wanted to go. I told her that's what I was doing and she kind of went along with it, barely.

I was off the radar screen when my mother remarried, when I was in college. They paid for a year of school, then they told me I was on my own, that he was closing his business and they didn't have money to help me anymore. I already had one job to help with tuition. Meanwhile, they moved to the coast and bought a seven-acre spread on the ocean. Whether I had enough money to live on or finish school was just irrelevant. It was what they wanted to do, so that's what they did. I didn't even question it, I was so used to it being that way. So I found other jobs and bartended nights and got through on my own.

Lee: I went off to college, and my father would have been saying—he was just like that—that things at home were fine, go and enjoy school. I'm very grateful for that, and it helped me just concentrate on my new life in a new place.

Jerri: Going to college was hard because my dad wanted me to stay home. He thought any change would upset my mother. I did stay home for a while because school was close enough, but then I really wanted to live at the dorm, and I finally convinced him it was a good idea. I found out later he told the dean about my mother, and then they let me in the dorm. I was so angry. I just hated the fact that we had to use it. It was like sneaking in the back door. I felt that it was unfair. It was, like, "You taught me all my life not to talk about it, and now you're using it as a weapon to get what you want." I thought, "Everybody has issues. Why do I have to be different?"

Once I was in college, I just didn't let anything stop me. I got a sports car—that shocked my dad—and I dated, and I became this totally independent person. I got married early to a man in the military because I knew we would travel a lot, but I guess I was still influenced by home, because I never had the thought that I could travel by myself, I don't have to get married to do that.

Rose: I was in a complete fog when I went off to nursing school. The world was like a bad dream. My father had died, then my mother had gone crazy. It seemed surreal. Nothing was solid anymore. I was drawn to nursing school because of the adrenaline rush of working with patients and life-and-death problems—that was what I was used to, by that time. I felt comfortable when the adrenaline was flowing. I didn't like it when things were quiet or calm.

Rachel's mother continued to undermine and belittle her as she went off to college, and Rachel continued to feel that her home was like a prison. But when she left, unfortunately her mother's voice followed her for many years. So her escape, although a strong indication of her resilience, was only physical, not emotional.

Rachel: I went to college nearby, and my mother gave me the hardest time about living on campus, even though I was paying for everything. She bad-mouthed me to people, telling them how stupid I was to waste money on the dorm when I could live at home. I think if I had kids, I would be proud of them if they wanted that independence. I did come home on weekends because of a job I'd had for several years, where I made good money. But I was drinking a lot at the same time. I felt free during the week in college. I felt like I had broken out of prison and escaped. When I went home, I had to live in a box. At home I couldn't have my feelings or my freedom. Neither one of my parents ever showed the slightest interest in what I was doing, much less pride at my good grades.

What was so great was, I was successful at things I did, and I put a lot of effort into things, so I felt I deserved the success I got. I had fun for the first time in my life and wasn't always afraid of what was going to happen next.

June was on her own, although continuing high school, and made her way through her last high school years with some help. She carried with her, however, the pattern of simply moving on when there was a situation she couldn't handle.

June: After I told my mother I couldn't take care of her or live with her anymore, she stayed in hospitals for a couple of years. I packed up the apartment, because I didn't have enough to pay the rent. It wasn't because I was fifteen and I shouldn't have been living on my own—I didn't think that, just that I couldn't pay the rent. Then, just by happenstance, I ran into a woman in town who had been a counselor of mine a few years before. I told her what was going on, and she offered to have me live at her house. So I moved in there with her—I thought it was like a roommate, and she thought more like being a foster mother. I remember being depressed for about a year. I didn't know what to do, I didn't have that purpose anymore—I lost that focus on my mother. The lady who had taken me in was really a good person and tried to make a normal home for me, but I know I didn't talk to her. I didn't talk to her not because *she* wasn't there but because *I* wasn't there.

At some point in there, I don't even remember when, she went on a trip overseas, and I just moved out. Later on, when we connected again, she wanted to know if I left because she went on that long trip, and I said no—the problem was she was trying to provide me with something very normal and I didn't know what to do with it. It was just too alien. I couldn't deal with it. She asked why I didn't come back to explain that, and I said, "It never occurred to me." If something didn't work out with somebody, it would never occur to me to go back! It wasn't an option any other time in my life.

Tess went to college for a while, more or less by accident, as her immigrant parents weren't knowledgeable about how to help her beyond high school. She wasn't suited for it at that time and found much more satisfaction in work. As an adolescent, too, she always found a refuge in jobs rather than in school. In her work, she got a lot of positive feedback and recognition and exercised healthy responsibility. So, the source of her resilience seems not to have changed during this period.

> **Tess:** My parents didn't know a thing about it. I didn't know a thing about colleges either. I just went because this guy that I dated said, "Oh, come on and apply to my college." So I went for two years. It was a waste. I wasn't a good student. What really helped me was getting a job in a kitchen with Portuguese people. I learned to be very responsible and I loved it.

Danielle got away to school but ended up mentally taking her family with her, in some ways. She kept track of what was happening at home and carried the guilt of leaving her sister behind. Things weren't going well for her parents, but she resisted the pull to run home and try to fix things.

> **Danielle:** When I left to go to college, I felt really guilty about leaving my younger sister there alone with my parents. It was awful for her. I would go home for vacations, but I really didn't want to be there at all. My mother was just totally depressed, even though she was still working, and they were both drinking all the time. Even not being there, I kind of took it with me mentally anyway.

Alice floundered along the way, as her chosen profession demanded more inner rather than outer focus. And Barbara found old patterns, with her mother cropping up in a very unexpected place.

> **Alice:** When I was twenty-three I was going into really intensive training in my field, and I knew that the next year coming up was when you didn't work, you didn't run around—you studied, you looked into yourself. I knew I was not ready to go there. I decided to take a break from that for a while. I was having a lot of trouble with drinking, but it was more under control right then, but was a problem on and off for years. So I wasn't really able to go into the career I wanted to, because it just required more self examination than I could do, at that point.
>
> **Barbara:** When I left for college, my mother started divorce proceedings, and she also had just one hospitalization after another. It was the time of women's liberation, and I think she wanted more for herself. I think my father just went along with it because that's the way he was. He would just do whatever he was supposed to do.

One thing that was really telling, when I was out and on my own, I was taking an improvisation class in acting one time, and the scene was that this other person was supposed to come at me, attack me. Well, he started, but I kept trying to talk him down, get him to stop, divert his attention, all that. Well, the teacher stopped it and said to me, "This is totally unrealistic. Nobody would keep going like that." Well, guess what—somebody *did* keep going like that! I was trained by a master—my mother!

STAYING CONNECTED WITH HOME

When kids or young adults from dysfunctional families go out into the world, they either go as far and as fast as they can, without looking back, or they leave and experience some freedom but maintain connections. Juliana formed a relationship with her father, but it had its own problems. Both Alice and Maggie were very concerned about their younger siblings and remained in a mothering role long after they left home. Cynthia knew about ongoing and new problems at home, although she stayed in school.

Juliana: When I was older and on my own and living in Chicago, my father would visit often because he had business there, and he wanted to be closer. But I realized he wanted me to know *him* better, he didn't care about knowing *me* better. And he would introduce me to his friends, like, "Look at my daughter. Didn't I do a great job raising her?" and that pissed me off. He had nothing to do with it. So I had a fight with him and told him, "You weren't there at all. Not when I was upset, not when Mom was being awful to me, not when my brother was beating me up—you weren't there." So we didn't talk for a couple of years after that.

Alice: Once I went to college, my younger sister had already started to take over the mother role more and more. My mother got a lot more crazy at that point, too. I would take the kids up to the dorm with me for the weekend. There was a way to have them come visit, and I did that as much as I could. So the four kids would come up and stay overnight. They had fun—they were out of the house and with me, and I looked forward to it, too. The two littler kids were afraid they'd never see me again once I went to college, so it was important to them. I was really their mother—they didn't rely on Mom at all. How could they? And when I did well in school and got any attention for that, she would get jealous and say things that were undermining. Like, she was the only one who could ever be in the spotlight.

Cynthia: I was okay going off to college, even though things were the same at home. But then my dad had another affair with someone, and there was a lot of upset about all that. He decided to stay with my mom. But that was when I was a freshman in college, so I was really torn about where I should be and how my mom would cope with all this.

Sandy had left home when she was sixteen and maintained a pretty independent existence, while her family continued to deteriorate. Here she describes that deterioration, which affected every member of her family except her. In retrospect, it looks like she escaped just in time.

Sandy: From the time of my father's death, which was one week before I graduated college, she lost the house, then she lived with my older brother and all hell broke loose. My brother was using and selling hard drugs at that time. My mother was enabling that and housing him— losing the house had to do with all the drug stuff, losing money there. My younger brother was involved in drugs, too. It was this rampantly sick system.

Later she got this little apartment with, literally, a path through the boxes, and she had this huge refrigerator from our home, which didn't work. She had it filled up with jars and boxes and containers. At some point along in there, I just cut off contact and would just send a card now and then. I needed to be away from them, and it was just too crazy.

Both Barbara's and Maggie's brothers had some serious problems. Barbara's brother got into drugs, but despite this she was able to maintain a connection with him, whereas Maggie's developed serious psychiatric problems.

Barbara: He got very messed up and became a heroin addict, but he would tell me it was okay to feel whatever I felt. Once he wrote me a letter trying to tell me that our parents' divorce was their deal, that I shouldn't take it on myself. But there were no adults to put it in perspective.

Maggie: My brother started having really manic episodes in his early twenties. He was in the hospital, he was arrested, you name it. He thought he was supposed to save the government in Washington; he got arrested for wandering around there. I was frantic with worry and trying to help him and make him realize he was sick and had to take his medicine. We'd get him hospitalized, and then they'd let him out because they couldn't hold him. He married a wonderful woman, but he could talk her into anything. So I would be saying, "He needs to stay in the hospital to get stable," and she would sign him out.

My mother was no help, even though she would try to participate. She treated him being sick the same way she was when she was sick. Just pity and "Oh, he's so sick. Isn't it terrible? He can't help it that he won't take the medicine." Meanwhile, he had also developed OCD [obsessive-compulsive disorder] like her, in addition to the bipolar.

I was the only one who really saw what was happening.

Although Eleanor's parents divorced and her mother had significant problems during Eleanor's early twenties, she didn't feel responsible for what happened, or for fixing it. As a child, she had felt rather invisible, and this apparent liability had a silver lining: It translated into her ability to keep her distance when other people's disasters threatened to suck everyone into a whirlpool of chaos. She didn't feel compelled to act, but did feel compelled to say what was expected and to provide emotional support for both parents, usually without knowing what she herself actually thought or felt.

> **Eleanor:** When I was in college, my parents moved several times, so I didn't really have a home base anymore. Then, when I was about twenty, my mother divorced my father—just locked him out of the house and wouldn't let him in, and then changed the locks. She was seeing a psychiatrist who evidently encouraged her to "assert herself." Even though I knew that she was in this holy war with my father, always feeling controlled and trying to overthrow him as the family dictator, I didn't see this coming. My father was devastated but said he never would have left her, no matter what. He told me he was her "life preserver." It's really strange that she's the one that divorced him, not the other way around.
>
> My mother lived on her own, but she was in bad shape—pretty crazy and also drinking, trashing their house. She lived on the alimony my father paid for decades. She set the place on fire once, smoking in bed. Almost lost the house because she wasn't paying the bills. I was out of touch with her at that time, but my older brother, who had become a psychiatrist, was trying to take care of her. She was hospitalized a couple of times, once with malnutrition, but after being a mess for a few years, she somehow stabilized and moved into a little apartment, and then she did better for five or six years. I really don't know how she did it.

MOM IN THE HOSPITAL

Hospitalizations continued mostly to be emergencies for everyone in the family, whether they were still living at home or not. There were no stories about their mothers collaborating in their own care or seeking voluntary hospitalization or treatment to prevent a relapse. Mother would have to get "really bad" before the decision was made to put her in the hospital, and this very ineffective way of going about things only guaranteed that the next time would be worse.

Some women felt they always had one ear cocked for troubles at home. Most felt they had to be there to help out when things got bad and didn't know how to handle the cost to themselves. Since these were now young women, they had more information and more history about their mother, the mental health system, and so forth, and concomitantly more responsibility. Given all the family issues that converge on the decision to hospitalize a parent, what's particularly appalling is the way the mental health system responded far too many times. There was no help for young adults torn between handling repeated emergencies and trying to make a go of their own lives.

Barbara had many encounters with her mother around hospitalizations and medication. Part of setting boundaries here relies on other people doing what they're supposed to be doing—for example, mental health professionals, who can be enormously useful to families who've brought someone to the hospital or the ER. Right there, on the front lines, is a chance to listen to what family members have to say, collaborate with them in figuring out what's going on, and help them make a smooth transition to the next stage, whether it's hospitalization or sending the patient back home.

> **Barbara:** Nobody was helpful to me in dealing with her for years and years. Once, after I was out of college, I was living in an apartment and she just showed up, totally crazy, not making any sense at all, and me and my sister took her over to the hospital to get her admitted. When we got there, there was a social worker there who actually remembered us from other times she had seen my mother, and she said we needed to make sure we could keep our boundaries around this stuff with her. I said, "What boundaries?" not to be sarcastic but because I wasn't even sure what she meant. Certainly nobody had ever said anything remotely like that before.
>
> She was hospitalized many times after I started college. Once I went by myself to visit her, and she picked up a lamp and tried to throw it at me. There was nobody there to tell me what was going on with her. They just told me she was in room number whatever, and that was it. Once I took her out of the hospital for a visit, for a couple of hours. She got in the car and started screaming at me, telling me to follow certain license plates because our lives depended on it. Nobody told me she might act like this. They just said, "Fine, take her out for a few hours." So we get to this restaurant, and my mother is getting messages from the flies on the wall. It was totally bizarre.
>
> Another time, when I was in my early twenties, they called me from the hospital. When I got there, they wanted me to sign her in. No conversation, no awareness that I was her kid and I was pretty young, and I was very upset about the whole thing. Like they just needed a signature on a piece of paper, and they didn't care what the fallout would be for me or for her. Okay, she needed to be in the hospital, but how was she going to feel toward me when she realized I signed her in? That I was the one that put her there?

Once in a while, professionals are helpful and see beyond the patient to the family. When they take the time to solicit questions and offer direct answers and reassurance, people certainly remember. A little of this goes a very long way.

Barbara: When I was supposed to commit her, they had to have somebody interview her before it was legally completed. So this doctor comes
in to where we're sitting and starts talking to my mother. Well, she
totally pulled herself together and was sounding oh so normal. I'm thinking, "Oh, shit, they're going to buy this." Then he started asking her different kinds of questions, and the craziness came out, like how important
it was that the two sides of a bed are different from each other, and a lot
of other stuff. So he takes me outside and says, "Your mother is a very
sick woman." I was relieved and upset at the same time. He was con-
firming what I knew was true, but it made it more real. You'd think it
was obvious after all this time, but nobody had ever just said it like that
to me. He seemed sympathetic, so I asked him something about whether
I was going to end up like her. He just talked to me and reassured me,
and it was really helpful.

When the family isn't involved in making the decision about treatment and is expected to accommodate decisions made by others, the
fallout can be very difficult.

Helen: Another time she went to the hospital, but this time they decided
to give her shock treatments as an outpatient, and my sister—who had
young kids—was supposed to take her there and pick her up and take care
of her. I was living out of state at that time, and my father had died, so my
mother was alone. I know it was extremely hard on my sister. She had to
talk her into going each time, which wasn't easy, then leave her there and
pick her up afterwards. Mom was a mess afterwards, like a sick child you
had to take total care of. The staff evidently didn't care in the least.

Lee's discovery of her father's taking matters into his own hands
was shocking to her—and also to me, during Lee's interview, but less
so after several other women mentioned that they thought their fathers
may have done the same thing. The temptation to stockpile medication
and, unbeknownst to her, slip it to someone who's unraveling right in
front of you must be enormous, especially when you know the only
other option is to drag that person to the ER and sit for hours while
she berates you for thinking there's something wrong with her.

Lee: My father told me something that horrified me: Mom always had
this big bottle of soda in the fridge that she would drink, and if he
thought she was getting high, he would put in Mellaril [antipsychotic
medication]. Once, when he was getting really sick with cancer—this was
when I was older—he called me and was whispering on the phone saying, "Lee, you've gotta come over and put some medicine in Mom's
soda, she's getting high."
  When I went to college, she went to the state hospital for the first
time. She was in very bad shape, very manic. When I was growing up

that was always, like, "You'd better watch out or you're going to State," like it was the Snake Pit. It was for crazy people.

Because Lee went into mental health as a profession, she had the misfortune to be working at the same place her mother was hospitalized during a manic phase. Going back and forth between her job on one floor and being in a family meeting with her mother on another floor was quite a challenge to this person who had been so very private about her mother's illness.

Lee: I ended up working there at my first job as a psychiatric nurse. She was admitted there, and I knew from my father it was the same deal— the police and the ambulance. I remember going over and seeing her and being in a family meeting with social workers for that unit. That was really, really hard. It was awful, just awful. I remember the woman there tried to make it less humiliating, but the look on her face didn't help a lot.

After years of seeing her mother go downhill with deepening depression, chronic facial pain, and covert drug dependence, Pat left home to go to social work school. Shortly afterward, her mother was hospitalized for the first time, but Pat knew little about what happened to precipitate it.

Pat: She went to the local hospital, and I don't even remember who told me, my father or my sister. I remember going with my father to the hospital, and I remember being in the car, and he went in there. The car radio was on, and there was a particular song on the radio. Even today I cannot hear that song without thinking about sitting in that car in the darkened hospital parking lot. That forever will be my association. I know we were given some information, that she might have some memory loss from the shock therapy. What I heard that really surprised me was that she and two other women got into some kind of trouble for playing a prank—pretending to escape or something. That was so completely out of character for her, it was weird to hear about it. It was like there was this other person inside her that was not depressed, that would do something like that.

I spent years trying to help her and figure out what in the world was really wrong with her. For me, the clincher was that, after the shock therapy, she didn't have any facial pain for a long time. She didn't even remember having it. That said to me it was psychosomatic. She consulted every neurologist in the state, but there was the proof that it wasn't neurological, it was psychological.

Rose was in her late teens when her mother was in the hospital, and then lived at home with her mother for a few months.

Rose: I got to the point of saying, "I'm going to end up in prison because I'm going to kill her," or "I'm going to end up in the loony bin myself because she'll drive me there." She would wander downtown and not know who she was or where she was, and somebody would bring her back. She would tell me how much she loved me, and then in the middle of the night come in and try to strangle me. I couldn't sleep, I couldn't concentrate. Her doctor wouldn't say what they thought the diagnosis was. My sister and I decided that we would find a nursing home for my mother, and my aunt thought that was disgusting and "How could you do that?" It was kind of assumed that I was the one who would stay there, but I said, "I can't go on."

I just blurted it out—what I had been thinking about was Louise, this strange woman that lived by herself, and the story was that she had taken care of her mother for years and years, and after her mother died, all Louise did was sit in church with her rosary and talk up a storm—to herself. I would see Louise's grinning face, and that did it for me—I'm not doing that. So even though my aunt was angry, once my mother was in a protected environment she started to do much better with a routine schedule and getting the medications on time and having the right care. And the expectations were zero.

Before that, though, I confronted one of the psychiatrists at the hospital and demanded to know what had happened to her. He finally admitted that he shouldn't have treated her with shock treatment, but he really didn't know what exactly was wrong. I mean, we still don't know the whole thing. There was a point where I was obsessed with it, looking it up and trying to figure it out. One doctor said psychotic depression. And no one else in the family was talking about it. I just thought it was so strange and so complicated, and nobody really talking about it. It was a big blur to me. My mother disintegrated right before our eyes. She died four years after my father died, but as far as I'm concerned, they both died the night he had that heart attack. She was never the same after that. I was scared to death that something like that could happen to me.

Alice's mother deteriorated after Alice went off to college and was finally diagnosed bipolar after years of disruptive behavior. This still didn't quite explain her profound neglect of her children, though, and didn't erase Alice's suspicion that her mother's flair for the dramatic was often a factor in the scenes that the family endured. Other daughters of a bipolar mother found that the "drama queen" element in their mother's behavior made it harder to see her as sick and stirred up feelings of bitter resentment about having to care for someone who seemed to enjoy leaving chaos in her wake and being the center of attention. The question of their own need for maternal attention seems to have been discarded long ago.

Alice: After I went to college, my mom had her first real psychotic break. She did the whole thing—she acted like she was stretched out on a crucifix, she was saying over and over, "I sacrificed one of my sons to help save the world." It was horrifying to see her like that, totally around the bend. And she was screaming at me to not go back to school and saying that I had to stay home, that she needed me. It was at finals time, and I remember sobbing on the train back to school. I felt I had abandoned her.

Then it would be that every time my brother and I were around, she would get psychotic. So she was going into the hospital every few weeks and staying for a few days, then coming home, and the whole thing started over again. She was also medicating herself, in and out of the medicine cabinets constantly. As bad as I felt for her, I was also thinking, "Why do I have to have a family like this?"

I finally pushed my father to insist on longer-term care, and she did go into a hospital for about nine months. My sister was playing the role of "Mom" at that point, and my father turned the house back into a military camp. Whatever was wrong, if you just kept the floors swept, you were okay.

Whenever I saw him, though, he was just a wreck. I had to talk to him and encourage him and tell him he was doing the right thing. He was especially mad she had gone in the hospital on his birthday, so his priorities weren't exactly the most logical, either.

When she was in the hospital, they diagnosed her with manic depression, and she was on meds, but even after she got out, she continued to have scenes or breakdowns, or whatever you want to call them. When my brother and I were home, she would still throw rosary beads at us and do all this crazy religious stuff to prevent us from dying, she said. She would tell us we were all on stage and we had to do these things. I just removed myself as much as I possibly could, even though I stayed connected with my younger brothers and sisters.

June, having been on her own since fifteen or so, no longer had to care for her mother. She was also spared the ordeal of repeated emergency hospital commitments, because once there was no outside caretaker, the hospital staff apparently recognized that her mother needed intensive, long-term treatment for her dual illnesses of schizophrenia and dissociative identity disorder (formerly known as multiple personality disorder).

June: By the time I was out of high school, she was still living in controlled environments after she left the hospital. She was there for a couple of years. I would call her, but she'd just need me to convince her I was fine, which, of course, I wasn't. We couldn't talk about anything real, even though she wasn't psychotic at that point. I would go see her either at the hospital or, later, at various group home places that she lived. I didn't really want to, but I thought I had to. Even when she was a little better, she was never anywhere close to the mother she had been when I was young.

At this stage of the game, mothers seem mostly to have abdicated their mothering role. The relationships of the women in this project seem to be either disengaged, with the mothers letting their daughters go without much notice; maintaining a hostile and critical relationship with them; or becoming dependent on them as their daughters become young women. In Lee's case, she seems here to have become the mother herself.

> **Lee:** I went to the hospital to pick her up, because by then she was on pass to go home for Thanksgiving, and I was a little late. She told me she was afraid I had forgotten about her. To this day I can't imagine what that must have felt like to her.

BEGINNING HER OWN FAMILY

Few of the women interviewed here got married during their early adult years, which is unusual given the cultural expectations and statistics about marriage during that period. Some took longer to find relationships that seemed solid, and a larger percentage than one would expect were lesbian. Some haven't had long-lasting relationships of any kind, and it seems clear to them that the difficulties of growing up are still having an effect on their ability to form trusting and supportive primary relationships. In Gina O'Connell Higgins's book on resilience, in which she interviewed people who had had traumatic childhoods but who now had stable long-term relationships and meaningful work, many of the people who were interviewed said that they did not achieve these successes until they were well into their thirties or forties.[1] During the early adult period, they found life more difficult.

A solid marriage, or partnering, presupposes a secure attachment to a trusted, safe, protective person. When that hasn't happened in childhood, it's really a leap of faith in adulthood. I would speculate that the rate of divorce or breakup for adults who grew up in significantly dysfunctional families is much higher than the national average.

Eleanor's marriage ended in divorce after ten years. Although her parents did not disapprove of her marriage, neither were they especially supportive, and in fact they had little energy to invest in her life, since their own lives had been in turmoil around their divorce. When a marriage gets off to this kind of start, the lack of a strong foundation again proves to be a weakening factor.

> **Eleanor:** I got married when I was twenty-three. I think in retrospect I mostly needed to feel I was visible and important to someone. My parents were divorced, and my father had just remarried, and my mother was furious at him. She would rant at me on the phone, and she actually

threatened to disown me if I didn't take her side on something against him, and I refused to do that. My husband and I just went to a justice of the peace because I didn't know how she would act, and the idea of having the family together was just too overwhelming. Also, because I was pretty invisible to them, I wasn't sure they would be interested in my getting married.

But she told me she would have a party for me at her apartment in the city where both she and my father lived, and I thought that maybe she was going to come through this time. So we made the long drive there, and when we arrived at her apartment, she was gone. She had evidently been evicted, since her things had been put out on the curb by the landlord. She had some family china that she wanted to give to me, but she had just left it in cardboard boxes, and it was put on the street and stolen. I had no idea where she was. Somehow we connected on the phone the next day, and she was furious that I hadn't somehow found out where she was. I hung up on her, and we didn't talk for about five years. I felt stronger because of being married, and I just didn't feel I could put up with her anymore. It just confirmed my lifelong feeling that I was basically a nonperson in my family.

Helen and her husband, on the other hand, formed a very strong bond and remain married. She laughed when I asked her if there were any anxieties about having kids because of her mother's problems.

Helen: Well, I didn't have a lot of time to think about it, because I got pregnant on my honeymoon. Maybe that was a good thing. I was terrified. We were on the West Coast with no family nearby, because my husband was in grad school. I was very lucky that I had a very nice doctor and I had a roommate at the hospital who was a terrific person. She said, "Call me anytime—this is my second baby." I think that was a help. My husband was also terrific with me, and with the baby. He was able to be home a lot with me.

The thing that interfered, really, was my fear that it was too big a challenge and I wouldn't be able to handle it. That's the same thing I had kind of been taught—that my mother was like that and I was like that, too. She kind of wanted me to be like her in that way. Turns out, I'm not—but it's taken a long time to know that.

Another problem, although not insurmountable, is how to tell one's prospective mate or in-law family about the psychiatric history in your family. Jerri recalls how the topic of her mother's illness and psychiatric history came up with her in-laws-to-be.

Jerri: When I was twenty-one, my husband and I were planning our wedding. We were sitting around with my in-laws-to-be, and my mother just got out the phone book and started calling people out of the blue, people she hadn't talked to in years. This is really strange, because she hated to use the phone, and here she is calling all these people. I remember thinking, "Holy shit, what's happening?" And my father told me then that he was worried she would have another breakdown, and I had to tell my mother-in-law that. My mother had been okay for a few years, so I hadn't talked about it. But now she was embarrassing herself. So I had to tell my new mother-in-law that she would have to handle the shower by herself, because we were afraid my mother would have another breakdown. So then I had to explain the whole history and everything. So that was my in-laws' introduction to my family, and I could see they were thinking, "Who is this girl our son is going to marry and have kids with? What kind of crazy family is this?"

What I did find out, years and years later, was that my father got the doctor to give her tranquilizers, and he just insisted that she take them before the wedding. All I knew is that my mother made her own dress for the wedding, and it was the most beautiful blue dress. I still have it; it means a lot to me. Maybe that's really all she could give me.

But again, it's the secret, "Don't tell Jerri anything." I always disliked that about my dad. He would not give me full information, because he thought he was protecting me. I guess it was typical for that era, but I'm the type of person who wants to know exactly what I'm dealing with, and then face it and resolve it.

Danielle: When I got married, my in-laws didn't really know about my mother, and they didn't know about my parents' problems with alcohol. So I really arranged the whole wedding and all the other social things in such a way that it would minimize the possibility that they would drink. We had one event as a breakfast instead of a luncheon, that kind of thing. So that was a major preoccupation—how I would manage their behavior.

FALLOUT AND RESILIENCE

Rachel paints us a picture in two tones: fallout and resilience. The way she managed to live in both places at once, or alternated between the two, shows clearly the way she felt she was living two separate lives.

Rachel: By the end of freshman year, I was anorexic, hardly eating, exercising a lot. The next couple of years I would binge and then starve, and it was horrendous, just keeping the secret of it. I was maintaining straight As, president of three clubs, working thirty hours a week, and paying my way through college.

Despite everything I was doing, I still felt I was really bad. I couldn't let anybody get to know me, because they would see what an evil, wretched person I was, whose own mother didn't love her. I had a lot of friends, but they really didn't know me.

I believed what my mother said to me about myself. I just couldn't dismiss it, and I still to this day have a lot of that belief still stuck in my mind, and I'm still trying to deal with that.

I wanted to have a boyfriend, but I couldn't be intimate, couldn't have sex, and I didn't know why. I hadn't yet remembered the sexual abuse from the next-door neighbors. I didn't want people knowing I had that problem, so I just stayed away from boys, too. Underneath, I was ashamed and embarrassed about myself in so many ways. That was just one more way. And I didn't even know why. I was just the friendly, bubbly person who kept all of this stuff to myself.

Once again I felt so different from the rest of the world. I felt like a Martian dropped off on the face of the Earth. The only way I could cope was with the eating disorder—that gave me a feeling of being kind of in control of something. I was always afraid someone would find out about my binging, and that just furthered my embarrassment.

I was leading a double life. I was a good friend, people would talk to me about their problems. I was a straight-A student at school. My professors really liked me. And then I would go home, where my mother told me how bad I was.

But on the other hand, despite all that, when I got to college I blossomed in a lot of ways. I started to find out who I was, what I liked, what I didn't like, what I could do, what I couldn't do. I didn't know any of those things. My parents really controlled us and limited us so much that there was a lot I didn't know. I'd never gone to McDonald's, because my mother thought it was so awful if kids ever ate fast food and the proof that she was a wonderful mother was that she cooked every night.

Now I could be somebody else. I had my own space. I didn't have to worry about somebody going through my stuff. I had my own space that was mine. For the first time in my life, I could decide what I wanted to do. It was amazing.

Juliana, like Rachel a daughter of a personality-disordered mother, began to have serious trouble before she finished college and wasn't able to continue her upward trajectory. She was off her parents' radar as they immersed themselves in their own lives, and it's clear to her in retrospect that a long-standing depression surfaced during this period.

Juliana: I just couldn't keep it up. I got depressed, and it was a bad depression. I just sort of fell into it. I had to quit school, and I never regrouped enough to finish. After I dropped out of school I lived on popcorn and Coca-Cola. When I was working, I might call in sick to one job to put more hours in on the other job. I went out with a guy I found out was alcoholic, and I was devastated. There were very long periods of depression after that. I was trying to figure out what I wanted to do. Finally, I got a job in an art studio. I hadn't been in therapy at all, and I just carried that feeling that I was worthless, that my mother was right to hate me, because I was just a rotten kid and now I was going to be a rotten adult.

The only good thing I did was just pick up and move across town when I realized I was surrounded by druggies and people who were just going down the tubes. I didn't tell anyone, I just moved, changed my phone, and started over.

Tess, too, carried a lifetime of confusion into adulthood.

Tess: I remember when my youngest sister—she's been angry at me for a long, long time. I went through, like, every stage: the disco stage, the hippie stage, the drug addict stage, the good little girl stage, the good little Catholic girl, the traditional Italian stage. And she said—I remember her having an argument with me—"I don't know who you are. You're always changing, I don't understand." And it was actually very telling. I was completely lost. I had no idea who I was or what I thought or believed.

Eleanor and Danielle had similar ways of handling (or not handling) their feelings about themselves and their assumptions about how they had to function in their social worlds. Both found that walling off their own histories, which had shaped them, really walled them off from themselves. To the outside, they both looked fine. While some people's fallout is more visible and costs them more, or at least differently, we tend to overlook the invisible survivors. Emotional constriction isn't dramatic, but it's painful and debilitating nonetheless.

Eleanor: I didn't really think about trusting people or not—I just didn't do it. It was just part of the way my world was, to not talk about certain things that I felt I had successfully escaped. I didn't have to talk about my family, because I was in a different world, and nothing about that world had a place for them. I didn't realize until much later that when I did that, I basically stopped talking about anything important. I was just frozen. I went through the motions, and was pretty good at my job, but it was all built on nothing. Now that I'm older, I know that what I went through growing up is so much a part of me that if you don't know something about that, you don't know me.
Danielle: I just didn't talk about anything relating to my family or my growing up. That meant I just didn't talk about myself, period. Very little personal stuff. Other people talked to me, and I liked that, but they didn't seem to notice I didn't say much back, or it was only superficial. It was important to escape all that, to put a wall between me and it, between me and my family. I could visit and try to help my parents, but the wall was still there.

June saw herself simply disappearing from one place and reappearing elsewhere, without even being aware that she was doing it. It's as though she absorbed some of her mother's "switching" from one personality to another, in simply switching from one person or place to another without being able to acknowledge much connection.

June: My biggest regret—and I learned that in twelve-step programs—was that I just disappeared from people's lives. I'm not over there anymore, I'm here now—so that's in the past. I didn't make many conscious choices about not talking to someone again, but it would just happen that I would realize I hadn't seen a certain person for five years or something. Or if something went wrong, or if the other person was upset with me for any reason, I would just move on. That would be over. It would never occur to me to go back, to talk to the person, to try to stay connected. There just weren't any connections.

Only in the last couple of years do I have my feet on the ground. I really wasn't there all that time. I spent a few years waiting to go crazy, like they said I was supposed to—or that's what I thought. I remember being relieved when I turned twenty-two and wasn't schizophrenic yet.

Although Tess says she didn't know who she was or what she believed, she continued to find a refuge and a place of resilience for herself in work. Here she describes a job she had during her late teens.

Tess: I worked with Portuguese people in the kitchen. I learned to be very responsible. I was always basically responsible, but I got rewarded. I developed a sense of identity. It was like my second family there. And it got me out of that craziness in my house. It was an escape, and I loved it.

Many of the women in this book had fears, whether they voiced them or not, about becoming ill in the same ways their mothers had. Some mentioned passing the critical age at which their mothers first got ill, and some simply had a lingering fear about losing control or being too emotional.

Barbara: That time after I signed her into the hospital, I ended up staying at her apartment for whatever reason. I didn't live in the same city at that time. So in her apartment, things were insane. Like, everything was unplugged because she had this thing about electricity, and her jewelry was in the garbage cans—it was just nuts. And it was frightening to see this evidence of how unraveled she was. I called my boyfriend and he came to stay with me, and I just started to cry and I couldn't stop. I just sobbed and sobbed. I got freaked out because I really didn't know if I was going over the edge like my mother. We ended up calling some older friends, who were really comforting and reassuring.

Then, later in college and after college, I would just throw my life into chaos whenever she would call and need me for something. That went on for a long time. I would also try to catch it before she got really manic, when I could see it. But when she's in that state, she's pretty out there, and if you didn't do exactly what she wanted, she'd get really verbally abusive and the whole artillery would come out.

Jerri continued her determined flight into independence and made the best of whatever situation she found herself in. Her strong and secure attachment to her grandmother, beginning early on, no doubt stood her in good stead. And although she bitterly resented her father's secretiveness about her mother's illness and symptoms, it may have been a good protection in her younger years.

> **Jerri:** When I got more on my own and got a car, I took trips with my friends, and all that. I was off and running! My husband went overseas in the service, and I wound up meeting him in Hong Kong. That was who I was, and I wasn't going to let my mother put a lid on it. It wasn't like a conscious thought, it's just that I knew who I was and what I wanted to do. I wasn't going to let anything hold me back. But it kind of went against everything I had done up to that time, against the rule about not doing anything that might upset my mother.
>
> When I think of some of the things that I was able to do despite what was going on at home, I'm pretty proud of myself. I never used that to tie me down.
>
> I find myself pretty amazing. I wonder to myself if I just got a lucky set of genes, or what. I really have to marvel at the little kid that I was. You know, I got mad, and I got upset, and I missed having a mother, but I never felt sorry for myself.

Chapter 6

Adulthood

It's hard to consider adulthood as a "developmental period" like child-hood or adolescence, and therefore harder to draw a straight line between the experiences of the child and those of the adult. By the time the "daughters of madness" reached adulthood, they'd been man-aging their unusual identities for a long time, and most had found some creative ways to deal with their problems. One of these ways is psychotherapy, and when it's effective, it can alter that developmental trajectory and enable people to make major changes in direction.

All of the women in this book have been in therapy long-term, usu-ally starting in their late twenties or thirties. Since I'm a psychothera-pist, I'm certainly biased in favor of the process, and this is a sample of women likely to agree with my bias. That said, it's difficult to imag-ine how someone with so many layers of nonverbal and verbal mem-ory, and so much early instability and deficit, can come to integrate all of this into some coherent whole sense of self without having a good therapist at some point. When good therapy is part of the mix, it becomes possible to strengthen the foundations, create secure attach-ments, and as we now know, actually grow new neural connections where they didn't exist before. Scars remain, and the early years are never forgotten, but it's possible to find freedom and wholeness nevertheless.

As we follow these women into their adult lives, we hear their reflections about, and insights into, their mothers and themselves. Most have a hard-won ability to step back a bit and see their mothers and themselves more clearly, even as they may still be caught up in the ongoing task of trying to help them get the right treatment or medication or living situation.

MOTHERS' LIVES, CONTINUED

The trajectory of some mothers' lives seems to have leveled off in later adulthood. Problems remained, but either the crises were fewer or people in the family handled them more easily. It's common that some of the symptoms of schizophrenia can "burn out" over time, leaving someone like Tess's mother still holding to the old paranoid beliefs but able to move beyond them and enjoy being a grandmother. Depressions tend to continue recurring, and it's unclear whether these are the same old depressions as in younger days or if some of the normal issues of aging play a role. The mothers who were personality disordered seem to have continued along their well-worn path, as detailed in the next section. Here, four women talk about their mothers' later years.

> **Alice:** Her mood swings are still there, and as she's gotten older she's stopped any kind of regular medication regimen and hasn't stayed on meds the way she should. She still has these crises and will call her psychiatrist when she feels she can't handle stuff, or if she thinks we're not paying enough attention to her or being respectful to her. She hasn't had a consistent therapist; she goes from one person to another. But she's pretty social, and she goes to the senior center, the theater, Bible studies, that kind of stuff. These are not intimate or close relationships with anybody, but it works for her. We tease my father, saying if he dies first, "Gee, Dad, no offense, but she's going to be remarried within three months of you being in the ground!" But if she died, I don't think my father would last more than a month. His whole life has been to protect her, and he really doesn't know what to do without that.
>
> **Tess:** She told me that she resigned herself to how things were and that she had to help herself and nobody else could help her. But she never stopped believing that she was right about people hating her and trying to spy on her. I know she probably still has those moments, but she's able to lift herself out a little bit better now. When the kids come over, for example, that helps her put those memories aside. She knows she was sick. But to her, sick means depressed. She doesn't think she was crazy at all.
>
> **Helen:** She had shock treatments when she was older, and they made her worse. But in her seventies, she pulled herself together and lived in the apartment for a few years, and she did okay. She was very strong in that way. Eventually she had another bad depression, and after that she went into a nursing home. She couldn't be alone, and we couldn't find anyone who would take care of her. She was very difficult to be around at that point.

She reverted back to when she used to volunteer at the same nursing home, so she was getting dressed up very nicely every day and pushing wheelchairs. Then she met another resident and they fell in love! That was amazing! She was smiling and happy for about a year, and then, even despite that, she fell into a bad depression and had to be hospitalized again. She never really recovered very well from that last depression, but did go back to the nursing home until she got cancer and passed away.

Eleanor: There was a period of five or six years, when she was in her sixties, when she was much better. She had divorced my father and had some very bad years in there, but then, for whatever reasons, she was better. Her thinking was clear, and I actually enjoyed conversations with her. She was very perceptive about people, she was interesting to talk to. Her apartment was very well cared for—good art and interesting pottery, all that. I saw her in a way I hadn't seen, much—smart, interesting, insightful. Not very warm, but nice enough. That's who she was when she wasn't sick. That's the mother I didn't have until I was thirty.

But then she started to slide downhill, and she really couldn't maintain anymore.

The biggest decision Eleanor had to make was whether to have her mother declared incompetent legally or to let her live in the way she preferred as long as things didn't break down beyond repair.

Eleanor: The apartment that she'd fixed up so nicely became an unbelievable mess. There was stuff everywhere and a few inches of stuff covering the floor—papers and old bills and canceled checks, mixed in with pictures from family photo albums she had taken apart, mixed in with tubes of hand cream that had leaked all over, and then, of course, mice got in there as well and nibbled on the edges of things. She never wanted me to move anything, because she was just on the verge of "getting organized," but I just snuck all the baby pictures of me and my brothers and put them in a bag while she wasn't looking. I have eight or ten pictures of myself as a kid, and all of them have grease marks from hand cream, and a lot of them are torn or have nibble marks from the mice.

She lived that way for about eight or nine years. I cleaned up sometimes, and she'd just get it back in the shape it had been before. I don't know how she functioned. She'd kind of creep down to the store a block away and buy things. Sometimes she would leave unpacked bags of groceries in the bathtub, and the building manager would complain. But she seemed okay—she wasn't overtly psychotic and she wasn't depressed. And because she was getting older, people just thought of her as an old lady. She just kind of puttered around, and she never complained.

I had a hard decision to make, and it took me a few years. She was living there, just barely getting by, and I knew it wasn't a good way for anybody to live, but the only way to get her out of there would have been to have her declared incompetent and have her removed and put somewhere else. She refused to go voluntarily, and trying to talk her into anything was completely pointless. She never said no point-blank, but she could lead you around in a maze until you didn't know which end was up.

Once I hired a social worker who specialized in difficult elderly people to go visit her in her apartment and see if she would consider other alternatives. The social worker assured me that she could handle anyone, but after a few visits she called me and said she'd never met anyone like my mother and she had to give up, there was no way to move her one inch. I felt a little vindicated at that point.

Other people were saying to me, "How can you let your own mother live like that?" I finally decided that she was relatively safe, she was as happy as she was going to be, and that I wasn't going to put us both through some legal process of having her declared legally incompetent and moved to some facility. It would be a huge blow to her, and she'd probably never speak to me again, and what would be the benefit? She'd live in a cleaner place with someone telling her what to do. And this may sound overly dramatic, but for her I thought it would be like soul murder. So I made a decision to do nothing, to let her live in peace, as long as I could. That gave me some peace of mind, and thankfully, I didn't regret it. Eventually her apartment got even worse, after my brother died, and the health department said she had to move, and they evicted her. Then she finally accepted going into assisted living.

GETTING ALONG, OR NOT

The most daunting developmental challenge for these adult daughters was to disengage in a constructive way from entanglement in their mothers' problems. This didn't mean disconnecting completely, or condemning or blaming their mothers. Rather, it meant—and still does, to these women—that they needed to establish clear boundaries with their families, and especially their mothers, so that the relationship was no longer dominated by guilt, anger, or the chaos of constant emergencies.

Sticking to firm boundaries in the face of protest isn't an easy task for a person who's learned early on to keep peace at any price. It requires boat-rocking and egg-breaking. However, it doesn't require anger, confrontation, or blame. Many of these women first learned how to "do boundaries" in therapy, with the therapist as coach. It became apparent in the interviews that even bright, well-educated women, if they grew up with mentally ill mothers, need help with their own "reality meter." It's hard for them to judge how "off" a situation is, because they grew up learning to accept crazy situations as normal and their skewed view was often confirmed by others who were part of the same crazy situation.

Many women in this book, and other adults from dysfunctional families, benefit enormously from becoming strong enough to consciously reject their families for a period of time, then reconnecting in a better way, if possible. The very act of rejecting, of cutting off contact, is powerful in and of itself and establishes a feeling of adult equality. If the parent is powerful enough to reject and wound the child, the child grown up may need to retaliate, powerfully, when she is strong enough.

This kind of cutoff is not usually a good permanent solution, although there are cases in which it seems the only reasonable option. At some point, the adult child who has distanced herself needs to try reconnecting, but this time setting some terms. When the parent has been abusive in some way, that behavior has to stop. When the parent has pulled the adult child into chaotic situations of the parent's making, that's what has to stop. Juliana talks below about feeling bombarded by her mother's communication and unable to get her own bearings even as an adult, until she suspended contact for a while. Barbara discusses setting limits about her mother staying on medication, and Eleanor talks about the feeling of being the rejecter, and the reconnection that happened afterward.

Juliana: I struggled with how to deal with her for years. She would beg me to come visit, and every time I would have this big fantasy that it was going to be great. I would think, "This time she's going to be nice," and that it would be like the movies. And every single time it was awful, and the longer I stayed there, the harder it was to breathe. Finally I got into therapy with somebody who's really helping me. I finally realized I just had to not have contact with her for a while if I was going to ever heal from all this stuff.

A call or e-mail from her still just throws me. Hopefully I can have some contact in the future, but not right now. At one point I e-mailed her and really tried to explain what I was struggling with, and it was as nice as I could make it. Not sweet, but not nasty or accusatory. She immediately shot back this sarcastic e-mail saying, "You had a wonderful childhood, the best childhood a person could possibly have, and I don't know why you're making this stuff up. I did my best with you in spite of you being selfish and mean and just wanting to make everybody else unhappy." Same answer as always.

The last time she was supposed to come for some holiday, I just wasn't in a place where I could deal with her, where I could brace myself enough to withstand her. So my therapist said, "Look, you're going to call her and tell her she can't come. You're going to make up some reason why it's not good for her to come up. And you're going to ask your husband to help you if you can't do it yourself." And I did. It never occurred to me I could say no to her. If I ever even tried in the past, she would just plow right through anyway.

She's amazingly self-centered, and not only with me. Her own sister called and said her husband was just diagnosed with cancer, and my mother's reaction was, "Oh, this is just what I need to hear on my first day back from vacation." My aunt told me this.

Barbara: A few years ago she got me and my sister together and asked us what it was like to grow up with her. So we told her, the good and the bad, and she kind of heard it and it was okay. She said, "Look, I don't want to take the medication, and does that mean I can't be a part of your lives?" We agreed: She could do what she wanted with the medication—it's her life—but if there was another episode, she was on her own. We wouldn't turn ourselves inside out for her again. We actually had a very good year. She was actually able to be supportive about some things, and there was some closeness. One time she came to visit and brought some fresh fruit, and I was blown away. And then the reality hit me why this was such a big deal: She was acting like a normal mother would act.

It would be nice if that was the happy ending. But then, once I was saying how glad I was we had that conversation last year, and she said, "Oh, I didn't mean that stuff. I was just saying it." So who do you trust? I just don't let her get that close to me. I try to stay in touch, and I write, but I just can't give her that opportunity to get to me, to get close to the part of me that is real.

And then, of course, it all started up again, and I really tried to stick to my guns. I did drop everything to run and take her to the doctor once because she was in a panic and thought there was something physically wrong. So we saw the doctor, and there was nothing really wrong, and when I took her home, the craziness and drama just started right up again. She falls down on the floor, she's saying, "Help me, I can't make it," and I thought I was sunk. Long story short, she was fine. She got up and made herself something to eat the minute she got hungry, and that never would have happened if I had started taking care of her.

Eleanor: During the time I stopped talking to her for a few years, she did call me sometimes, like on my birthday. The first few times I just hung up the phone. Then once I told her she never should have had children and hung up. It felt incredibly powerful to just hang up the phone instead of getting pulled into her conversations that just went around in circles. And it was good she kept calling me. I give her a lot of credit for that. She didn't force it, and she wasn't angry. She just called and took the chance I would hang up on her. I needed to do that until I really felt, from inside myself, that I wanted to talk to her.

After we were in contact again, we both visited my older brother. We were having dinner out one night, and my mother and brother got into an argument about something. It was just like she would be when I was a kid. He acted like a jerk, too. I completely lost my ability to speak, literally. She asked me at one point what I thought, assuming I'd be on her side—there were always sides in these conversations; every word you said was political, it had to be put exactly the correct way to stay in the middle and not take sides. I literally couldn't speak. I felt I was walking on land mines—one wrong step and everything would blow up. I was amazed I went right into that frozen position, just like when I was a kid.

Alice's mother was unrealistic about what to expect from their relationship, and Alice's weariness with her mother's behavior comes through in the tone of her comments. She seems to have come to terms with her mother's limitations, but evidently has to hold the line pretty firmly to avoid getting pulled in again.

Alice: She used to treat me like—well, the only way I can describe it is like a sponge. She would wring me out and I'd have nothing left. I wasn't married, so she felt she could just call and have a crisis and I had to take care of it. She would get kind of crazy, or depressed, or just totally focused on religion, or on food, either one.

She had this idea we were supposed to have this great close relationship, and she kept complaining that we didn't have it. I got to the point where I could say to her, "That's a nice idea, but you can't create it at this stage. I'm sorry you see other people with their children having such a great relationship as adults, but we don't have any of that history. That comes out of the relationship they had as parents and children, you don't just make it happen all of a sudden." I'm past the point of thinking of her as being evil or bad, and I don't blame her any longer, but there's just nothing there that would make me want to be any closer to her.

Both Helen and Pat found their mothers difficult to deal with because of their seeming complicity in acting the sick role in their chronic and recurring depressions. However, Pat made some inroads with her mother when she was able to ask directly for what she was missing.

Helen: She was hard to be with. My son was getting married and we were meeting the family of the girl, and they were eager to meet my mother. But she just sat like a lump. She didn't like them, for whatever reason, and just ignored them. I was embarrassed even at this age. She would often sit at the table, never listen to anybody, and then out of the blue come up with something that was on her mind. My husband and I took her for the weekends for many years, and my relationship with her didn't change much because I just couldn't trust her. She would still be manipulative. I still thought, "If she would be more direct about things, I bet she wouldn't be depressed." But I felt I was being manipulated all of the time. I just couldn't trust this woman. I never called her Mom. I always called her Mother.

Pat: I would invite her to come, and then feel relieved when she wouldn't come—and then guilty that I felt so relieved. I would be very nasty about all the pills she had. I was worried the kids would get into them, and I just laid down the law. Of course, I was furious about the pills myself. There were a lot of times that I wasn't nice to her. She was this poor beaten thing, and I don't think I did much to make her feel better. She did visit alone a couple of times after my dad died, and that made things a lot easier.

I love my mother, and I always hoped she would be happy to see me. Sometimes she seemed to be, but then we went through times when I just wasn't getting anything back from her. It was rare for me to be able to say what I wanted from her, but I guess I had just sort of had it and I said—not in an angry way, though—I said to her, "Mother, you know I wanted to come to visit you. I'm really happy to be here with you, and yet I feel you're not here with me." She looked at me and she said, "I'll try to do better." This was kind of a marker moment, because I could admit to myself and also tell her that I wanted something from her. And it was amazing that she got what I was saying and understood.

Sandy had to make a much more radical break with her family, not only because of her mother's problems but also because both brothers had become drug addicts and her mother was enabling them in this enterprise. She felt the only hope she had of keeping some stability in her own life was to minimize contact as much as possible, but she was self-critical about her difficulty being more loving with her mother.

Sandy: During my late twenties and early thirties, I broke ties with the family for a whole bunch of reasons. My father had died. My mother and brother were living together, and she was enabling him to sell and use hard drugs out of the house. My other brother was using drugs. Before that, she could rally at times and get things together, but after my dad died, she just lost it. I did take care of her when she got older, and I was the one visiting her in the nursing home, but I needed some time away from the whole scene.

I'm a loving person, and I feel shitty about myself in relation to her. Why couldn't I be more loving, more giving, more present with her in spite of how she was? She had a way of getting to me. She would just provoke the hell out of me. I only hit her that one time, but we had a lot of screaming matches. She knew how to grab your heart and just twist it around. In relation to me, she had a wicked cruel streak. In all truth, I hated her more than I loved her.

Danielle continued for years to worry about her mother, but without much hope of having any positive effect. The boundaries she built between her and her mother were internal, so that she stayed as far away emotionally as she could, while still being concerned about her mother's well-being. Her mother showed little if any awareness of her own problems or the problems in the relationship, and she died before there was any resolution for either of them. Danielle reflects, with regret, on the last few years of her mother's life.

Danielle: She had trouble walking, at one point, and was visiting and needed a wheelchair at the airport, so I ordered it. She kept bugging me about it, and I snapped at her. I was completely insensitive to her vulnerability and not being able to walk and not being able to be in control. She would always be the one in control, and now she couldn't be, she had to depend on somebody else.

This was the same trip when she came and tried to hug me and I just turned away. I don't know if I could do it any differently today. I guess she wanted to be motherly, but she was completely inadequate and self-conscious and insecure about it. I never quite allowed myself to see that in her. The day that she died, I was in the room but I didn't want to cry in front of her, but I knew that she was going to die and that this was good-bye. I asked her if she was scared, and she nodded yes, which startled me, and it took me so off guard, I just don't think I tried to comfort her. I tried to be reassuring, and I did say to her that I was sorry but I can't hug you. And then I was glad she wasn't suffering anymore.

I don't know if she were here today if it would be any different, because it was so awful, but I think in retrospect, talking about her and the situation, I feel bad that I couldn't see her as the person she was. I was too young, and now that I'm an adult I am still trying to wrestle with this stuff. I had to defend myself against her so much that I couldn't see her vulnerability.

Tess's mother's schizophrenia faded somewhat in her later years, but the tumultuous early years left their mark on Tess. Here she tries to describe her mother, but in a way that's reminiscent of people whose attachment styles are fairly disorganized. Somehow the positives and negatives of her mother's personality are so mixed up that it's hard to get a clear picture.

Tess: She's such a nice little lady if you met her. She's very kind. She can be selfish, too. She's so gentle. And now she's a lot more assertive, and she can be cutting, too. She would slice anybody into bits with her mouth and her anger, even her own husband. She'll let people have it when it's too much. But she doesn't necessarily know the difference between being assertive and being aggressive.

ELDERLY MOTHERS

When an elderly parent begins to fail mentally, the adult children are often embarrassed and don't know how to manage this change in their parent's personality and ability to think clearly. Daughters of mentally ill mothers finally get a break, at this point, though, because mild dementia, which is acceptable in an elderly person, can "cover" mental illness. Irrational thinking or behavior can easily be passed off as "a little dementia" so that other explanations are unnecessary. Society is much more accepting of the eccentricities of elderly people, so for some of the women here, their mothers seemed "normal" for the first time. Several of the women found it much easier to talk to other people about their mothers, even sometimes to *be with* their mothers, when their mothers were in their seventies and eighties.

Lee's mother, for example, suffered from a progression of her diabetes and eventually became quite ill and stopped participating in her health care. Lee says she "turned her face to the wall" and died after a series of setbacks. Lee found it easier to explain this to other people as a reaction to Lee's father's death and to her mother's own aging, rather than as a resurgence of the depressive side of her mother's bipolar disorder.

Eleanor's mother mellowed considerably as an elder, and there turned out to be some humor in her aging.

> **Eleanor:** As her dementia got worse, she got very sweet and easy to be with, and all the paranoia just melted away. Once, when I was sitting with her in the nursing home, the thought popped into my head, "I'm not afraid of her anymore." She was about seventy-eight, in a wheelchair, and weighed about ninety-five pounds. I had gotten so used to feeling on guard, it was background noise, until it got turned off and I noticed the silence. One funny thing—the owner of this small nursing home took a liking to my mother because my mother was very smart and could still carry on an intelligent-sounding conversation, even if she had no idea who you were. So the owner says to me one day, "I have this theory about older people, that as they age they get more and more like the way they always were. So your mother must have really been a sweet, wonderful person." Long pause. I didn't contradict her, but I did think, "If she had been sweet and wonderful, it was when she was a child, sure as hell not when she was raising us kids."
>
> I found myself mentioning my mother to people at times, saying she was in a nursing home. That was fine, lots of people's mothers were in nursing homes because they needed care. I could never have said that when she was in the mental hospital because she needed care.

Some mothers were still incredibly difficult to deal with, and some of the worst were the mothers who always presented well to the outside world and were volatile and nasty only at home. At this point in their lives, the public-private distinction seemed to break down, leaving the children to deal in public with the mother they'd always dealt with privately.

> **Sandy:** My mother acted out in the nursing home, and she would go into these rages; she would be horrible and throw things at people! Then she would start saying, "I love you, love you, love you," and telling me how

important I was to her, and then in the next breath it would be all the things I had forgotten to bring to her and what a rotten daughter I was.

She died last year, and I keep thinking I wasn't a good enough daughter. I run into these women who do everything for their mothers. They visit them every day, they shop for them—they do everything for them. In the later years, I just—I helped her out financially, I would visit her erratically. But it was hard to visit her, it was hard to be with her, and the best that I can do with that is have compassion for myself for how hard it was for me to be in her presence. That was the best I could do.

MOTHERS AS GRANDMOTHERS

More than half of the women interviewed here chose not to have children, for various reasons, and a few haven't made a final decision. The women who did have children had to decide how much to involve their own mothers in helping or advising about pregnancy and delivery and in caring for the new baby. Later on, they kept a watchful eye on the relationship between their children and their own mothers. Some women from dysfunctional families want very much to protect and foster whatever good feelings and good relationships their kids can have with grandparents and will not disclose negative information unless it's absolutely essential. Further along, they may make different decisions about how much to tell their kids. In these women's stories, when becoming a grandparent coincided with a lessening in the severity of the mother's mental illness, everybody got a bit of a new lease on family life. Seeing a very difficult parent become a loving, attentive, and kind grandparent brought some sense of healing to all involved.

Jerri addresses many of these issues in talking about having children.

Jerri: When my kids were old enough to understand, I would tell them whatever they wanted or needed to know. She was just their Gramma, and there wasn't any bizarre behavior when they were little. When they got a little older, old enough to understand, I would explain why Gramma had put on weight, or why Gramma sometimes says things that don't make any sense. I wanted them to know what was going on, without being negative about it, just realistic. Now, of course, they know the whole story, because they're adults.

My mother started to get better as she got older. My parents did some traveling, and they became a little more social. When the grandchildren came along, I could always guarantee that she would babysit and have them overnight. My mother got an enriched life after I had my kids. That was the one thing I knew she needed, when I got to be a mother. She needed to have something of mothering. She couldn't mother me, but she could mother my kids. It helped everything to see her turn into a good grandmother.

Tess: When my sister had kids, my mother really did more of a turn-around. She was so sick when we were little, but she had gotten better over time, and since the birth of the grandchildren, the last seven years or so, that has been her best medication. It's like they ground her, she's solid with them. She doesn't do any of that crazy stuff with them. She still gets suspicious sometimes, but she really enjoys those kids and the time with them, and she's made a good grandparent. She's pretty stable, more stable than she's ever, ever been.

Unfortunately, it doesn't always work out so well. Juliana found that her mother began to treat her son in the same way she had treated Juliana as a child, and it was as disturbing as it was validating.

Juliana: I went to visit more often, because she was great with my son when he was a baby. I didn't mind going down then, she enjoyed him and it was okay. But as soon as he was about two and could say no, as soon as he had his own opinion, that was it. Then she called him a spoiled brat, a stubborn kid, other names. He just thinks she's mean and not just to him. He doesn't like her. I didn't even say anything to him about her, because I wanted him to have a good feeling about his grandparents.

Once, when he was about six, I left him there for a couple of days because I thought it would be okay, even though I had seen her change toward him. I think I was still in that place of hoping, every time I went, that this time it would be fine. When I came back, he ran up to me from the swimming pool and put his wet hands on my face and said something like, "Mommy, you have to save me from this evil grandma." I couldn't believe that I had left my child with her. I just fell apart. He was devastated, and so was I. I told him he'd never have to go back there. When he gets older, I'm going to have to explain more, because I don't want to repeat the pattern of telling him it's his fault that she's mean to him. I won't trash her, but I'm not going to sugarcoat things, either.

My biggest fear is that my son will feel about me the way I feel about her. It's not realistic, because I'm so different from my mother, and he and I have a good relationship. I couldn't stand it if he felt about me the way I've ended up feeling about her.

HOSPITALS AND PSYCHIATRIC TREATMENT

As adults, the daughters began to have more choices about how to respond to psychiatric crises with their mothers, but still felt emotionally exhausted from the experience of trying to handle their mothers' problems and simultaneously live their own lives. Although they knew that their mothers had serious psychiatric problems, it seemed universally difficult not to be angry about some aspect of the illness, from the timing of a flare-up to the drama and the resistance to treatment. The impaired mothers seemed to have little awareness of their impact on others, even in the family.

Eleanor: Remember that old Mr. Magoo cartoon where he's this little man who doesn't realize he's blind? In one cartoon, he just steps off the curb—he's completely unaware of where he is—and he's crossing the street in front of oncoming traffic, and causing one accident after another. The cars are swerving all over the place to keep from hitting him, they're running into lamp poles and up on the sidewalk and crashing. And he just calmly walks away, oblivious to all the damage he's caused while everybody is honking their horns and yelling and cursing. That was my mother.

Barbara: With the help of my therapist, I wrote her a letter trying to say what was important to me. I asked her to take her medication. Well, she promised she would, and the minute she was discharged from the hospital, she took off for the West Coast and ditched her medication completely. I realized that I just couldn't deal with never-ending crisis situations, and when I would get calls from hospitals and ERs saying she was having cardiac problems or whatever, I would just tell them straight out, "She has a psych history, and this is probably the beginning of a manic episode." She'll hate me, but she'll get the proper treatment faster. Last time it happened, she told me I betrayed her. But she got put on a mood stabilizer for her mania, and there were no more chest pains or any of that.

You know, I try to be compassionate and remember she's sick, and sometimes I can be, but I think she's just worn me out. There have been so many times she's been in the hospital, so many episodes, so many times she wouldn't take her meds and we were just all at the mercy of whatever she did next. I just can't live that way, and I can't keep feeling guilty about it, either. Generally, I don't enjoy being around her that much. She's usually just very self-centered and demanding. It's draining.

Tara Elgin Holley writes of coming home from Europe to find that her mother had disappeared and no one knew where she was. The police finally found her in a hospital several hundred miles away. Holley spent time with her and helped her find a place to live, but after a while her mother wandered away and became homeless again.

This is what it had come to. After all we had been through together ... after the hospitalization and the therapy and the effort to impose a routine, after all the weekends we had spent together, all the efforts to find a half-way house that would accept her, after all my pathetic obsessive efforts to rescue her, and after all the hope and the hard-won signs of progress, my mother had decided that she preferred the street. Decided, I suppose, is not the word. Maybe I should say that she had succumbed to the street. She spent her days wandering the crowded sidewalks, with no place to rest ... at the mercy of muggers.... She spent her nights curled up on a flattened cardboard box behind a trash bin or beneath a railroad bridge near downtown. Her skin toughened, her hair became straw, she wore every article of clothing she owned. This life—unimaginable to most of us, unimaginable to the person she had been—was the life she now preferred. I lived in dread of being exposed, of someone finding out that the strange woman on the street corner was my mother.[1]

She was also worried that her boyfriend might not want to get married and have kids with her because of the chance that she could become ill or pass her mother's illness on to their children. Eventually her mother disappeared, and after seeing no sign of her for months, she assumed her mother was dead. "I can't deny that I ... felt relief. My mother and the burden she represented were out of my life." It also meant—despite her own mothering of others—that "I would be unmothered for the rest of my life."[2] Her mother resurfaced much later, was homeless again for a while, and finally settled into a small group home.

Lee's story is an especially hard one to hear, since her mother demanded, via her symptoms, that Lee come to her rescue at just the time that Lee's father most needed her. Caring for an impaired parent rarely happens in a vacuum; there are almost always hard choices about where to be, who to help, whose priorities are most important. Helen and her sister continued to try to understand exactly what was wrong with their mother, to no avail.

> **Lee:** My father had cancer, and my brother and I both went home to see him. We were horrified when we saw him. He was in bed, very jaundiced, in the late stages of liver cancer, and my mother was floridly psychotic. She thought he looked just fine. I called his doctor and told him my father needed to be in the hospital, and he sent an ambulance over. Meanwhile, my brother had taken my mother out shopping to get her out of the way. Now, anybody who's dealt with a person who's manic knows that they can get into collecting bizarre things sometimes, and this time she had hundreds of these plastic tulip-shaped wastebaskets of various nauseating pastel colors. I remember this perfectly clearly.
>
> So I got my father situated at the hospital and came home, and we told her he was in the hospital. She did manage to visit him once before getting thrown out because she caused such a ruckus. She was revving up, and at that point we took her down to the ER. They said, "Well yeah, she's high, but she's not a danger to herself or anyone else, so why don't you take her home?" So I was walking her out of the ER and she's telling me how all the doctors are angels, and all the nurses are angels—and she means, like, *real* angels. So I took her over to her own doctor, and he took her right into the office and I could hear him through the door. He said,

"Ann, I think you're having another breakdown," and he got her to agree to a voluntary admission. That was the first time ever. The admission was for the next afternoon, so my brother and I had twenty-four hours that we had to manage her at home.

When I got home from that, I called the hospital to see how my father was doing, and they told me he had just died. It took me a lot of therapy to get through that one. I was taking care of this crazy woman, and he was alone and he died alone.

We decided not to tell her because she was already off the wall, so we had a whole day now to keep her occupied, pretending everything is fine, when our father had just died. My brother kept her distracted somehow, while I went to the funeral home and picked out my father's casket.

She had an excellent psychiatrist, this time around. He actually asked me about what dosage of med she should be on, based on my twenty years of experience with her—imagine that!

Helen: My sister and I went to talk to the psychiatrist when she had been in the hospital for a few months. He came out with a statement that "everything that you put into her comes out brown." He said he had tried everything and nothing was working. He didn't think she was suicidal, although she had threatened many times, and he listened to us and he was really nice about answering questions, but the bottom line was—there weren't any answers.

MORE FALLOUT

There can be many causes of the psychological problems some of the women here had as adults, but what follows are stories of some of the fallout that these women feel is directly related to their mothers' illnesses. Some is painful and constricting for the person involved and those close to her, affecting the quality of life and relationships in a significant way. These are "high-functioning survivors," who look fine to the outside world. For others, the long-term effects of early maternal impairment have interfered with their ability to function. Some of the women have been hospitalized or have been on disability for a period of time, a few have had significant substance abuse problems requiring treatment, and several have serious psychiatric diagnoses as well.

Maggie's work life has always been very solid and a source of satisfaction and pride. However, her wish to deny both to herself and to others that there had been any problems in growing up no doubt related to two failed marriages, as she herself recognizes.

Maggie: I pretended that I had the perfect home life. I blocked out all of it. I didn't talk about it until I realized—hey, I'm not having feelings about anything; something's wrong here. I knew I had just shut down, so I went to talk to somebody about it, and then talked to my dad and my sister and brother. We hashed it all out. I realized I was just repeating the pattern from my adolescence, when things were crazy. I made some bad decisions. I married the wrong man, twice. When my second husband treated me very badly, I would forgive him and think, "If I only do this, then I can make it better," when I couldn't. I know where that came from! I can't control everything. My second husband was capable of great love and was capable of great abuse. What I had learned from my mother's craziness was the roller coaster: I love you, I'm crazy, life is good, life is bad. What I grew up with was a roller coaster. Roller coaster is not good for children. A little up, a little down, but not this. That's what I thought was normal.

Juliana talked about the problems she still has with trust and with relying on anyone for any reason. Her general silence about her mother costs her a sense of freedom in her relationships, and the stakes are high for her when she confides anything of real importance to a friend.

Juliana: I don't trust people. I don't depend on anybody for anything. I don't ask anything, I never ask for favors. I don't usually say anything about my mother to anybody. It just doesn't work out. For example, after I left the first interview [for this book], I had lunch with this woman who's become kind of a friend. So she asked me what the interview was about, and I told her some basic overview. She asked me what my own life was like growing up, and I didn't give any detail but just the gist of it. We agreed we would have lunch the next time I came up, and she was supposed to call to confirm the date we set. She never called me, and I haven't heard from her since. Maybe my reaction is extreme, but it just confirms to me—don't talk about this stuff to people.

Both Rose and Barbara talked about being afraid of sudden changes in relationships, of things just falling apart into chaos without warning. And Barbara talked about her sensitivity to denial, which comes directly from her mother's inability to give her consistent realistic feedback. For them, the shadow of the past is cast onto the future.

Rose: I've been afraid in relationships that everything is just going to fall apart like things did with my mother. Now I know enough to talk about it.

Barbara: I have a fear of someone going bad on me. What happened to my mother is kind of mysterious to me, and I don't really know how it happened. It's hard to realize that, normally, things don't change that fast. People who grew up in a more normal family are probably more comfortable with the natural ups and downs of things. But it's hard for me to tell the difference between normal and emergency.

I'm probably too sensitive to people denying what I think is true. And that does happen, and it's not always crazy—it might be just a different way of seeing something. But I just go bonkers if I know something is true and somebody denies it. One time my mother said to me, "If you think I have a mental illness, I don't want anything to do with you." What are you supposed to do with that? To have a relationship with her, I have to pretend she's not who she is? That's pretty crazy.

Both Rose and Tess expressed fears of becoming like their mothers, and Rose especially points to her fear of being unaware of even having a problem, like her mother was unaware. It's common to have some anxiety about developing an illness that affected a parent, but the difference here is that denial and lack of awareness are also part of the picture when there's a mental rather than a physical illness. In this way it's similar to the fear of getting dementia, because it's a fear of losing not only one's health but also one's self and identity.

> **Rose:** I was afraid that I might get to be like my mother, and that nobody would do anything. That I'd just be unavailable to life and people and that I wouldn't know it, and that no one would have the good sense to bring me to the vet and have me put to sleep.
> **Tess:** I've been afraid of being like my mother, although I'm now past the age where she was first ill. I've tried to fight that all my life. I suffer from paranoia at this job that I'm at now for the last eight years. Very, very similar thoughts that people were trying to get me, trying to trick me. Of course, nothing as intense as my mother, but still, the thoughts are very present and bother me a lot. I've been in therapy for a long time.

Helen had a serious depression when she was in her late forties and was treated very effectively for it. The depression itself probably reflects some biological predisposition in combination with life stressors, and she doesn't see the depression itself as an aftereffect of her early experience; however, her *reaction* to the depression is clearly related to her earlier life experience with her mother.

> **Helen:** I had a really bad depression myself when I was forty-seven. I had some medical problems, which resulted in a problem with chronic pain for a period of time, and there wasn't really anything that helped. I was terrified that nothing was helping. I think my husband got scared, too. I went to a psychiatrist, and not only did she help with the depression, she was very reassuring that I was going to get back to normal and we could resolve this. She put me on medications and found one that worked so I could sleep, and then I started eating again. I felt she saved my life. That's how bad I felt. I really thought of suicide, but never had the courage to do anything. Then I understood my mother in a completely different way. I had always thought it was so much psychological with her and didn't buy that it could be biochemical, but after this I saw how much it could be both. I told her what was going on, and she was

very nice to me. She said, "I knew what was happening to you, but I didn't know how to tell you." She was almost motherly.

When I got depressed, I was so scared I was going to be just like my mother. I needed to hear over and over from my friends "You're not like your mother, you're not handling it like she did." Nothing helped her. She never went into therapy. She refused to talk. I'd never really seen somebody come out of a depression. She was like my negative role model! When I had medical problems later on, I realized my biggest fear was not that I would die, but that I just wouldn't be able to handle whatever happened.

Juliana and Rachel, both of whom grew up with personality-disordered mothers, have had many difficulties. Both have been in therapy for a long time and have climbed out of very deep holes. Both have struggled with suicidal thoughts and, in Rachel's case, suicide attempts. Rachel has also been hospitalized several times and has had a very hard time making a satisfying life for herself. For both women, these problems are a direct continuation of what they grew up with. Both have had insecure attachments with their mothers (characterized by rejection, neglect, and intrusion) and feel they've never had solid ground to stand on. They exercise maximum effort just to keep their emotional balance, and both have trouble modulating their feelings—all feelings seem very intense and threatening, and there are no gradations between "on" and "off." A secure childhood attachment and good-enough early mothering are the contexts in which this is "learned" or absorbed, and its absence is very obvious.

Juliana: I have a hard time with my feelings not just going out of control. I have very intense reactions to minor stuff. I'm way too guarded with people, and I have my antenna up all the time. I just read people in terms of whether they're safe or not. When I was a kid, I could tell what mood my mother was in by the way she closed the car door.

A small disagreement with someone makes me feel I'm about to be abandoned, and it's very painful. I always think people are about to leave. I can't see how relationships can go on after an argument. You can't sneak up on me or walk into a room without making a noise to warn me you're coming, otherwise I freak out. If anything falls on the floor, I jump. Any loud noise, I jump. If my husband or my son come into the room and I don't see them, I just freeze and have trouble breathing.

Rachel: I did really well at work. I worked with a lot of different people in all positions and everybody liked me, and I was commended for doing a good job. But at some point I started to get depressed again and my fears just got the best of me. I realized that my job was all I had. I didn't have a family or anyplace to go if something happened to me. It started to get to me, because I realized I was doing okay, but nobody really knew me. I imagined ending up on the street. It got so bad I over-dosed on my medication when I was at work, and someone realized what happened and took me to the hospital. After that I just felt suicidal all the time and made other suicide attempts.

I've been in and out of the hospital several times, in good programs, and had some good therapists. But when things change I have a hard time adapting, and I'll fall into depression again. I've been anorexic again. In treatment it's like I have to learn from square one how to feel more secure, how to handle it when I feel bad about myself. My mother's voice is in my head all the time, telling me how bad and stupid and worthless I am.

One really good thing is I finally started to talk to some of my friends about what was really going on with me. They've been great. Some of them are amazed I lived through it all without becoming a serial mur-derer! They're really good friends, and it's a relief that people know me. I couldn't keep that facade up forever.

Alice and Sarah were both diagnosed bipolar in their adult lives, and both have handled it well. Growing up in a family where a devas-tating illness is the elephant in the living room seems to have made them determined to be more forthright and take more personal respon-sibility for their own illness.

Alice: My mother started to have severe emotional problems when she was in her mid-thirties, and that's when I started to have problems, too. I knew I was an alcoholic and was hospitalized for that, and had mood swings for a long time. I finally got diagnosed bipolar. That's when I thought, "Oh God, I'm totally fucked now." I never had the manias like she did, just the depression, from childhood. But I've definitely handled it differently from how she did—I'm up-front about it and I take meds and I do what I have to do. I don't lay it on other people like she did.

Sarah: I knew I had more problems than just from growing up with my crazy mother and grandmother, which was bad enough. My emo-tions were just out of balance. I was finally diagnosed bipolar, which, ironically, is probably from my father's side of the family, the side that thought so badly of my mother. But I identified the problem myself, I asked for help, and I take care of it with medication and therapy. It's an illness, and I take care of it.

FALLOUT FOR SIBLINGS

The fallout of major family dysfunction isn't confined to one child, even when siblings seem to escape unharmed. Rachel felt deeply for her two adopted brothers, who were mistreated and then returned to foster care by her mother, and Sandy talked about her brothers both getting into drugs very early on and having major legal and other problems as a result. Alice virtually raised her siblings, and she talked about how they were able to be good parents to their own kids, but not without cost. In two cases, however, a brother was a major casualty of earlier family problems.

> **Maggie:** My younger brother really got the full brunt of it after I left and went to college. And what nobody realized was that he actually had OCD [obsessive-compulsive disorder] also and was bipolar. He got into all kinds of trouble being really manic. When he was in the service, he'd get into these states where he thought he was supposed to change the world. He'd get arrested or he'd be put in the hospital.
>
> I kept wanting him to stay in and get treatment and stay on some meds, but my mother was always sympathetic and said, "Oh, he can't help it, he's doing the best he can," and she would encourage him to leave. She treated him the same way she wanted to be treated—with kid gloves. She would never say, "Look, you have a serious problem and we have to fix it."
>
> Eventually, about ten years ago, he committed suicide. He had told his wife he thought he was a burden on her. And they had already decided not to have children because of the genetic load for OCD and now bipolar. It was devastating. I know I blame her for a lot of his problems. I don't really blame her that he got the OCD like she did, because there wasn't anything she could do to change that. But she just denied and ran away from her own problems and encouraged him to do the same thing. That I blame her for.
>
> **Eleanor:** My older brother struggled with depression for a long time and he played with a lot of medications. He eventually ended up, twice, in a psychiatric hospital. He had seen the long-term effect of shock therapy on our mother. She had lived on her own for about eight or nine years and just deteriorated, and it seemed obvious that part of that was due to her memory loss and the long-term effects of the ECT [electroconvulsive therapy]. During one of his most depressed periods, he ended up visiting her in the city where she lived. According to his wife, he couldn't even set foot in her apartment because he was so horrified at how chaotic it looked and how she had just gone downhill. He got more depressed after that, was hospitalized again, and his psychiatrist starting recommending shock treatment, since nothing else had worked. They knew he had been suicidal on and off, but they gave him a pass to leave the hospital, and when he left, he went to a motel and committed suicide. The hospital never even knew he was missing until the police called them eighteen hours later.
>
> There are always a lot of reasons why someone kills themselves. But I know that if my brother thought he was going to end up living like our mother, he would not have wanted to do it. I think when he stood in the door of her apartment and looked inside, and couldn't even go in, I think he was seeing himself twenty years down the road.

REFLECTIONS

Danielle expresses a sense of regret about the poor quality of her mother's life.

> **Danielle:** As I look at my whole life with her, I can see she was so miserable for so long—her whole life, really. I never allowed myself to feel that until now. I was angry and repulsed, and I just couldn't see her, really. I guess there is more there. I'm just surprised. I don't know if she were here today if it would be any different, but I think in retrospect, from talking about her this way, I can see her a little differently. I just couldn't do it before, when she was still alive, so now that I'm an adult I'm still trying to wrestle with this stuff. Her vulnerability might have been more visible when she got older.

Despite the insights and thoughtfulness of the women I interviewed, many still needed, or responded strongly to, external validation of their experience. Their reactions confirm that it takes many years to put together a complete picture of what happened in their families and to begin to come to terms with it. Cynthia had the common experience of keeping her two lives (home and work) separate and having them come together unexpectedly in a way that ultimately proved to be positive.

> **Cynthia:** I went to a friend's wedding in her backyard, and it was just packed with kids and parents who grew up within the neighborhood. And the mom of one of my best friends growing up made reference to "the craziness"—I mean, she used the word "craziness"—and how difficult it must have been for us kids, because she could see how Mom struggled all the time. It was one of those times when my two lives suddenly became integrated, because none of these people had seen me for years. And so I just talked a bit about my story: about how lousy it had been and how important some of the people there had been in showing me there was another way.
>   When she said it, I cannot tell you how validating it was. But my other reaction was, "How dare you—you saw that and you didn't do anything or say anything?" And since it was a small neighborhood, I realized they must have all talked about it but never said anything to us kids.

Pat still struggles with her own perception of her mother's illness, partly since there was so little real validation for it in her growing up. She knew she felt loyal to her mother, but alienated at the same time, so the relationship continued to be confusing to her.

> **Pat:** Once when a close friend of mine met my mother, my friend said to me afterwards, "I see no connection between the two of you." I couldn't

get over it. It was the first time anybody had said anything objective to me about her. I was at once troubled by it but also thrilled, because there was this whole sense of not wanting to be like my mother, but somehow thinking either that I was or that out of loyalty to her I should be.

I had another good friend who met my mother once, and she said it was so sad that "she can't see what a wonderful daughter she had. She can't see you, she doesn't see you." Then someone else said, "I have never seen anyone's eyes filled with so much anger and hate." Both women commented that it was absolutely chilling to be around my mother. These were two people who were friends of mine that cared about me, who liked me, where I had some kind of validation.

Adult children from dysfunctional families frequently talk about not knowing ordinary things other people seem to know, and being embarrassed by those holes in their awareness. Along with this, they find themselves discovering their own traits as though they were a surprise. Helen's mother seemed to want her to be fragile and sensitive, like she herself was, and this perception took many years to dissolve. Here Pat and Helen look back on their younger selves from an adult perspective.

Pat: There were a lot of normal things that I just didn't know, that I never learned about, partly because we were socially pretty isolated. I never had a fantasy of myself walking down the aisle and getting married. It was never part of my script. So when I was getting married, I didn't have any plan, and of course my mother couldn't be any help at all. I thought you pretty much had to march down the aisle with a long white dress, and the only exception to that was my aunt and uncle, and she wore a suit when they got married. So somehow it was in my head that if you didn't wear a long, flowing white dress, then you wore a suit. I went to buy a suit. Even now it's somehow embarrassing to me, to think that I got married in a wool suit because that's what I thought you did. I just did things on my own and never thought of asking anyone for help or advice.

Helen: It was only later in life that I found out, hey, I'm pretty strong. My kids gave me a surprise birthday party, and I loved every minute of it. I always got this message that I was fragile and couldn't withstand anything unexpected, and it's something I always have to test myself against. But actually, nobody has to protect me. In fact, I don't like to be protected. I want to know what's going on.

Jerri reflects on the powerful insights she had when she had her own children, and when she herself became a grandmother.

Jerri: I had a big realization after I started having my own children. My biggest connection was when I gave birth to my first daughter, and

I started to realize all of the things that my mother had missed. I never felt sorry for myself, and I never saw how much I missed. But I saw how much she missed as a mother—she never made that kind of connection to me at all. It was overwhelming.

My daughter has just given birth, and it's like we've really made a connection, and I could never do that with my mother. I couldn't connect. I couldn't ask her what it was like when she had me, what did she feel like, any of that. I almost wondered if my mother didn't have a kind of a breakdown when she had me. My father later on had told me that the doctor had come out and said, "Make sure your wife doesn't have any more children." I could never get a straight answer out of him about that. So I don't know what her experience was like, but I had natural childbirth with all my kids, and I was aware of everything going on. It was great, and I really feel sorry my mother couldn't have that.

Eleanor talks in retrospect about her decision not to have children, and Alice talks about mothering her own younger siblings and relinquishing having her own children.

Eleanor: I never had the strong desire to have kids, for a bunch of reasons. Part of it was because of my own mother being so distant and remote, and part was just seeing how incredibly hard it is emotionally to be a good mother.

I thought I understood my own reasons, but then I got a jolt when I was in my forties, talking to a friend whose kids were just going off to college. She started talking about times she and her kids just hung out together and had fun and talked about all kinds of stuff, and the kids liked to come home and hang out with her. And it just hit me—parents and kids can actually *like* each other, can actually *want* to spend time together. How weird! I just assumed that kids wanted to get away from their parents as soon as they could, which is what I did. So why would I have wanted to have kids if we wouldn't even like each other?

Alice: When I was about thirty I really wanted to have kids, and I struggled with it, but I realized I wasn't healthy enough. I give myself credit that I didn't just indulge my own selfishness so that I would just have a kid to meet my needs. I wasn't going to go there. I'm very grateful that I knew I couldn't do justice to a child if I had one. I was strong enough to say no to myself on that one. My mother should have done that, and she didn't. It would not have been for the benefit of the child, but just for me. I think of my brothers and sisters as my kids, and they have been, in a way.

What's tremendously important to me is that my sisters and brothers got what they needed to be healthy enough to have kids and be good parents. And they got that from me. I was more their mother than anyone else, and I was a good role model, and looked after them and protected them, and taught them what they needed to know. My mother didn't do that for me, but I did it for them.

My sister is going to have a baby, and her husband has to be away—he's in the service—and he said, "If you need help, call your sister." Again, it's not "call your mother," it's call me. My mother was told not to come for two months after the baby was born. So I guess now I get to have "grandchildren"!

Even now all of us kids stay together, we always get together for the holidays and see each other as often as we can. Since we all have other obligations on Thanksgiving, we schedule our own Thanksgiving the week before. We love the grandkids, and they get a ton of attention from all of us, and they all know there's something wrong with my mother. They sense it—she isn't affectionate at all with them.

REFLECTIONS ABOUT FATHERS

Issues of control and domination continued to be part of the relationship between some impaired women and their husbands. In Rachel's case, her mother continued to dictate the kind of relationship Rachel and her father could have. Rachel continues to see her father in a positive light, partly because of her real love for him and his gentleness with her, and partly because, as she has said, she can't afford to be angry with him. If she were, she would be without any parent at all. Her mother cut off contact with Rachel about six years ago, as she had cut off contact with her own parents and siblings when they crossed her. Still, Rachel's disappointment in her father's distance over the past few years is apparent.

> **Rachel:** Because my mother disowned me, my dad isn't supposed to have contact with me, either. I haven't seen him in over five years. When he got cancer, she allowed him to talk to me, but now he's better, so she clamped down again, and he can only call from work on his cell phone for a couple of minutes. He won't cross her. Obviously our conversations are completely superficial at this point.
>
> The way I figure it is, my father grew up in a foster home with only one of his real brothers, and so this is his family and he'll never do anything to rock the boat. He needs my mother to love him and he needs the family to be there, even on her terms. He stood by her no matter what. He would never confront her about anything—well, only once, and then she threatened him with suicide. I've had a very hard time getting angry at my father, and to this day that's still true. He and I get along fine if we can spend time together, but he absolutely cannot cross my mother.

Helen came to feel that her father was happy with the degree of control he had in his marriage, and that, in fact, her mother, while seeming to need this control and protection, actually did better on her own after Helen's father died. This isn't to say that she wasn't ill, since she clearly was, but that her illness and her husband's need for control meshed in a way that served both of them reasonably well. In the following vignette from Helen, it's interesting to note that he doesn't ask either of his daughters to pick up where he had to leave off.

Helen: When my father got sick and then died the following year, she did take care of him. That was when she tried to go in the hospital and her psychiatrist blocked it. My father and I also got closer. What happened was that I finally got permission to not be like her, not to be her. He said one thing to both my sister and me—he said, "When I die, don't take her in. Make sure she gets care, but if you take her in, she'll ruin your life." That was pretty strong. And we didn't take her in, and in fact she did better on her own, even though she still had severe depressions from time to time. That was a real gift that he said that, instead of begging us to have her live with one of us. He really protected us there. It did make me wonder at times what he might have done to encourage her to be so incompetent, how much maybe he needed her to be sick.

Cecily: I asked my father to talk to me once about my mother, on tape, and he did. What he repeated over and over was, "Your mother was a lady." There could be no other lady. In a way, he really idealized her, and so did I. She was quiet, she never raised her voice. She had spent a few years in a convent after her mother died when she was in her teens, and we kind of related it to that.

He was very protective, and as I look back on it now, I wonder if she got to develop as much as she could have. But on the other hand, she didn't seem unhappy. A lot of things, I think, are buried with him that I'll never know, because I didn't know the right questions to ask at the time.

I do remember feeling very lucky because he had total access to a cute little girl. Total access. He could have had his way; he could have really screwed me up for life. He could have brought girlfriends in, he could have smacked my mother around, all those kinds of things. I just thank my lucky stars that I had a father that would love his wife and his kids as much as he did. Maybe he did have girlfriends, or something; I wouldn't have blamed him in the least. But if he did, he kept that secret really well.

I always felt really very lucky to have my father as two parents. I remember thinking when I was younger, "Good, I have him, and he can be both." I really feel like he really lived up to that.

Tess: I just think the world of my dad. He was both mother and father to us. He did everything—worked long hours, cooked dinner for us when he came home, took us places with him, everything. He would always tell us, "Your mommy is good, she just needs help," and he would just try to be nice to her, even when she was so paranoid about him and his family. Everybody in town knew him and loved him, and they knew what was going on at home. He would be out doing the grocery shopping, and people would be friendly to him. He never, ever gave up on her. His own father died when he was seven, and he was the old-est of the four kids, so he became kind of a father to them very young. They all remained very close, and his sisters would help him with my mother.

Barbara: I think my father just did what he thought was the right thing to do, or what he was supposed to do. I think he didn't know what else to do, and that he wasn't really very aware of what was going on with him. I once asked him, "Were you there when I was born?" He said, "If I was supposed to be there when you were born, then I was there."

Several women speculated, as Cecily did, about whether their fathers had affairs or "other lives" apart from the family. Both children and spouses in very dysfunctional families often live two parallel lives, finding enough satisfaction in their other life to sustain them in the tri-als of their primary family. The women who wondered about this were all in agreement that they would have understood their father's need for something outside the marriage and wouldn't have blamed him at all.

Jerri: The other thing that I never really thought about until I got much older was I often wondered what my dad's sex life was like. I don't even know if there was one. When I got older, I wondered, even, if my dad had another woman. It was possible—who knows? I would never ques-tion him on it, but I could understand why. I would never put him down for it.

Eleanor: I know a lot of history on my father's side of the family, and emotionally it's not so good. So from what he told me, he kind of made up a fantasy family life that he would want, and then he kind of imposed that fantasy on our family. In a way, it was helpful structure, but a lot of it was based on pretending everything was wonderful when it was very screwed up. He had adored my mother and admired her, and also dominated her an incredible amount. After she divorced him when he was in his fifties, I asked him once if he would ever have left *her* and he said no, "I felt I was her life raft." I thought he was being a little dramatic, but looking back, I can see it both ways. He provoked some of her craziness by being so controlling of everyone, but he also held things together when otherwise the family would have come unraveled.

Many years later, it dawned on me that he could have had a second life that we didn't know about, he could have had a mistress or what-ever. He could have worked that out, and it would have been to preserve the family and not rock the boat. He would definitely have seen it that way, and I think he would have been right. And nobody ever would have known about it.

Lee: I went down to the restaurant with him one time to get his check, and I had this haunting experience: I could swear he was sitting in a booth holding hands with someone. And I have this memory, and I don't know if it's real or not, but the other strange thing that happened was that after my mother came home from the hospital, this woman started coming around, and she was clearly crazy. And my mother wouldn't sleep with him in the bed again. I wondered if my father was fooling around with this woman, even though I thought it was unlikely.

Maggie: My dad and I were very, very close as a result of all of this, but I was also his caregiver. In later years I remember asking my dad, after I went to therapy, "Why did you leave us there? What were you thinking?" As I learned, there were alternatives. One time he said to me, "It would have killed her if I had taken you, and I couldn't do it." So he sacrificed me for her. He didn't see it that way, at the time—"I was hoping it would get better. I knew she loved you." I felt, "Well, thanks Dad."

I was running a house at thirteen, fourteen years old. He and I have really talked a lot about that. He could never just say, "I'm so sorry," or see that even though he tried his best, it just wasn't enough to stop the damage she did. He'll talk about it, but all he can say is, "I did the best I could at the time. I did the very best I could."

Chapter 7

Afterthoughts

SOME FINAL REFLECTIONS ON MOTHERS' LIVES

Helen said something most of these women could endorse: "It was an ongoing project to try to figure out what in the world was going on with my mother." As the reader now knows, none of these mothers fits neatly into some category or diagnosis that clarifies everything. The daughters whose mothers had a confirmed diagnosis did feel some relief, but still, the label doesn't define the person. In the last chapter, we saw how things changed over time, and how the whole family needed to keep adjusting to the changes. Most of these women, even those who ended up curtailing contact with their mothers, wanted to understand as much as they could about how their mothers came to be who they were. As a family therapist, I often advise clients to learn enough about their parents to write a book (okay, a magazine article) about each of them in which the client appears only in the last chapter (or last paragraph, as the case may be). By the time the writer gets to that last chapter, it's pretty clear that the parent was a fully formed person, with his or her own history, childhood experiences, role models, and decisions before the child was ever on the scene. Listen to June's further reflections, recalling that her mother brought a lethal dose of pills to her bedroom when June was fifteen and asked June to join her in committing suicide, based on her paranoid delusion that they were going to be murdered.

> **June:** After the last interview [for this book], I realized how central that night was, when she asked me to take the pills, and that was it for me living with her anymore. I've always felt a huge amount of guilt and

responsibility for not wanting to live with her after that. But I see now that she was responsible for that. She made a lot of choices in her life along the way that brought her to that point. I've always felt so guilty when I do volunteer work and what I hear in my head is this dark voice-over saying, "I'm helping these strangers, and I won't even help my own mother." But I see now—I help people who want help, who are asking for help. My mother's not asking for help. She's sitting in her apartment with the blinds drawn, watching TV. She doesn't use the help I've tried to give her in the past. She never really asked for help for herself, and she flat-out refused it for years. I didn't put her there—she put herself there.

Pat and Cynthia share some sadness that their mothers' lives were so painful, and they seem to have some perspective on what happened. Danielle and Cecily put information together to make a coherent picture of what might have happened to their mothers and families, but only from an adult perspective does this really sink in.

Pat: I wish she had a better life, but I think she did as well by us as she could have, and probably in some ways at great costs to her. It may not have been what we wanted or what we needed, but it was the best she could do. I believe that. I think her own life was very sad.

I wish I had known at the time that there was no pill in the world, or no diagnosis in the world, that would have changed or would have made any difference. I just don't think anything would have changed my mother's circumstances, and I think she was unwilling to change them herself. This was a pattern she fell into with my father, out of desperation, and she got locked into it. I don't think I've ever said that so clearly.

Cynthia: I remember finding my mother sitting on the couch crying and tearing up all these letters, reading them, then tearing them. I asked her what they were, and she said they were letters she had written as a little girl to her mother pleading with her to love her, and she never let me read any of them, but she gave me about a five-minute explanation about it, and we talked about it later, and it was just excruciating for me.

Danielle: When I was about six and I had a younger sister, my mother had another child, a boy, who lived only a few days. I think he was in an incubator. It was clearly very traumatic for my parents. It kept coming up over and over when they were fighting with each other. They blamed each other, really got nasty about it. But it came up for years. So I think in retrospect it may have been a turning point toward grief and depression that was never addressed or resolved in any way.

Cecily: My mother's own mother died when she was a teenager, and she was the oldest of three kids. According to my father, her mother asked her on her deathbed to "take care of my babies," and I think that might have put her right over the edge. She went to a kind of convent or convent school for a while, which was why she was so quiet and dignified. When they married, my mother just got taken into my father's family, and I never met her brothers or her father, and it seemed her family just fell apart. So I don't really know what else happened.

June put together some of what she knew of her mother's history, but there was an additional twist: Which personality's history could she believe?

June: As the story goes, both my mother's parents were criminally insane. Her father had murdered people, and my mother was terrified of him. Her mother brought her to a courthouse when my mother was five years old and said, "Now you wait right here," and that's the last time she ever saw her. So my mother grew up in foster homes and orphanages.

One of the problems is trying to figure out what's true and what's not. If I only hear something from one of her personalities, then I'm not sure. If I hear it from several personalities, then it's more likely true.

I don't know for sure if that's true about her father, but I'm pretty sure both of them were very abusive, and she would say, "He's going to come kill me, and I have to kill myself first." And her psychotic breaks were often around the fear that he was coming to get her. That's what she was saying when she gave me the pills to take with her when I was fifteen, that he was coming to kill both of us.

Several of the older women in this book wondered about the cultural expectations for women during the 1950s and 1960s, when they grew up, and how their mothers would have fared after, rather than before, women's liberation. If their mothers had had more options, less isolation at home, would depression have hit so hard? Similar questions came up in relation to medication and treatment, with regret that some of the better current treatments and medications weren't available when they might have made a big difference.

Mental illness doesn't occur in a vacuum, and some of the mothers in this book were pretty isolated stay-at-home moms for many years at a time when that was less of a choice. Women with young children were often very isolated from other adults, and of course the expectations of the fifties are well known: Mom should stay at home doing housework enthusiastically (in high heels), preparing nutritious after-school snacks for her children, effortlessly producing meals, doing the laundry, and creating a soothingly harmonious home atmosphere around the clock—and loving every minute of it.

Helen: I can't help thinking that maybe if she came along at a different time in the women's movement that maybe she would have been depressed in her own way but not suffered quite as much. She spoke four or five languages. They didn't have money, but they cared about learning.

I think she always missed that in her life, because she had had to drop out of school, and that was a sadness in her life. As a much older adult, she took some classes and just kind of came to life when she had that intellectual stimulation. I wished she had done more of that. It would have been so good for her if she had just done more of that. But once she got sick, that was it. She never got past it, she never was well again.

THE BEST AND WORST OF BEING A "DAUGHTER OF MADNESS"

My last two questions of the interviews were "What is the worst that came out of being your mother's daughter?" and "What is the best that came out of that?" Sometimes these questions required some thought, and at other times, answers were readily available.

June: There were so many violations of trust, and so much isolation, where no one even saw what was happening to us. But probably the most damaging thing from growing up with my mother was the feeling of being completely robbed of myself—to have no idea what I'm feeling, what's real for me, who I am.

To be robbed of my parents and my sisters is horrible, to be robbed of my childhood is horrible, but to be robbed of myself is the most devastating. It's the hardest to reclaim, because I've had to learn how to even pay attention to my own self. I used to not even know when I had to go to the bathroom. My own body and my own mind weren't even on the radar. I couldn't have even had this conversation a few years ago before I worked with a good therapist. You have to reprogram yourself completely to know even how to trust yourself. It's as though I have a fleet of small children inside me that know I'm their only hope, and they don't trust me. They have to, but they can't, and they have to. And they can't. Slowly, slowly, I'm earning their trust back.

The biggest positive impact—hmm. It's as if the pendulum swings both ways. Because I've been so devastated, I feel I have the capacity to love beyond what most people can. It's like my sensory self had to grow more nerve endings or something in order to survive and figure it all out—and now I have this capacity to be more positive. The pendulum goes both directions the same amount, so when I had to go to the negative so incredibly far, I now can go to the positive incredibly far. I feel like my range is broader than most people's.

Eleanor: The best and the worst are probably the same. The worst effect is that there's some fundamental root connection that most people get in the beginning that was missing for me. And you don't really get that back. And that has meant to me that there's some sense of belonging or security in the world that most people have automatically, that they take for granted so completely that they don't even know they have it. And when you don't have that, life can be pretty hard work. But I have a depth of understanding that's invaluable to me.

Rose: The worst is probably losing those years after my father died and my mother just fell apart. I lost both parents when he died. But I've worked hard to see it as a strength and make it a part of my work with people. I tell people I know they can survive because I know that I was wrung out and run over and I survived. I just say that it's like a flame—things can bring it down to just a flicker, but it definitely can come back.

Danielle: I don't think I even know overall what the worst long-term effect has been for me. The best effect might be that I have a tolerance and a capacity to be able to connect. I haven't ever really tried to talk about this. Some of that has to do with the way I connected to my mother. Many people saw her at her worst outside the house, and I just wanted others to be understanding, and wanted others not to judge her or not stick holes in her, and yet they did. And so did I, I'm sure. So my ability to hang in there with people and accept them even at their worst, that's probably what I value the most about my own experience.

Barbara: There's been a lot of chaos in my life, and it's hurt my relationships. But the worst thing, if I think about it now, is that I lost a mother. If I ever even had her. And there's this sense of lingering shame about it all.

The best thing, though—and ironically this probably came out of her manic side—was that I got directly from her the idea that "anything is possible" and that I can do whatever I want to do. It's allowed me not to feel bound by conventions. So I got some of her gusto, some of her strong will. I got some of her spunkiness, so I got a little benefit of that manic grandiosity without having to be manic. In that area, I've accomplished a lot of what I've wanted to, and I have a lot of confidence in myself. I've done things in a short time people can't usually do.

I'm a strong person, and growing up with her has given me a lot of insight. And my relationship with my sister was forged in my mother's mental illness. That closeness with her is incredibly important, and it probably wouldn't have happened if things had been normal.

Lee: The hardest thing I continue to deal with is having a hard time believing things are going to be there when I need them—people, other supports. If they're right in front of me, okay. If not, I can't count on them. There's still a lot of shame. If something happens, I just don't talk about it—that's just automatic. Later on I can talk about it, thanks to therapy, but there's an automatic shutdown. That's the biggest negative to growing up with my mother—I detach from things before they get out of hand. And there's still that irrational fear that, if you know my mother was crazy, will you think I'm crazy, too? How will you judge me?

The most positive thing is I feel like if I got through that, I can get through anything. When she was okay, she was a very sweet woman. I'm sorry I never really had a chance to know her. She loved to read, and I got that from her, and it's such a positive thing that I value her for.

Jerri: The biggest negative, I would say, was she wasn't able to be my mother. I didn't really have a mother. I know now what that means because of my own kids. She just couldn't connect with me, and maybe I couldn't connect with her. That's the hardest thing to grieve over.

The biggest positive is that I learned how much an invisible illness, an emotional illness, can affect you. So I've always been open and not kept stuff secret, because that's the worst thing you can do. I was with some kids the other day and a topic came up, and as the kids were talking I could tell that somebody in that discussion was dealing with a mentally ill parent. I could just tell. So I just said very matter-of-factly that my mother had been mentally ill, and we left it at that. But some kid in that group got something positive from me saying that.

Juliana: The most profound effect for me is my belief that nothing good ever comes without a price. Payment will be expected, in some form or another. And I can't see myself in the future, I can't make plans. I grew up not knowing if I was going to be here next week. To be able to plan ahead and have any confidence that something good could happen? Forget it. I'm still just acknowledging to myself that there really are other ways to live, and I have a lot of therapy still ahead of me. I have to undo so much damage and then figure out what to put in its place.

I guess I'd have to say there's more than one "worst" effect! The biggest effect of all of it was that I've spent my whole life wondering "Is it really me? Am I really the bad one? Am I so bad and crazy that she had to treat me that way? Is that why I get depressed and angry? What if she was right, that I was just a bad kid, and I'm still bad?" Then I pull myself off that edge, but it's still there.

The best effect—I guess you'll have to ask me that again in a few years.

Cynthia: The worst effect? That's easy. I feel like I didn't have a mom. I didn't have a mom to go to when I was a kid, and I don't do it now. She was there, but she wasn't there. There's just that emptiness.

The best is, in my work with people, I have a level of compassion and sensitivity to people who also have that kind of feeling, for whatever reason. I have a soft spot for people who didn't have a mother, for whatever reason.

Cecily: The long-term effect is a sadness and a longing for a mother who couldn't help herself. It's like she was born with an illness, or it descended on her in her life, and she was lucky because she had the husband she had and the support she had. But the fallout for me is ... not that I'm jealous exactly, but when people talk about their parents, I have a feeling of longing. "I wish I had that. Do you know how lucky you are to have a mother?" Losing her to the illness and then to cancer, those two things collided. If she had been ill and gotten over that or managed that, then it would have been a different story, but she died when I was seventeen. So that's why I have trouble with death, dying, and suffering. It just brings up all the losses. I would have to say loss is a major thing. The way that I've tried to compensate for that is hold onto the things that I love.

The best, I guess, is the family that I did have. I always felt really very lucky to have my father as two parents. I remember thinking, when I was younger, "Good, I have him, and he can be both." I feel like he really lived up to that.

Pat: The biggest negative impact overall? I think I've had to generate my own fuel. I never thought of it that way before, but I've never felt I've had anybody behind me. I feel like I started with an empty tank. I never felt entitled to my own happiness. I think being happy is a scary feeling for me. It's like, if she's in so much pain, literally and figuratively, how can I be disloyal and be happy? That lack of entitlement is part of the rhythm of my everyday life.

The positive, I guess is my resilience. If there was strength somewhere, I could spot it a hundred yards away and draw it out. If there was any resource to be had, I could find it. But that's not the same as having someone behind you.

It's given me a kind of a hyperawareness, a sensitivity to mood, to dynamics, to whatever. Kind of a hyperalertness, I guess.

After talking about a lack of entitlement, Pat's automatic reaction to the end of the last interview was, "I'm sorry, I'm afraid this has been more about me than about my mother." I had to remind her, laughing, that its being about her, and all the other "daughters of madness," was the entire point.

Chapter 8

What Do We Need to Learn?

June wrote the following piece several years ago and has published it elsewhere. Hard as it may be to read, I think what she has to say is something we all need to learn.

> **School:** you would not see me behind deep circles under eyes big knots in hair tied in unfashionable bows torn stained clothes pulling here sagging there you scolded me for all those missed school days you would not hear my mommy beg me to stay with her stay close by her side keep her safe until she did not recognize me and ordered me to leave her house and until she would not see me at all that was the same as death you killed me each time you denied my pain each tear you did not see was one of millions of deaths my many deaths at your hands i remember when i used to write suicide notes how i would carefully excuse all "my blood is on no hands but mine" well i will not write any more notes and i will no longer excuse the millions of times you killed me because you were leaving it up to god or the courts or the system or the family cuz god knows the family is sacred and should stay together no matter what and i did everything i could to tell you i was dying i was fading to death every moment of every day and you took attendance or brought a food basket or did not do anything at all i died in your arms and you felt nothing i died in your office and you did nothing you joked about adding my name to the door since i spent so much time dying in your office calling my lawyer i wrote about my many dead moments and you said i wrote well and nothing more you just wanted me to keep on dying you wouldn't see me no matter what i did no matter how i died before your eyes it was as if you did not see me at all so i must not be dying because you have to exist before you can die.

Mental health professionals didn't do very well with these women and their mothers, except for Cecily and her family. Cecily's mother's psychiatrist guided Cecily's father through telling the kids, in a very matter-of-fact way, about schizophrenia and reinforcing the fact that the illness was no one's fault. As Cecily said, "There was no shame. It's not a secret and it's not a main event. It was never in the spotlight, and it wasn't in the closet. It was just a fact." This psychiatrist was on hand, in a supportive and consulting capacity, for many years, guiding the family through the course of Cecily's mother's illness. She was as enlightened a professional as anyone could hope to find, whether three decades ago or today.

That one positive encounter, out of about twenty stories, accounts for 5 percent of the women interviewed for this book. Two other women recalled a psychiatrist or psychologist being helpful and supportive somewhere along the line, in one or two instances. This is a pretty paltry showing for my profession.

Family therapists have worked for decades with families of people who have chronic physical and mental illnesses. Unfortunately, there aren't enough family therapists, and they're not in the right places to catch situations in which a mentally ill parent is admitted to a psychiatric hospital or unit. In most cases, those being admitted are still treated as though they are solo individuals, until there's a question of who will take care of them after discharge. Although some psychiatric facilities now have family meetings, only one woman I interviewed mentioned such a group, and she remembered little about it.

Families of alcoholics have much more visibility now than they did twenty-five years ago, so much so that it's common knowledge that alcoholism affects everyone in the family and that treatment doesn't end when the alcoholic stops drinking. If we were as knowledgeable about the effects of mental illness on the whole family, children would be in much better shape. The National Alliance for the Mentally Ill (NAMI) has tried to reduce the stigma of mental illness and encourage education, but NAMI is not exactly a household name, and it focuses most of its attention on parents of young people with schizophrenia. Many books written about families coping with mental illness have a similar focus, rarely devoting more than a page or two to the effects of parental illness on children.

An international, multidisciplinary team of professionals has collaborated on some of the best research now available, focusing especially on ill parents and their children. What's notable is how rare this research is, and how little we really know about how to do things right.[1]

Some of these researchers ran groups of mentally ill people who were parents, as well as groups of their families. The first and maybe most obvious injunction is simply to notice and ask, when a patient is admitted to a psychiatric hospital or ward, whether he or she has children at home! It seems obvious, but generally it is only one of many questions on lengthy official forms, and the main issue of interest is whether there's another adult at home looking after the children. Patients who are parents have said this over and over, and their children have, too: As soon as the emergency aspect of a hospital admission is handled, professionals need to turn to the family, give information and support, get and give information, and encourage collaboration. It doesn't make sense to assume that the parent is automatically a bad parent or that another adult looking after the children is handling the situation well. It *does* make sense to talk to the whole family, speaking to the children in terms they can understand, appropriate to their ages. It makes sense to explain the illness and its possible course, as well as what the treatment will be and the possible side effects of medications or other treatments.

We do all of this when someone has a heart attack, cancer, or multiple sclerosis. Why can't we do this with mental illness? When mental illness is seen as a secret and shameful condition, it only makes sense to keep everything hush-hush, pretend nothing has happened, and ignore its impact. Children, however, are not stupid, even if they may be uninformed. Children of impaired parents, giving feedback to researchers, emphasized that they wanted to be included in fact-finding, since they spent more time with their parent than anyone else did and usually knew best how to spot early-warning signs, as well as how to help the parent. They wanted to be included in the explanations, and they wanted to work *with* the professionals in figuring out how to help. Once children knew, in a factual way, that their parent had an illness that was not their fault, they were more than willing to offer what they had and to ask for what they needed.

Parents in these groups stressed how supported they felt when they knew that professionals were helping their children. They were open to learning more about child rearing and to figuring out where they were being good parents and where they were falling down on the job. These researchers then put together a very comprehensive assessment protocol based on their knowledge of parenting, child development, likely deficits associated with various mental illnesses, and the feedback they got from parents and children in these discussion groups.[2] In it, there are questions about the security of children's attachments to the ill parent, the availability of other competent adults, the level of understanding the children have about the illness, the way the child is coping in school and at home, and so forth. If we included this kind of assessment in the hospital admission information, we would be light-years ahead of where we are now in helping families deal with the family impact of mental illness.

Based on some of the experiences of the women in this book, I would add one important note. It was monumentally important to these women on the rare occasions when a mother could say, "I know that my illness made things hard on you. Maybe I was hard on you, or ignored you, or acted weird around you. Maybe I embarrassed you. I'm sorry that happened to you." This is a far cry from saying, "I'm sick. Don't blame me." It's a simple acknowledgment that one person's behavior affected another person.

When mothers of these women even came close to this, it made a big difference and went a long way to healing some rifts. We underestimate, I think, how willing children are to forgive, to help, to understand—if they are also understood. When a parent is able to say, "I see that what I did affected you," she is "keeping the child in mind." It says to the child (or adult): "I see you as you. I can acknowledge that I've affected you and my illness has affected you, without having to defend myself." It would take a very reflective parent to be able to say this, and it might be asking too much at some stages of mental illness. However, a sensitive therapist could help coach parents to be able to say it, and could coach children (or teenagers or adults) to hear it. Parents with mental illness are sometimes so overcome with guilt and shame about themselves and their parenting abilities that all they want to do is erase everything that has happened. They need to know that simply acknowledging the reality of what happened goes such a long way. There's a world of difference between a parent who's just plain scary and one who's scary but can say, later, "I think you must have been scared when you saw me acting that way." The validation of the child's reality and the willingness to have the child in mind is something a parent can do, without being able to undo anything in the past. Alcoholics Anonymous (AA) provides a framework for its members to do something like this, called "making amends." The AA member acknowledges his or her behavior and its fallout to people whom they have hurt. Without that step in the twelve-step program, few people would think of doing this or know how to do it. Professionals can and should help in a similar process when a family member is mentally ill.

Based on these interviews, I would also reiterate something that's come up repeatedly: Even as mature, intelligent, psychologically sophisticated adults, these women needed to hear from me, a professional, that their experiences were indeed crazy, abnormal, not to be expected, not just a product of "stress," and not something everyone experiences sometimes. As professionals, then, we need to remember that this simple reassurance is very important and needs to be repeated. Telling the story seems to bring back the old coping mechanisms of making the best of things, minimizing the craziness, redefining it so it doesn't seem so bad. Growing up in a very dysfunctional family really does skew a person's idea of what's normal and what isn't. I'm not suggesting that there's some rigid line dividing "normal" from "crazy"—life would be very boring, indeed, if that were the case! But children, or adults who are vividly remembering their crazy childhoods, need to know there *is* a line, and that somebody out there knows where it is.

Beyond this, and beyond the scope of this book, is the politics of stigma, especially the stigma of mothers who are too impaired to care for their children. If mental illness is hidden and shameful, and if a "good mother" would never harm her children no matter what, there's the setup for the kind of horror show that happened when Andrea Yates, while psychotic, killed her five children. She will live out the cruelest punishment that could be devised: being helped, with medication, to become sane enough to know what she did. If we look at the history of her illness, there were more warning signs than anyone could have wanted pointing to the fact that this was a women in deep trouble. She was desperately trying to cope, with minimal help and intervention from her family or from professionals who might have been able to protect her and her children from what happened. I think Andrea Yates probably *was* a good mother—when she was well. But being a good mother doesn't prevent psychosis from taking hold.

If Andrea Yates had been in a car accident and was paraplegic, or if she had cancer, people would openly and legitimately have been concerned and caring about her and about her ability to care adequately for her children. They would have asked if she needed help. Her husband wouldn't have blithely gone off to work, assuming she was fine. Yet being diagnosed with a postpartum psychosis doesn't bring out the casseroles or the offers of help with babysitting.

What happened to her and her children didn't have to happen. It wasn't inevitable. As June says: "The most dangerous part of my upbringing was that there was no one to say, 'This is strange' or 'This isn't right.' We were totally isolated that way. There was dangerous stuff, but by far the most deadly was that there was no one to see what was going on, to say anything about it."

Appendix: Short Biographies of Women Interviewed*

Alice: Alice was the oldest of five children. Her mother was quite neglectful, leaving Alice to care for the younger kids. Her father was passive, although present. When Alice was an adolescent, her mother had psychotic periods and began to have times in and out of psychiatric hospitals. Her diagnosis is unclear. Alice currently has a distant relationship with her mother but is close to all her siblings. She has chosen not to have children herself.

Barbara: Barbara's mother began to have serious psychiatric problems when Barbara was about ten, and was in and out of hospitals for many years, diagnosed with bipolar disorder. Barbara tried to take care of her mother and learned only in adulthood to draw firm boundaries so that her own life wouldn't constantly be disrupted. She had some very disturbing encounters with her mother in and out of the hospital, without preparation by mental health professionals. She's very close to her sister and her nieces and nephews, but has no children of her own.

Cecily: Although Cecily's mother was schizophrenic, Cecily's father handled this in an almost ideal way with the help of a very enlightened psychiatrist. Cecily didn't feel responsible for her mother's illness or for making her get well, and the topic was handled matter-of-factly by the whole family. Cecily's mother died of cancer when Cecily was a young adult, and this loss looms large as well. Cecily is grateful that her father was a good and responsible father who took over the roles of both mother and father during times of her mother's illness.

---

*All names have been changed to protect privacy.

Cynthia: Cynthia's mother was never hospitalized, although she was chronically depressed and very visibly unhappy for her entire life. Cynthia's family was oriented around making her mother happy, or at least more content, and Cynthia felt that if only she were a better child, she could succeed at this. Her mother's unhappiness pervaded the mood of the entire family for many years.

Danielle: Danielle's mother was depressed throughout Danielle's life, whether she was drinking or not. Both Danielle's parents abused alcohol, which only exacerbated her mother's underlying despair. Danielle took on a great deal of emotional responsibility for helping her mother, but also tried to keep emotional distance from her. Danielle's mother died ten years ago, and their relationship remained unresolved.

Eleanor: Eleanor's mother had several psychotic episodes and was chronically paranoid or suspicious, even when not psychotic. She was hospitalized several times and diagnosed with schizophrenia. Eleanor's father was very involved in family life, and he provided structure that was generally positive, despite his insistence on pretending that the family was happy and normal. Her parents eventually divorced, and Eleanor struggled with questions about how best to care for her mother during a long decline in her mother's older age. Eleanor's brother developed severe depression and eventually committed suicide.

Helen: Helen's mother's illness was something of a mystery to the whole family, although she was always "sensitive" and clearly not someone who could tolerate any stress. She developed severe depressions when Helen was an adolescent, and was hospitalized several times as an adult and an elder. After Helen's father died, Helen and her sister tried to care for their mother. Helen still feels a bit mystified about exactly what was wrong with her mother. Helen has a long and stable marriage and several grown children.

Jerri: Jerri's mother had a series of psychotic episodes and hospitalizations during Jerri's earlier years, up until about age ten. Jerri was protected by her father's whisking her away to relatives' homes, and Jerri detached from her mother and made an especially strong attachment to her grandmother. She feels strongly that being kept in the dark about her mother's condition was a negative experience and tries hard to reverse that in her own family, with her children and grandchildren.

Juliana: Juliana's mother fits the description of someone with a borderline-narcissistic personality disorder but was never hospitalized—or, in fact, treated at all. There was no recognition that she was seriously disturbed, as she presented well to the outside world and confined her cruel, demeaning behavior to her home and her daughter. Juliana always experienced her mother as intrusive, critical, demeaning, provocative, and rejecting, from her earliest years. Juliana's parents divorced when she was young, and her mother was a single parent through much of Juliana's growing up. Juliana found refuge in work but struggled after she left home, and she has battled depression and self-doubt for many years. She's successful professionally and is married and has two children.

June: June's mother was diagnosed with schizophrenia and multiple personality disorder and began to be very disturbed when June was about ten. June's father was sexually abusive and out of the house when June was quite young, although visitation continued. June's mother was essentially unable to mother her children at all during June's middle childhood and adolescence, and June was either on her own or parenting her mother during these years. Her mother was hospitalized frequently, being either psychotic or suicidal or both, and June's visits to the hospital were harrowing. She finally stopped living with her mother at fifteen. She maintains a distant relationship with her mother, who lives in supervised housing.

Lee: Lee's mother was diagnosed bipolar and began having episodes requiring hospitalization when Lee was about eleven. Her behavior went beyond manic at times, and she seemed to show some psychotic features as well. Lee filled in for her mother at home, since her mother experienced long periods of depression and passivity between her manic episodes. One of Lee's most harrowing experiences occurred when she was an adult, as her father was in the terminal stages of cancer at the same time her mother became manic and required hospitalization.

Maggie: Maggie had a relatively normal upbringing until she was about twelve, when her mother suddenly developed obsessive-compulsive disorder. This took over the family for a number of years, especially when Maggie was an adolescent. Maggie ran the household and filled in for her mother during this time and also tried her best to make her mother act normal again. Maggie's brother became psychiatrically ill when Maggie was an adult and eventually committed suicide.

Pat: Pat's mother was chronically passive and depressed and was hospitalized after Pat graduated from high school. Pat's father was emotionally abusive, and her parents' conflicts no doubt contributed greatly to her mother's dependence on prescription drugs. Psychiatric treatment was ineffective, although Pat was involved for years in trying to find people who could help her mother. Pat is in a long and stable marriage and has children and grandchildren, and her mother died about ten years ago.

Rachel: Rachel's mother fits the criteria of someone with a borderline-narcissistic personality disorder, although she was never diagnosed, treated, or hospitalized. She has been critical, demeaning, and rejecting to Rachel for as long as Rachel can remember. Rachel's father was present but passive throughout Rachel's youth and is in minimal touch with Rachel at the present time, since Rachel's mother disowned her about six years ago. Rachel's parents adopted—and then returned to foster care—two boys, and in the process of doing this, Rachel's mother also disowned her own parents and siblings. Rachel has shown remarkable resilience in many ways but at present is struggling with depression.

Rose: Rose's mother, father, and siblings were a "typical" medical family for much of the time as Rose was growing up, with her father more or less in control and her mother apparently happy in the role of doctor's wife. When he died quite suddenly, when Rose was an adolescent, Rose's mother became completely unable to cope. Not only did she not recover from her husband's death, she continued to fall apart, was unable to handle the finances, lost the family house, and ended up in a nursing home, where she died four years after her husband. Rose's adolescence was chaotic as she tried to live alone during the times her mother was in and out of the hospital.

Sandy: Sandy's family did well for the first few years of Sandy's life, living an upper-middle-class life in which her parents' charm and good looks were in evidence. When Sandy was about seven, her mother became quite erratic, with mood swings and instability in her relationships. Sandy's parents began to fight violently, wrecking the house, and her mother began to threaten suicide when she was upset. Things deteriorated when Sandy was eleven, as her father moved in and out of the house unpredictably. Sandy fought with her mother and moved out before she graduated from high school. After her father died when Sandy was twenty-one, her mother deteriorated and finally died in a nursing home, leaving Sandy feeling guilty and, once again, like a bad daughter.

Sarah: Sarah's father died suddenly when Sarah was a child, and her mother became psychotic shortly thereafter. Sarah and her mother went to live with Sarah's grandmother, who was physically abusive. Sarah felt trapped, as she was repeatedly told that the government payments for her care were the only money her mother had. Her mother was abusive to her when psychotic, but this was dismissed as unimportant until her mother assaulted someone outside the family and was arrested. Sarah was able to free herself in adolescence and got a good education, despite family discouragement and criticism of her on all fronts. She herself has been diagnosed as bipolar but takes responsibility for handling it appropriately.

Tess: Tess's mother was hospitalized many times, sometimes for long periods, and seems to have been quite psychotic for many years, with little relief. She screamed at people in public, with her children in tow, causing deep humiliation and shame for Tess. She barely managed to function at home, getting the children off to school in their uniforms but being disheveled herself. Tess's father was present and carried the family, remaining loyal to his wife and encouraging the children to help her. He was well loved in the community, and Tess admires him greatly. Tess's brother also became psychotic when Tess was an adolescent. Tess has struggled with depression and suspiciousness herself for many years. At present her mother is doing somewhat better as she focuses on her grandchildren and as her schizophrenia has evidently "burned out," to some extent.

Notes

INTRODUCTION

1. Victoria Secunda, *When Madness Comes Home: Help and Hope for the Children, Siblings, and Partners of the Mentally Ill* (New York: Hyperion Press, 1997), 1.

2. Minrose Gwin, *Wishing for Snow* (Baton Rouge: Louisiana State University Press, 2004), 179–180.

CHAPTER I

1. Daniel Stern, *The Interpersonal World of the Infant* (New York: Basic Books, 1985), 50–70.

2. Ibid., 71.

3. Donald Winnicott, a British psychoanalyst, coined the term "good enough mothering," and it's now in general use.

4. Urie Bronfenbrenner, *The Ecology of Human Development*, 24.

5. John Bowlby, *A Secure Base: Parent-Child Attachment and Healthy Human Development* (New York: Basic Books, 1988), 129–133.

6. Joseph LeDoux, *The Emotional Brain: The Mysterious Underpinnings of Emotional Life* (New York: Simon & Schuster, 1996), 18.

7. Marion F. Solomon and Daniel J. Siegel, eds., *Healing Trauma: Attachment, Mind, Body, and Brain* (New York: W. W. Norton, 2003), 53.

8. Allan N. Schore, *Affect Regulation and the Repair of the Self* (New York: W. W. Norton, 2003), 3.

9. Bowlby, *A Secure Base*, 1–19.

10. Ibid.

11. Minnesota Parent-Child Project.

12. Bowlby, *A Secure Base*, 132.

13. Alyson Hall, "Parental Psychiatric Disorder and the Developing Child," in *Parental Psychiatric Disorder: Distressed Parents and Their Families*, 2nd ed., ed. Michael Göpfert, Jeni Webster, and Mary V. Seeman (Cambridge, U.K.: Cambridge University Press, 2004), 34.

14. Christine Puckering, "When a Parent Suffers from an Affective Disorder: Effect on the Child," in Göpfert, Webster, and Seeman, *Parental Psychiatric Disorder*, 177.

15. Susan Goldberg, *Attachment and Development* (New York: Oxford University Press, 2000), 48.

16. Mary Sykes Wylie and Richard Simon, "Discoveries from the Black Box," *Psychotherapy Networker* 26, no. 5 (2002): 26.

17. Solomon and Siegel, *Healing Trauma*, 10.

18. Schore, *Affect Regulation*, xv.

19. Ibid., xvi.

20. Wylie and Simon, "Discoveries from the Black Box," 33.

21. Solomon and Siegel, *Healing Trauma*, 32.

22. Stern, *The Interpersonal World of the Infant*, 196–200.

CHAPTER 2

1. Tara Elgin Holley, *My Mother's Keeper: A Daughter's Memoir of Growing Up in the Shadow of Schizophrenia* (New York: William Morrow, 1997), 107.

2. Ibid., 18.

3. Laura Love, *You Ain't Got No Easter Clothes* (New York: Hyperion Press, 2004), 200.

4. John Bowlby, *A Secure Base: Parent-Child Attachment and Healthy Human Development* (New York: Basic Books, 1988), 99–119.

5. Ibid., 132.

CHAPTER 3

1. Antonia Bifulco and Patricia Moran, *Wednesday's Child: Research into Women's Experience of Neglect and Abuse in Childhood, and Adult Depression* (London: Routledge, 1998), 50.

2. Kernberg, *Pathological Narcissism*.

3. Christina Crawford, *Mommie Dearest* (New York: William Morrow, 1978).

4. Ibid., 187.

5. Bifulco and Moran, *Wednesday's Child*, 19.

6. Margaret J. Brown and Doris Parker Roberts, *Growing Up with a Schizophrenic Mother* (Jefferson, N.C.: McFarland, 2000), 152.

7. Ibid., 47.

8. Tara Elgin Holley, *My Mother's Keeper: A Daughter's Memoir of Growing Up in the Shadow of Schizophrenia* (New York: William Morrow, 1997), 90.

9. Minrose Gwin, *Wishing for Snow* (Baton Rouge: Louisiana State University Press, 2004), 33.

10. Laura Love, *You Ain't Got No Easter Clothes* (New York: Hyperion Press, 2004), 67.

11. Ibid., 28.

12. Brown and Roberts, *Growing Up with a Schizophrenic Mother*, 44.

13. Love, *You Ain't Got No Easter Clothes*, 15.

14. Brown and Roberts, *Growing Up with a Schizophrenic Mother*, 44.

CHAPTER 4

1. Tara Elgin Holley, *My Mother's Keeper: A Daughter's Memoir of Growing Up in the Shadow of Schizophrenia* (New York: William Morrow, 1997), 173.

2. Sandra Bilsborough, "What We Want from Adult Psychiatrists and Their Colleagues: Telling It Like It Is," in *Parental Psychiatric Disorder: Distressed Parents and Their Families*, 2nd ed., ed. Michael Göpfert, Jeni Webster, and Mary V. Seeman (Cambridge, U.K.: Cambridge University Press, 2004), 3–7.

3. Joseph P. Allan and Deborah Lund, "Attachment in Adolescence," in *Handbook of Attachment: Theory, Research, and Clinical Applications*, ed. Jude Cassidy and Phillip R. Shaver (New York: Guilford Press, 1999), 319–336.

CHAPTER 5

1. Gina O'Connell Higgins, *Resilient Adults: Overcoming a Cruel Past* (San Francisco: Jossey-Bass, 1994), 69.

CHAPTER 6

1. Tara Elgin Holley, *My Mother's Keeper: A Daughter's Memoir of Growing Up in the Shadow of Schizophrenia* (New York: William Morrow, 1997), 279.

2. Ibid., 319.

CHAPTER 8

1. Michael Göpfert, Jeni Webster, and Jila Nelki, "Formulation and Assessment of Parenting," in *Parental Psychiatric Disorder: Distressed Parents and Their Families*, 2nd ed., Michael Göpfert, Jeni Webster, and Mary V. Seeman (Cambridge, U.K.: Cambridge University Press, 2004).

2. Ibid., 98–99.

Index

Memory loss, 61. *See also* ECT; shock therapy
Memory system, 3, 4, 12, 13, 16, 98
Menstruation, 82, 102, 103
Mental health professional, 64, 92, 98, 176. *See also individual professions*
Mental health system, 126, 127
Mommie Dearest, 45, 46. *See also* Crawford, Christina
Multiple personality disorder, 42, 46, 99, 131, 169, 183
My Mother's Keeper, 21, 22, 151, 152. *See also* Holley, Tara Elgin

Narcissism, 27, 44
National Alliance for the Mentally Ill (NAMI), 176
Nature-nurture, 10
Negative states, 13, 14
Neglect, 2, 29, 35, 50, 70, 76, 78, 95, 113, 130, 156
Neural pathways, 6, 13, 139
Neurological development, 6
Numb, 110
Nursing home, 130, 140, 141, 146, 148

Obsession, 43, 82, 83
Obsessive Compulsive Disorder (OCD), 82, 106, 125, 158
Orphanages, 7
Out-of-sync, 9, 15, 16

Paranoia, 20, 21, 26, 32, 34, 39, 40, 43, 51, 95, 96, 140, 148, 155, 167
Parentification, 56, 57, 74, 92, 93, 94, 95, 132. *See also* Role reversal
Partnering, 132–34. *See also* Marriage
Personality disorder, 27, 28, 30, 44, 64, 65, 84–86, 135, 140, 156, 180, 182–84
Postpartum psychosis, 179
Pre-verbal, 13
Privacy, violation of, 73, 85, 102
Psychiatric medication. *See* Medication
Psychiatrists, 64, 94, 95, 99, 113, 126, 130, 153, 155, 163, 176. *See also* Social worker

Psychosis, 9, 10, 19, 21, 22, 25, 40, 41, 43, 44, 51, 54, 89, 90, 96–99, 101, 130, 131, 152, 169, 179, 181–85

Research, 2, 4, 7, 10, 11, 13, 17
Resilience, 4, 17, 34, 35, 48, 49, 78–80, 114–17, 120, 122, 123, 132, 134, 137
Right brain, 11, 12, 14, 15
Rites of passage, 101–3
Role reversal, 23, 56, 57, 92, 94, 95, 97, 132. *See also* Parentification

Schizophrenia, 21, 22, 41, 42, 46, 51, 64, 72, 78, 140, 147, 176, 182, 183, 185
Schore, Allan, 6, 12
Secrets, 23, 32, 54, 60, 68–71, 90, 106, 109, 110, 116, 134, 138, 172, 177
Secure base, 8, 9, 109
Self-harm, 44, 75, 109–11
Self-regulation, 13, 109. *See also* Affect regulation
Self, sense of, 3, 10–12, 139
Sexual abuse: maternal, 30, 46–47; paternal, 44, 46, 60, 72, 105, 183; sibling, 28, 31; stranger, 135
Sexual acting out, 110, 112, 113
Shame, 52, 69, 91, 106–8, 135, 171, 177–79. *See also* Embarrassment
Shock therapy, 61–63, 69, 94, 97, 98, 104, 128, 129, 140, 158. *See also* Electroconvulsive treatment (ECT)
Siblings, 28, 72–76, 103, 105, 106, 124, 125, 157, 158, 161, 162
Siegel, Daniel J., 10, 15. See also *Interpersonal Neurobiology*
Social worker, 70, 129, 142
Spiritual connection, 118
Stern, Daniel, 3
Stigma, 2, 62, 92, 108, 176, 179
Substance abuse, 47, 75, 109–12, 153, 157
Suicide, 76–78, 158, 167, 175, 182; attempts, 22, 44, 69, 77, 156–58; thoughts of, 110, 156; threats, 53, 69, 76, 77, 88, 98, 120, 153, 162

Tardive dyskinesia, 61
Template, 3, 14, 16, 20, 25
Therapy, 2, 10, 55, 62, 75, 94, 113,
    135, 139, 142, 143, 151, 155, 156,
    170–72, 178
Thorazine, 51, 93, 97
Trauma, 2, 6, 71, 132, 169
Treatment, psychiatric, 51, 61, 91–99,
    151–53
Trust, 1, 17, 25, 154; of others, 1, 17,
    32, 42, 69–71, 101, 132, 136,
    144, 145, 154; of self, 25, 26,
    32, 170

Undermining, 27, 32, 39, 53, 54, 85,
    111, 116, 121

Wednesday's Child, 44, 50. *See also*
    Bifulco, Antonia
Wishing for Snow, 66. *See also* Gwin,
    Minrose
Women's liberation, 123, 169
Working models, 4, 14, 55, 116

Yates, Andrea, 179
You Ain't Got No Easter Clothes, 22, 69,
    77. *See also* Love, Laura

About the Series Editor
and Advisers

MICHELE PALUDI is an adjunct full professor in the Department of Psychology of Union College and the Graduate College of Union University. She has been a full and tenured, associate, or visiting professor at Franklin and Marshall College, Kent State University, and Hunter College. She is on the editorial boards of *Sex Roles, Women and Aging,* and *Mentoring International.* In 1994 she earned the Outstanding Academic Book Award from the American Library Association for her work *The Psychology of Women: A Handbook.* She earned the Thurgood Marshall Award for Teaching in 1996 and 1998. She has written, edited, or co-edited ten books and presented at numerous meetings, including those of the American Psychological Association, the Association for Women in Psychology, and the American Association of Affirmative Action.

SUSAN A. BASOW is Charles A. Dana Professor of Psychology at Lafayette College, a social clinical psychologist, and the author of a textbook on gender. She currently is secretary of Division 35 of the Society for the Psychology of Women.

NANCY E. BETZ is a professor of psychology at Ohio State University. She served for six years as the editor of the *Journal of Vocational Behavior* and currently serves on the editorial boards of several scholarly journals.

LAURA S. BROWN is a professor at the Washington School of Professional Psychology at Argosy University, Seattle. She has published widely on the topic of feminist therapy, theory, and practice, twice winning the Distinguished Publication Award of the Association for

Women in Psychology. She was the 2005 recipient of the Sherif Award from the Society for the Psychology of Women.

NICOLE T. BUCHANAN is an assistant professor in the Department of Psychology at Michigan State University. Her research focuses on the intersections of race/ethnicity and gender in sexual victimization, with an emphasis on racialized sexual harassment targeting African-American and Latina women.

DARLENE C. DEFOUR is a social psychologist/community psychologist and currently an associate professor of psychology at Hunter College of the City University of New York. She is a member of the board of directors of the New York Association of Black Psychologists.

JANET SIGAL is a professor of psychology at Fairleigh Dickinson University. She has made more than one hundred conference presentations focused primarily on women's issues, including sexual harassment and domestic violence.

About the Author

SUSAN NATHIEL is a psychotherapist treating individuals, couples and families. She has been in practice for more than thirty years, and has a special interest in helping families deal with problems. Nathiel is a founding member of the Connecticut Guild of Psychotherapists and founding member of the Center for Illness in Families.

CPSIA information can be obtained at www.ICGtesting.com
Printed in the USA
LVOW071606230112

265192LV00007B/1/P